IFIP Advances in Information and Communication Technology

687

Editor-in-Chief

Kai Rannenberg, Goethe University Frankfurt, Germany

Editorial Board Members

IFIP Advances in Information and Communication Technology

The IFIP AICT series publishes state-of-the-art results in the sciences and technologies of information and communication. The scope of the series includes: foundations of computer science; software theory and practice; education; computer applications in technology; communication systems; systems modeling and optimization; information systems; ICT and society; computer systems technology; security and protection in information processing systems; artificial intelligence; and human-computer interaction.

Edited volumes and proceedings of refereed international conferences in computer science and interdisciplinary fields are featured. These results often precede journal publication and represent the most current research.

The principal aim of the IFIP AICT series is to encourage education and the dissemination and exchange of information about all aspects of computing.

More information about this series at https://link.springer.com/bookseries/6102

Gilbert Peterson · Sujeet Shenoi

Advances in Digital Forensics XIX

19th IFIP WG 11.9 International Conference, ICDF 2023
Arlington, Virginia, USA, January 30–31, 2023
Revised Selected Papers

 Springer

Gilbert Peterson
Department of Electrical
and Computer Engineering
Air Force Institute of Technology
Wright-Patterson AFB, OH, USA

Sujeet Shenoi
Tandy School of Computer Science
University of Tulsa
Tulsa, OK, USA

ISSN 1868-4238   ISSN 1868-422X (electronic)
IFIP Advances in Information and Communication Technology
ISBN 978-3-031-42990-3   ISBN 978-3-031-42991-0 (eBook)
https://doi.org/10.1007/978-3-031-42991-0

This Springer imprint is published by the registered company Springer Nature Switzerland AG
The registered company address is: Gewerbestrasse 11, 6330 Cham, Switzerland

Paper in this product is recyclable.

Preface

Digital forensics deals with the acquisition, preservation, examination, analysis and presentation of electronic evidence. Computer networks, cloud computing, smartphones, embedded devices and the Internet of Things have expanded the role of digital forensics beyond traditional computer crime investigations. Practically every crime now involves some aspect of digital evidence; digital forensics provides the techniques and tools to articulate this evidence in legal proceedings. Digital forensics also has myriad intelligence applications; furthermore, it has a vital role in cyber security – investigations of security breaches yield valuable information that can be used to design more secure and resilient systems.

This book, *Advances in Digital Forensics XIX*, is the nineteenth volume in the annual series produced by the IFIP Working Group 11.9 on Digital Forensics, an international community of scientists, engineers and practitioners dedicated to advancing the state of the art of research and practice in digital forensics. The book presents original research results and innovative applications in digital forensics. Also, it highlights some of the major technical and legal issues related to digital evidence and electronic crime investigations.

This volume contains fourteen revised and edited chapters based on papers presented at the Nineteenth IFIP WG 11.9 International Conference on Digital Forensics held at SRI International in Arlington, Virginia, USA on January 30–31, 2023. A total of 24 full-length papers were submitted for presentation at the conference. The papers were refereed in a single-blind manner by members of the conference program committee and other individuals, all of them internationally-recognized experts in digital forensics. The fourteen post-conference manuscripts submitted by the authors were required to be rewritten to accommodate the suggestions provided by the referees and by the conference attendees. The manuscripts were subsequently revised by the editors to produce the final chapters published in this volume.

The chapters in this volume are organized into five thematic sections: Mobile Device Forensics, Forensic Data Collection, Image and Video Forensics, Novel Applications, and Legal Issues and Applications. The coverage of topics highlights the richness and vitality of the digital forensics discipline, and offers promising avenues for future research.

This book is the result of the combined efforts of several individuals. In particular, we thank Kam-Pui Chow and Gaurav Gupta for their tireless work on behalf of IFIP Working Group 11.9 on Digital Forensics. We also acknowledge the support provided by the U.S. National Science Foundation, U.S. National Security Agency and U.S. Secret Service.

June 2023

Gilbert Peterson
Sujeet Shenoi

Conference Organization

General Chair

Laura Tinnel   SRI International, USA

Program Chairs

Gilbert Peterson   Air Force Institute of Technology, USA
Sujeet Shenoi   University of Tulsa, USA

Program Committee

Stefan Axelsson	Stockholm University, Sweden
Harald Baier	Bundeswehr University, Germany
Nicole Beebe	University of Texas at San Antonio, USA
Kam-Pui Chow	University of Hong Kong, China
Fred Cohen	Cohen and Associates, USA
Yong Guan	Iowa State University, USA
Gaurav Gupta	Ministry of Electronics and Information Technology, India
Al Holt	U.S. Department of Defense, USA
Umit Karabiyik	Purdue University, USA
Alan Lin	Air Force Office of Scientific Research, USA
Jigang Liu	Metropolitan State University, USA
Michael Losavio	University of Louisville, USA
James Okolica	Air Force Institute of Technology, USA
Martin Olivier	University of Pretoria, South Africa
Huw Read	Norwich University, USA
Mason Rice	Oak Ridge National Laboratory, USA
Vassil Roussev	University of New Orleans, USA
Anoop Singhal	National Institute of Standards and Technology, USA
Hein Venter	University of Pretoria, South Africa
Robin Verma	Marshall University, USA
York Yannikos	Fraunhofer Institute for Secure Information Technology, Germany
Philip Craiger	Embry-Riddle Aeronautical University, USA
Duminda Wijesekera	George Mason University, USA

Contents

Novel Applications

Legal Issues and Applications

List of Contributors

Harald Baier Bundeswehr University, Munich, Germany

Steven Baskerville U.S. Secret Service National Computer Forensics Institute Laboratory, Tulsa, Oklahoma, USA

Matthew Bovee Norwich University, Northfield, Vermont, USA

Chris Chao-Chun Cheng Iowa State University, Ames, Iowa, USA

Saheb Chhabra Indraprastha Institute of Information Technology, New Delhi, India

Kam-Pui Chow University of Hong Kong, Hong Kong, China

Jun Dai California State University Sacramento, Sacramento, California, USA

Trang Do Norwich University, Northfield, Vermont, USA

Kaushik Thinnaneri Ganesan Central Board of Indirect Taxes and Customs, Ministry of Finance, Mumbai, India

Pulkit Garg Indian Institute of Technology Jodhpur, Karwar, India

Thomas Göbel Bundeswehr University, Munich, Germany

Yong Guan Iowa State University, Ames, Iowa, USA

Garima Gupta Independent Researcher, New Delhi, India

Gaurav Gupta Ministry of Electronics and Information Technology, New Delhi, India

Darren Hayes Pace University, New York, New York, USA

Weiqing Huang Institute of Information Engineering, Chinese Academy of Sciences, Beijing, China

Nathan Hutchins University of Tulsa, Tulsa, Oklahoma, USA

Jianguo Jiang Institute of Information Engineering, Chinese Academy of Sciences, Beijing, China

Junye Jiang Institute of Information Engineering, Chinese Academy of Sciences, Beijing, China

Yubo Lang Criminal Investigation Police University of China, Shenyang, China

Nhien-An Le-Khac University College Dublin, Dublin, Ireland

Gengwang Li Institute of Information Engineering, Chinese Academy of Sciences, Beijing, China

Li Lin Iowa State University, Ames, Iowa, USA

Guojun Liu University of South Florida, Tampa, Florida, USA

Zhitong Lu Institute of Information Engineering, Chinese Academy of Sciences, Beijing, China

Duohe Ma Institute of Information Engineering, Chinese Academy of Sciences, Beijing, China

Shawn McKay University of Tulsa, Tulsa, Oklahoma, USA

Xiang Meng Institute of Information Engineering, Chinese Academy of Sciences, Beijing, China

Trevor Nicholson Royal Canadian Mounted Police, Surrey, Canada

Xinming Ou University of South Florida, Tampa, Florida, USA

Shenzhi Qin University of Hong Kong, Hong Kong, China

Pardon Ramazhamba Council for Scientific and Industrial Research, Pretoria, South Africa

Huw Read Norwich University, Northfield, Vermont, USA

Sujeet Shenoi University of Tulsa, Tulsa, Oklahoma, USA

Chen Shi Iowa State University, Ames, Iowa, USA

Anoop Singhal National Institute of Standards and Technology, Gaithersburg, Maryland, USA

Vishal Srivastava Raj Kumar Goel Institute of Technology, Ghaziabad, India

Xiaoyan Sun California State University Sacramento, Sacramento, California, USA

Rajani Suryavanshi KIOXIA America, Folsom, California, USA

Iain Sutherland Noroff University College, Kristiansand, Norway

Armin Ziaie Tabari OPSWAT, Tampa, Florida, USA

Leon Twenning Bundeswehr University, Munich, Germany

Hein Venter University of Pretoria, Pretoria, South Africa

Liming Wang Institute of Information Engineering, Chinese Academy of Sciences, Beijing, China

Xinzhe Wang Institute of Information Engineering, Chinese Academy of Sciences, Beijing, China

Yuanyuan Wang Institute of Information Engineering, Chinese Academy of Sciences, Beijing, China

Konstantinos Xynos Cyber Security Consultant, Stuttgart, Germany

Min Yu Institute of Information Engineering, Chinese Academy of Sciences, Beijing, China

Zhenchao Zhang Institute of Information Engineering, Chinese Academy of Sciences, Beijing, China

Mobile Device Forensics

Forensic Analysis of the iOS Apple Pay Mobile Payment System

Trevor Nicholson[1], Darren Hayes[2], and Nhien-An Le-Khac[3]

[1] Royal Canadian Mounted Police, Surrey, Canada
[2] Pace University, New York, New York, USA
[3] University College Dublin, Dublin, Ireland
an.lekhac@ucd.ie

Abstract. Mobile payment systems enable users to complete financial transactions with their smartphones, including contactless payments at retail stores. Because the financial transactions of individuals are indicators of their lifestyles, they are potential sources of data in criminal investigations. The items purchased and even the locations of transactions can constitute valuable evidence. However, mobile payment system data is intended to be interpreted by computer software not human investigators. As a result, a barrier exists between raw application data and their clear interpretations for evidentiary purposes.

This chapter describes research focused on Apple Pay, the leading mobile payment system for mobile debit wallet transactions in the United States. The research has sought to examine the Apple Pay mobile payment system and identify specific sources of forensic artifacts. This includes determining and interpreting the payment card and transaction data residing in the Apple Pay application and syncing across user devices, as well as the implications of deleting Apple Pay application data.

Keywords: Mobile Payment Forensics · Apple Pay · iCloud Backup Analysis

1 Introduction

Smartphones have replaced small devices from cameras and calculators to GPS navigation units and door keys. Just as cash has been largely replaced by payment cards in recent decades, trends suggest that smartphones are slated to replace payment cards. This is made possible by enabling users to store digital versions of payment cards in digital wallets and employ them to make contactless mobile payments.

Mobile payments employ mobile devices to initiate, authorize and confirm exchanges of financial value in return for goods or services [6]. One of the most widely used mobile payment systems is Apple Pay, which is included in current versions of iOS. First introduced in 2014 in the United States, the global adoption of Apple Pay continues to grow [7]. In 2020, the Apple Pay user base grew by 66 million, accounting for 92% of U.S. mobile debit wallet transactions [7].

© IFIP International Federation for Information Processing 2023
Published by Springer Nature Switzerland AG 2023
G. Peterson and S. Shenoi (Eds.): DigitalForensics 2023, IFIP AICT 687, pp. 3–19, 2023.
https://doi.org/10.1007/978-3-031-42991-0_1

Apple Pay combines the functionality of Apple Wallet that digitally stores payment and loyalty program cards with mobile payment functionality to use the cards at a growing number of merchants. Apple Wallet and Apple Pay are part of the same application, with Apple Wallet providing card storage and Apple Pay handling transactions. Apple Pay enables users to make online purchases as well as purchases at brick-and-mortar businesses via contactless payment at point-of-sale (PoS) terminals using near-field communications (NFC) technology, just like credit cards [11]. Apple Pay executes on Apple devices that run various versions of iOS, macOS and watchOS. The services include the syncing of Apple devices via iCloud [17], which enables users to add credit cards, debit cards and loyalty program cards, as well as drivers licenses, boarding passes, etc. to their Apple Wallets. Once a payment card is added, it can be selected within the Apple Pay application to complete transactions [2]. Information related to payment cards and transactions is protected in a secure encrypted environment on Apple devices [15].

Forensic artifacts related to mobile payment applications on smartphones can advance investigations because user transactions are consolidated on the devices. While transaction records have been available to investigators prior to mobile payment systems, services such as Apple Pay make the records readily available. Digital card usage information includes location- and time-related evidence that was not available previously. Transaction records provide evidence pertaining to where the phone has been and when specific items were purchased. The presence of digital payment cards on a smartphone also provides strong indications about the device user, which can be important in an investigation.

Mobile payment application data has evidentiary value. However, in the case of Apple Pay, forensic practitioners are presented with some challenges. First, Apple has employed industry-leading security measures on its devices that limit data access. Second, Apple Pay is not designed to present its information for analysis. Consequently, forensic practitioners must determine how to access the data and how to make logical sense of it. Meanwhile, other challenges persist. One is the lack of clarity about what happens to transactions when the associated payment cards are removed from Apple Pay. Another is the lack of understanding about the available data.

This research has focused on the underlying data in Apple Pay applications running on iOS devices. Experimentation was conducted to determine how data is presented in different circumstances. This was accomplished using iPhone test devices in practice to develop actual datasets and extracting the resulting data for analysis. The experiments provide insights into the available forensic artifacts as well as the limitations.

2   Related Work

Little, if any, research has been conducted on Apple Pay that could be used by forensic practitioners in investigations involving Apply Pay or other mobile payment services. While the literature discusses forensic analyses of Apple iOS operating systems, no research has focused on Apple Pay. Potential reasons are that mobile payment solutions are relatively new and the diverse technologies in the market are spreading research efforts too thin. However, Apple Pay has been the subject of research directed at assessing the security methods employed by its operating system.

Understanding the iOS operating system is beneficial when conducting forensic analysis of Apple Pay. Liao et al. [9] describe the iOS system architecture as having three levels, interface layer, business logic layer and data access layer. The interface layer is the software interface for user interactions, the business logic layer implements specific functions and the data access layer parses data for databases. In order to conduct experiments with Apple Pay, it is necessary to understand that an application presents an interface to a user, but a layer of data exists that is not visible, or even accessible, to the user; this layer is likely to contain much more information than what is displayed by the user interface.

Oesteicher [12] noted the relevance of iCloud data in investigations involving Apple devices. He identified that the primary purpose of iCloud is to function as a service that syncs data between a user's Apple devices. Cloud services offered by Apple are expanding in their capabilities and have millions of users. Indeed, the importance of cloud data in digital forensic investigations is more important than ever [8, 12, 13]. Clarity is needed about the presence of Apple Pay data in iCloud and its utility in mobile payment investigations.

Apple Pay is a leading mobile payment system, but it has not been studied by researchers. Therefore, it is understandable that little research has focused on alternative mobile payment systems. Bosamia and Patel [3] have examined security issues in Apple Pay, Google Pay and other mobile payment systems. They note that all the mobile payment systems function similarly as point-of-sale terminals and ultimately have similar vulnerabilities. However, they did not study the forensic artifacts existing in the mobile payment systems.

Sun et al. [14] focused specifically on security issues related to Samsung Pay. They proposed a method for securing transactions using encryption based on user fingerprints. While they did not conduct a forensic analysis of Samsung Pay, they note parenthetically that the security of Apple Pay is enhanced via the use of a Secure Element (SE) chip.

Every mobile payment application is expected to produce artifacts, some of them different, and store them in a unique manner that depends on the operating system. In the case of Apple Pay, the complexity is exacerbated by syncing a smartwatch with a smartphone and using the smartwatch to complete a transaction. Hence, the goal of this research is to obtain clarity about the payment-related data that can be recovered in devices running Apple Pay and interpreting the data for presentation in forensic reports.

3   Experimental Methodology

The experimental methodology involved setting up test devices with an Apple ID and generating Apple Pay data on them in a natural, real-world manner by

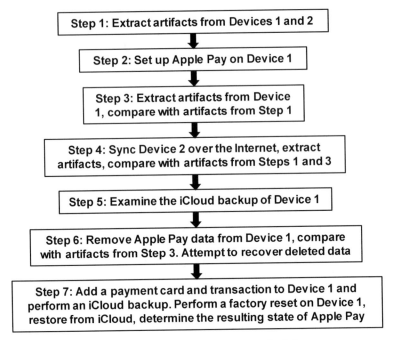

Fig. 1. Apple Pay experimental methodology.

adding payment cards and completing transactions. The test data was forensically acquired from the devices at different stages to identify changes. Forensic tools, including Cellebrite Physical Analyzer [4] and Magnet AXIOM [10], were used to analyze the data while maintaining its integrity. Data related to the payment cards and transactions was sought as well as evidence of syncing between devices. This included files related to the Apple Pay application and files that monitor device activity. Figure 1 shows the experimental methodology used in the Apple Pay research.

The datasets used in the experiments were created to closely resemble the datasets likely to be encountered in real investigations. During the testing process, records of events were maintained in an external log. The log helped track device setup, additions of payment cards, details of transactions and the stages when device data extractions were made. Recording the timestamps associated with device actions and events were critical to the task of identifying artifacts – connections between artifacts can be made using the timestamps. The record of timestamps also enabled artifacts to be assessed for their meaning, value and potential locations. The sources of forensic artifacts include the device as well as its connected cloud services.

4   Experiments and Findings

This section describes the experiments and findings.

Table 1. Experimental devices.

Device	Version	Apple Pay Application ID
Device 1: iPhone 12	iOS 15.1.1	03427D91-3263-4695-A79A-57F4DC342F5B
Device 2: iPhone 11	iOS 15.5	665A3775-52A9-48C1-8EF7-0D841730D56E

4.1   Experimental Devices

An Apple iPhone 11 (Device 1) and Apple iPhone 12 (Device 2) were employed in the experiments. These models were selected because they were released by Apple relatively recently and were in wide use when the research was conducted. Table 1 lists the two devices. Note that Apple Pay and Apple Wallet are essentially part of the same application and, therefore, use the same Application ID. They also fall under the same application bundle identifier, `com.apple.Passbook`.

Apple ID Setup In order to establish the cleanest possible testing environment, free of any unintentional synced data, a new Apple ID was created for the testing process. The email account `4n6computing@gmail.com` was created on Google Gmail. Apple services were used to create a new Apple ID using the email address `4n6computing@gmail.com`.

Device Setup Devices 1 and 2 were set up in the same manner. The devices were factory reset to ensure that they were clear of previous data. Standard device setup procedures were followed using the newly-created Apple ID associated with the email address `4n6computing@gmail.com`. Initial data extractions were performed on Devices 1 and 2. The extractions were identified by the containing devices and testing stages during which they were acquired. The Apple Pay application was not opened on the devices prior to acquisition. These extractions provided representations of uninitialized Apple Pay data.

Apple Pay Data Creation Apple Pay was setup on Device 1. The Apple Pay application is a feature of current versions of iOS, so no application installation was required. Apple Pay was initialized by adding a Scotiabank Visa credit card. The process of adding a card to Apple Pay is straightforward, however, not all cards are compatible. Attempts were made to add a pre-paid Mastercard, but Apple Pay indicated that the card was not compatible. Prompts were followed to validate the successfully-added payment card using the Scotiabank application. Device 1 was used to complete several transactions involving common purchases. The times, purchase amounts and locations were maintained in an external log. Data was extracted from Device 1, which was then analyzed.

iCloud Testing Device 1 was backed up to iCloud. Various iCloud extraction tools were used to recover data, which was subsequently analyzed. Additional

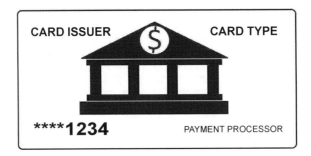

Fig. 2. Sample `FrontFace_embedded_1.png` image

.

iCloud testing was conducted later by returning Device 1 to the factory settings, restoring it from iCloud and then examining the results.

Synchronization Testing Device 2 was allowed to synchronize with iCloud and the data was extracted to determine what data was present. The same credit card was then added to Device 2 and the data was extracted again.

Deleted Data Testing Apple Pay data was deleted from Device 1 and the data was extracted to determine what information could be recovered.

4.2   Apple Pay Application Artifacts

Many of the forensic artifacts related to Apple Pay and the user interactions with it were located in the directories associated with the application. Numerous files containing forensic artifacts were located at the file paths identified in this section. Among these files were SQLite databases, PLIST files and images. The specifics of these files and the artifacts contained in them are described below. Much of the information about the card added to Apple Pay and the transactions completed by the card were duplicated across these files. Apple Pay does not store credit card numbers [6]. The experiments confirmed this as searches for the complete physical payment card did not return any results. Instead, Apple Pay uses a Device Account Number when completing transactions [6]. The Device Account Number is a unique number that Apple Pay assigns to a payment card.

Payment Card General Information At the path `\private/var/mobile/Library/Passes/Cards/`, images of the card, including one with the last four digits of the physical card number overlaid on it, were located. Several of the images were icons related to the card issuer that were located in the Preview subfolder. An image of the card with the name `FrontFace_embedded_1.png` was located in the FrontFace subfolder (Figure 2). Directories at this location were also named according to the unique card IDs of the cards in Apple Pay. After

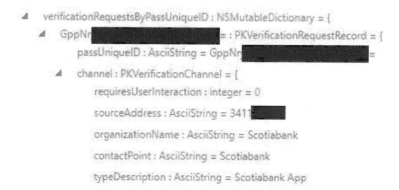

Fig. 3. Screenshot of file `PaymentWebServiceContext.archive`.

the basic card information has been collected for the card being investigated, the database files, PLIST files and JSON files can be reviewed for detailed information. These files can be exported from the device extraction data and opened in a viewer program capable of presenting the information for the file type.

Pass.json A JSON file `pass.json` located at `/private/var/mobile/Library/Passes/Cards/\{uniquecardid\}.pkpass/` was found to contain a significant amount of data for each card in Apple Wallet. Note that the file path includes the unique card ID. A viewer with a JSON formatter may be used to view the file. Some of the data was duplicated in the `passes23.sqlite` file whereas other data related to the card was only found in the JSON file. JSON files contain detailed information about the cards added to Apple Wallet, including the card issuers and relevant card numbers.

PaymentWebServicesContext.archive A PLIST file `PaymentWeb-Service Context.archive` located at private/var/mobile/Library/Passes/ was found to contain Apple Pay configuration and card validation information (Figure 3). The timestamps are in Coordinated Universal Time (UTC).

UserNotifications.archive The BPLIST file `UserNotifications.archive` was found to contain the configurations for Apple Pay notifications as well as detailed information about the transactions completed by the payment cards. Notification information for each card was found under the path PDWalletUserNotificationPass/ in the StateChanged:{uniquecardid} field. The notification configurations for Apple Pay included the content of the message and the timestamp (in UTC) for specific messages that were displayed.

During the experiments, it was observed that the message "X Card is ready for Apple Pay" was displayed when a card was validated successfully. Thus, the time that the message was displayed provides an indication of when the card was validated. Additionally, the `UserNotifications.archive` file contained a substantial amount of transaction information. The transactions were listed by their Service Identifier followed by `PDPassPaymentTransactionUserNotification`. The Service Identifier was found linked to the service_identifier field of the payment_transaction table in the `passes23.sqlite` file. In the case of multiple transactions with a single merchant, only the most recent transaction for the merchant was included in the file.

passes23.sqlite The SQLite database `passes23.sqlite` was found to contain a large portion of data related to the Apple Pay application, including a significant amount of data related to payment cards, expired transactions, merchants involved in the transactions and location data. The `passes23.sqlite` file can be exported from the device data extraction and viewed in a forensic SQLite database viewer. Timestamps in the database were found to be in the Apple Cocoa Core Data Time (Apple Absolute Time) format. The database contained 170 tables. Not all the tables were found to have been used by Apple Pay during the experiments. It was clear what some of the data in the tables represented, while other data would require further evaluation. The experiments indicate that the database is the main location where Apple Pay stores user card information and transaction data.

Temporary journaling files and write-ahead log files can be used by databases, including SQLite databases, to provide data resilience. During the experiments, no journaling or write-ahead log files were located for the `passes23.sqlite` database. Since many tables exist in the database, a process has to be followed to associate the data between different tables. The process begins by identifying the unique card ID of each card in Apple Pay. The `passes23.sqlite` file was found to contain many entries directly related to the cards added to Apple Wallet. As previously noted, card and transaction information were duplicated in multiple files. Apple Pay does not store credit card numbers, but instead uses a Device Account Number when completing transactions. This number is unique to a card. The last four digits can be located in the dpan_suffix field of the payment_application table. The `passes23.sqlite` file was also found to contain entries related directly to the transactions made by the cards in Apple Wallet.

ScheduledActivities.archive The BPLIST file `ScheduledActivities.archive` located at /private/var/mobile/Library/Passes/ was found to contain tasks related to Apple Pay. The tasks are scheduled by the system (Table 2).

Comparison of Database States The states of various Apple Pay related files must be considered to help identify iOS devices that were in use but did not have Apple Pay set up on them. The directory `private/var/mobile/Library/Passes/ Cards/` existed but contained no files, so the `pass.json` file was not present. The `PaymentWebServiceContext.archive` file was present

Table 2. Relevant fields of file `ScheduledActivities.archive`.

Field	Description
PDPaymentWebServicesCoordinator	Sub-fields contain data for scheduled tasks to conduct checks of the verification status and consistency of payment cards added to Apple Pay
PDMapsBrandAndMerchantUpdater	Sub-fields contain data for scheduled tasks to conduct checks for updated merchant information
PDMapsMerchantProcessingService	Sub-fields contain data for scheduled tasks to conduct checks for updated merchant processing data

and contained configuration data and a date in the registrationDate field. The `UserNotifications.archive` file did not exist. The `passes23.sqlite` database file existed with all 170 tables; however, the only tables containing data were cloud_store_database, cloud_store_zone, index_fetched_ metadata, index_ metadata, location_index_node and sqlite_master. The data in these tables was general, including version numbers and container names. The `ScheduledActiv ities.archive` file was present and its contents appeared to be very similar with the exception of card data.

4.3   iOS Artifacts

Upon completing the analysis of Apple Pay application files, additional artifacts related to payment cards added to Apple Pay and the use of the application may be found in files inherent to the iOS operating system or in files outside the application folders.

knowledgeC.db   The generic database file `knowledgeC.db` is maintained by the iOS operating system and can be used to determine the time frames when Apple Pay was used. The file is commonly analyzed by forensic practitioners during examinations of iOS and macOS devices because it contains many artifacts related to users and their use of applications [5].

During the experiments, `knowledgeC.db` was examined for artifacts relevant to Apple Pay. The database file `knowledgeC.db` has an associated write-ahead log (WAL) file that should also be considered because it may contain relevant database transactions that have not yet been applied to the database. Artifacts related to the use of Apple Pay and Apple Wallet were found in `knowledgeC.db` under its iOS bundle name `com.apple.Passbook` as well as `com.apple.PassbookUIService`. Note that Passbook is the former name of Apple Wallet.

In the experiments, Apple Pay was used to add payment cards, complete card validation and perform transactions. Figure 4 shows the contents of ZOBJECT,

ZVALUESTRING	ZSTARTDATE (UTC)	ZENDDATE (UTC)
com.apple.Passbook	2022-06-16 04:44:49	2022-06-16 04:45:00
com.apple.PassbookUIService	2022-06-16 04:45:00	2022-06-16 04:45:29
com.apple.Passbook	2022-06-16 04:44:49	2022-06-16 04:46:03
com.apple.Passbook	2022-06-16 04:45:29	2022-06-16 04:46:03
com.apple.Passbook	2022-06-16 04:46:30	2022-06-16 04:46:58
com.apple.Passbook	2022-06-16 04:46:30	2022-06-16 04:47:07
com.apple.Passbook	2022-06-16 04:46:58	2022-06-16 04:47:07
com.apple.Passbook	2022-06-16 04:53:48	2022-06-16 04:53:49
com.apple.Passbook	2022-06-16 04:53:52	2022-06-16 04:54:05

Fig. 4. Contents of the ZOBJECT table in database `knowledgeC.db`.

the main `knowledgeC.db` table, which contains data pertaining to the use of applications. Data related to the use of Apple Pay was discovered in this table.

key	daysSince1970	value
appBackgroundActiveTime.com.apple.Passbook	19159	4
appActivationCount.com.apple.Passbook	19159	6
appLaunchCount.com.apple.PassbookUIService	19159	4
appActivationCount.com.apple.PassbookUIService	19159	8
appActiveTime.com.apple.PassbookUIService	19159	97
appActiveTime.com.apple.Passbook	19159	165

Fig. 5. Contents of the Scalars table in database `ADDataStore.sqlitedb`.

ADDataStore.sqlitedb Similar to `knowledgeC.db`, the `ADDataStore.sqlite db` database file holds logs of iOS operating system activities [5]. This database can be used to determine when Apple Pay was last launched and how many times it was launched and activated in the recent past. Analysis revealed that the database only retained entries for about a week. Figure 5 shows the contents of the Scalars table in the database.

com.apple.passd.plist The PLIST file `com.apple.passd.plist`, located in the iOS preferences folder, contains data relevant to Apple Pay. Table 3 shows the relevant fields of the file and their descriptions. The content includes the configuration and states of the Apple Pay application as well as timestamps for payment card validation and removal.

Table 3. Relevant fields of file `com.apple.passd.plist`.

Field	Description
PDLastPaymentPassInsertionOrRemovalDate	Timestamp in UTC when a card was last removed or validated in Apple Pay
PDDefaultPaymentPassUniqueIdentifier	Unique identifier for the payment card that is the default card
PDLastUnlockedTime	Last time Apple Pay was unlocked and accessed (Apple Absolute Time); analysis revealed that this need not indicate that a user launched and unlocked Apple Pay, but it may have been a consequence of unlocking the device

Cache.db The database file `Cache.db` located at …/com.apple.passd/ was found to contain a small amount of data relevant to Apple Pay. The table cfurl_cache_response in the database contained a field request_key with the URL for a web resource related to Apple. In the URL was the serial number of a payment card that resided in Apple Pay. The same serial number was identified in the serial_number field of the pass table in the `passes23.sqlite` file. The timestamp appears to record when a key was requested for the associated card.

The name of the database suggests that it is used for caching data. Experiments also revealed that the database was susceptible to garbage collection. As a result, it is difficult to specify what relevant data `Cache.db` would contain at any given time, but it is a potential source of data. `Cache.db` was found to have an associated WAL file named `Cache.db-wal` that contained the locations where Apple Pay downloaded keys associated with its payment cards.

Apple Keychain and Safari Apple Keychain is a feature available to Apple device users. It is not directly related to Apple Pay and Apple Pay was not found to store its card information in Apple Keychain, but it may be an alternate source of artifacts for payment cards found in Apple Pay.

Apple Keychain stores sensitive information such as passwords and tokens as well as information about cards used in a Safari browser. The benefit of using Apple Keychain is that it securely stores sensitive information and allows the information to be synced with other Apple devices belonging to a user.

The option to store credit card information in Apple Keychain is presented to a user during the setup of an Apple device. If a user opts to store credit card information in the keychain, it is a potential source of artifacts. Credit card information is added via Safari for use within the browser and a user can manage the information using the browser.

4.4   Artifacts from Other Applications

This section discusses Apple Pay artifacts that are related to other applications.

Financial Institution Application Files While applications associated with the financial institutions of a user are not part of Apple Pay, a common method for validating a card for use with Apple Pay is to employ the financial institution application. Therefore, it is recommended to examine financial institution applications for artifacts. In fact, the presence of such applications alone could provide useful leads in investigations.

Third-Party Browsers As mentioned above, payment card information can be added to a Safari browser. Users often install and use third-party Internet browsers such as Google Chrome, which stores card information and processes payments via Google Pay. Thus, third-party browsers are also potential sources of artifacts.

4.5   iCloud Backup Artifacts

There are instances where a forensic practitioner may not have access to the data residing on an Apple device. An alternate data source is an iCloud backup of the device [16]. Experiments revealed that the default setting for iCloud backups on iOS 15 is for the feature to be activated. Also, most default Apple applications, including Apple Wallet, are set to be included in the iCloud backup. Thus, Apple Pay data could be recoverable from an iCloud backup.

Of course, judicial authorization would be required to access a subject's iCloud data in an investigation. One option is to seek judicial authorization to have Apple provide iCloud data for the investigation. Another option is for a forensic practitioner to access the subject's iCloud storage with judicial authorization and proceed to extract Apple Pay artifacts. Several iCloud extractions were performed to investigate this possibility. A test device with an active Apple Pay account and several transactions was backed up to iCloud. Three cloud forensic tools were used to analyze the iCloud backup. The extractions yielded several Apple Pay artifacts.

httpstorage.sqlite An empty database file `httpstorages.sqlite` was located in the iCloud backup at the path `com.apple.Passbook/Library/HTTPStorages/ com.apple.Passbook/`. While the extracted copy of the database file did not contain database entries, the fact that it is a database indicates that it could, under different circumstances, provide relevant information.

Financial Institution Applications Depending on the financial institution applications and their settings, data pertaining to validations of Apple Pay transactions made using payment cards could be included in an iCloud backup. Experiments confirmed that this is, in fact, the case, and the extracted data would be relevant in an investigation.

com.apple.passd.plist The PLIST file `com.apple.passd.plist` was found to be located at the path /mobile/Library/Preferences/com. This file contained less data than the version of the same file located on the device. However, it contained the unique card ID of the payment card added to Apple Pay.

Summary In order to confirm the findings listed above, experiments were conducted using a test iPhone. The iPhone was previously used to conduct Apple Pay transactions with a payment card and its Apple Wallet application was set for iCloud backup. A factory reset of the test iPhone was completed. The iPhone data on the test device was restored from the iCloud backup and the device was examined.

The experiments revealed that the original payment card appeared in Apple Pay as a suggested card, not an added and validated card. The payment card was then added to Apple Wallet again by entering its CVV number and verifying it through the card issuer. After the card was added, none of the pre-existing transaction data was present. This result is consistent with what was found in the iCloud extractions. It is also identical to what was found on an Apple device synced to the same Apple ID.

4.6   Investigative Scenarios

Two scenarios were examined to demonstrate the relevance of Apple Pay artifacts in real-world investigations. The scenarios led to additional experiments involving Apple device syncing and data deletion.

Apple Pay Data Targeting The first scenario involved a malicious entity targeting Apple Pay data in an iCloud backup of an iOS device and on the device itself. To assess the available iCloud backup data, the iCloud data of an iOS test device was extracted and analyzed. The device had previously used payment cards to conduct several Apple Pay transactions. Additionally, the Apple Wallet application on the device had the default setting for iCloud backups.

The analysis revealed that access to the iCloud backup would provide negligible information. Specifically, the malicious entity would be able to determine the number of cards in Apple Wallet, card types and their issuers, last four digits of the card numbers and the unique card IDs assigned to the cards by Apple. However, no transaction data would be available. Also, the malicious entity would be unable to further compromise the Apple Pay account or payment cards using the information obtained from the iCloud backup.

To assess the available Apple Pay data, the data residing on the iOS test devices was extracted and analyzed. When an iOS test device had not used Apple Pay but was synced to the same Apple ID as other devices that used Apple Pay, the results were identical to those obtained with the iCloud backup. Some data was available, but not enough to compromise the payment card or Apple Pay account.

However, when an iOS test device was used with Apple Pay, compromising the device would provide access to the data in the Apple Pay user interface. The data includes transaction data, location data and card data, such as its issuer and the last several digits of the Device Account Number and the payment card. However, the data would not enable the payment card to be compromised or transferred. In order to make purchases with Apple Pay, a malicious entity would have to re-authenticate the device with a passcode or alternate means such as Face ID.

Apple Pay Data Deletion The second scenario involved a malicious user attempting to delete transaction data by removing the payment card associated with the transactions in Apple Pay. To assess the consequences, a payment card was added to Apple Pay on a test iPhone and transactions were made. The card was then removed, the device was power cycled, following which data was extracted from the test device.

Analysis revealed that the main Apple Pay data files listed in this chapter were almost devoid of artifacts related to the payment card and transactions. However, some additional files were found to contain artifacts. These files would enable the unique card IDs of cards added to Apple Pay to be identified. The most valuable files contained the unique card IDs, card issuers and transaction information, including the merchants, merchant locations (cities) and purchase amounts. The files use timestamps as their names and would have different file names in different cases. The identified files were:

- File 677048032271198 located at `/DuetExpertCenter/streams/UserNotif icationEvents/local/`.
- File 677048032276680 located at `/Biome/streams/public/Notification/ local/`.
- File 677047489833466 located at `/Biome/streams/restricted/UserActiv ityMetadata/local/`.

5   Discussion

This research has identified a number of sources of forensic artifacts related to Apple Pay. Artifacts related to Apple Pay payment cards and transactions were forensically recovered from iOS devices. Also, insights were gained about specific Apple Pay artifacts syncing across iOS devices belonging to a user. This was assessed based on the various states of the Apple Pay applications on the synced devices. The experiments revealed that syncing does not work for Apple Pay in that transactions executed by a given iOS device reside only on the device. An exception is when an Apple Watch is used to execute transactions. Although the research did not focus on Apple Watch devices, the exception exists because an Apple Watch works in conjunction and synchronization with an iOS device to complete transactions.

This research also investigated whether users can clear their Apple Pay transaction histories and whether the details can be recovered. The experiments revealed that removing a payment card from Apple Pay removes the transactions from the main Apple Pay files. However, transaction details can potentially be recovered from other locations. Ultimately, the research results have value because they are likely to produce evidentiary artifacts that benefit real-world investigations. Using the artifacts identified in this research, a forensic practitioner could determine which physical payment cards were used within Apple Pay to make purchases as well as very specific details about the transactions completed by the cards using Apple Pay. A forensic practitioner could also use the artifacts identified in iCloud backups to determine the physical cards that users hold in their Apple Wallet applications.

The results related to deleted data would be useful in finding transactions related to previously-used payment cards on iOS devices. However, completing a factory reset of an iOS device would conceal evidence because it would eliminate the possibility of recovering the artifacts described in this chapter.

Direct comparisons of this work against other research in digital forensics would be challenging because no previous research has focused on forensic artifacts in mobile payment applications. However, comparisons can be made with some security research papers.

Margraf et al. [11] discovered that the security of Apple Pay was comparable to that of a physical credit card. This research supports the finding because it identified that Apple Pay has an additional layer of security that requires device authentication before a point-of-sale terminal transaction, which physical credit cards do not have on low-value transactions. Additionally, Oesteicher [12] identified the relevance of iCloud data in digital forensic investigations. This research also found that iCloud data is relevant to Apple Pay investigations, especially if the physical device is inaccessible because iCloud contained some payment card information. While iCloud does not currently maintain Apple Pay transaction data, future updates by Apple may change this situation.

6   Conclusions

The Apple Pay forensic artifacts identified in this research enable digital forensic professionals to identify payment cards used in Apple Pay and obtain details about completed transactions, including dates and times, and locations with latitude and longitude coordinates. The research has also provided clarity about Apple Pay data syncing between iOS devices connected to the same Apple ID. Additionally, insights were obtained about Apple Pay data at risk when iOS devices and iCloud accounts are compromised. The research also identified the payment card and transaction artifacts that remain after attempts have been made to delete Apple Pay data by removing payment cards from the application. Finally, sources for payment card artifacts outside of Apple Pay such as financial institution applications, Internet browsers and Apple Keychain were identified.

Future research will focus on enhancing the opportunities for forensic practitioners to access iOS device data. This includes forensically-sound procedures for handling seized iOS devices and comparing the results of different extraction tools. Although Apple Watch forensics has been investigated [1], the forensic implications of executing Apple Pay transactions on Apple Watch are not well understood. Future research will also examine this issue with the goal of identifying the artifacts that are synced between devices during Apple Pay transactions.

References

1. S. Alabdulsalam, K. Schaefer, T. Kechadi and N. Le-Khac, Internet of Things forensics – Challenges and a case study, in *Advances in Digital Forensics XIV*, G. Peterson and S. Shenoi (Eds.), Springer, Cham, Switzerland, pp. 35–48, 2018.
2. Apple, iPhone User Guide – Keep Cards and Passes in Wallet on iPhone, Cupertino, California (support.apple.com/en-ca/guide/iphone/iphc05dba539/ios), 2023.
3. M. Bosamia and D. Patel, Wallet payments: Recent potential threats and vulnerabilities with possible security measures, *International Journal of Computer Sciences and Engineering*, vol. 7(1), pp. 810–817, 2019.
4. Cellebrite, Cellebrite Physical Analyzer, Petah Tikva, Israel (cellebrite.com/en/physical-analyzer), 2023.
5. S. Edwards, Knowledge is power! Using the macOS/iOS knowledgeC.db database to determine precise user and application usage, *mac4n6 Blog* (www.mac4n6.com/?offset=1536804062230&category=iOS), August 6, 2018.
6. A. Jawale and J. Park, A security analysis of Apple Pay, *Proceedings of the European Intelligence and Security Informatics Conference*, pp. 160–163, 2016.
7. A. Julija, 10+ Apple Pay statistics that show mobile payments are the future, *Furtunly Blog Statistics* (fortunly.com/statistics/apple-pay-statistics), December 16, 2022.
8. N. Le-Khac, M. Mollema, R. Craig, S. Ryder and L. Chen, Data acquisition in the cloud, in *Security, Privacy and Digital Forensics in the Cloud*, L. Chen, H, Takabi and N. Le-Khac (Eds.), Wiley, Singapore, pp. 257–282, 2019.
9. Z. Liao, S. Wu, B. Xi, F. Wang, D. Ming and B. Chen, Digital forensic design of iOS operating system, *Proceedings of the Third High Performance Computing and Cluster Technologies Conference*, pp. 232–236, 2019.
10. Magnet Forensics, Magnet AXIOM, Waterloo, Canada (www.magnetforensics.com/products/magnet-axiom), 2023.
11. M. Margraf, S. Lange and F. Otterbein, Security evaluation of Apple Pay at point-of-sale terminals, *Proceedings of the Tenth International Conference on Next Generation Mobile Applications, Security and Technologies*, pp. 115–120, 2016.
12. K. Oesteicher, A forensically robust method for acquisition of iCloud data, *Digital Investigation*, vol. 11(S2), pp. S106–S113, 2014.
13. S. Schlepphorst, K. Choo and N. Le-Khac, Digital forensic approaches for cloud service models: A survey, in *Cyber and Digital Forensic Investigations*, N. Le-Khac and K. Choo (Eds.), Springer, Cham, Switzerland, pp. 175–199, 2020.
14. Y. Sun, R. Ruhl and H. Samuel, A Survey of Payment Token Vulnerabilities Towards Stronger Security with Fingerprint-Based Encryption on Samsung Pay, Project Report, Information Security and Assurance, Concordia University, Edmonton, Canada, 2018.

15. P. Teufl, T. Zefferer, C. Stromberger and C. Hechenblaikner, iOS encryption systems: Deploying iOS devices in security-critical environments, *Proceedings of the International Conference on Security and Cryptography*, 2013.
16. R. Thantilage and N. Le-Khac, Retrieving e-dating application artifacts from iPhone backups, in *Advances in Digital Forensics XVI*, G. Peterson and S. Shenoi (Eds.), Springer, Cham, Switzerland, pp. 215–230, 2020.
17. A. Yadi and F. Alfi, *iCloud Standard Guide*, Packt Publishing, Birmingham, United Kingdom, 2013.

Forensic Analysis of Android Cryptocurrency Wallet Applications

Chen Shi and Yong Guan

Iowa State University, Ames, Iowa, USA
guan@iastate.edu

Abstract. Crypto wallet apps that integrate with blockchains enable users to execute digital currency transactions with quick response codes. In 2021, there were more than 68 million crypto wallet app users [8]. As new crypto wallets and cryptocurrencies enter the market, the number of users will continue to increase. Mobile apps are commonly employed by users to execute cryptocurrency transactions and manage funds. As a result, sensitive information stored in mobile apps constitutes critical evidence in digital forensic investigations.

This chapter describes a forensic analysis method for Android cryptocurrency wallet apps that extracts evidence from the local filesystems and system logs. The results of forensic analyses of 253 real-world Android cryptocurrency wallet apps are interesting. A total of 135 crypto wallet apps store user account information in local filesystems that are accessible by malware. As many as 67 crypto wallet apps access and store user location information in a local database and log files, and twelve crypto wallet apps track the last used times of other applications installed on the devices. The research also reveals that, without resorting to deleted file recovery, various types of evidentiary data can be identified in local filesystems and system logs. Additionally, several types of evidence that were latent in previous studies are shown to be discoverable.

Keywords: Android Crypto Wallet Apps · Mobile App Forensics · Taint Analysis

1 Introduction

Mobile devices such as smartphones and tablets are hugely popular around the world. The global use of smartphones surpassed that of personal computers in 2013 [10]. Meanwhile, the mobile wallet industry is set to register profits of approximately $750.3 billion by 2028 [7].

Attractive features provided by crypto wallet apps on mobile devices have enabled them to dominate significant portions of cryptocurrency usage. Crypto wallet apps, which enable users to access their wallets anytime and anywhere, maintain private data and forensic artifacts that constitute critical evidence in civil and criminal cases. Analysis of cryptocurrency transactions provides insights into user activities and purchase history. Location data and the associated timestamps help construct chains of events.

© IFIP International Federation for Information Processing 2023
Published by Springer Nature Switzerland AG 2023
G. Peterson and S. Shenoi (Eds.): DigitalForensics 2023, IFIP AICT 687, pp. 21–36, 2023.
https://doi.org/10.1007/978-3-031-42991-0_2

Cryptocurrency wallets, especially web-based wallets and desktop wallets, have been the subject of research. Mirza et al. [20] presented approaches for extracting evidence such as private keys, IP addresses and timestamps from Web3 wallets on Android and iOS devices. However, forensic analysis approaches for crypto wallet apps on Android platforms are limited. Previous studies have not analyzed messages in Android logging systems that are written by crypto wallet apps. The studies have not focused on the key question of where evidence is stored. Additionally, since only a few crypto wallet apps – just three to five of the most popular apps – from among the more than 200 available apps have been investigated by researchers, the analysis results are not strong enough to generalize their conclusions.

This chapter describes an improved forensic analysis method for extracting artifacts generated by Android crypto wallet apps. The method, which involves live and offline analyses, was applied to 253 real-world crypto wallet apps on Android devices. The results reveal that more than 24 types of evidence are retrievable from the internal filesystems and system logs. This work is the first to include Android log messages in forensic analyses of crypto wallet apps. Additionally, it is the first to perform large-scale forensic analyses of Android crypto wallet apps.

2   Background

A recent Statista survey [24] revealed that there were more than 68 million crypto wallet users in 2022. The number of crypto wallet users is expected to grow with the increase of mobile device accessibility. While more and more markets are accepting cryptocurrency payments from consumers concerned about privacy, increasing numbers of cryptocurrency transactions involve illicit addresses. As a result, law enforcement personnel need better methods for seizing cryptocurrency and conducting forensic analyses of crypto wallet apps.

A crypto wallet contains pairs of public and private cryptographic keys. A key pair is used to track ownership and to receive or spend cryptocurrency. The public key enables other parties to make payments to the address derived from the key, which serves as a traditional bank account number whereas the private key enables cryptocurrency to be spent from the address.

To initiate a cryptocurrency payment transaction to another account, a cryptocurrency holder generates a transaction message and broadcasts it to the entire cryptocurrency network. Miners then proceed to validate the transaction. If the transaction is valid, the transaction is appended to the cryptocurrency blockchain.

Most crypto wallet apps claim to leverage methods that protect user privacy. Crypto wallets may be pseudonymous, but in their user agreements, they also include "Know Your Customer" protocols through which apps collect large amounts of user data. Each crypto wallet app has its own user interface and code implementation for storing and handling user data. At this time, dozens of trojaned cryptocurrency wallet apps target Android platforms [28]. These apps,

```
void getLastKnownLocation(Location loc)
{
    String prefix1 = "Lat-";
    String prefix2 = "Lon-";
    StringBuffer buff = new StringBuffer(prefix);
    double lat = loc.getLatitude();
    buff.append(Double.toString(lat));
    double lon = loc.getLongitude();
    buff.append(Double.toString(lon));
    String toStr = buff.toString();
    Log.d("Msg1", toStr);
}
```

Fig. 1. Method `getLastKnownLocation`.

which are distributed by websites that mimic legitimate services, steal user secret seed phrases by impersonating apps such as Coinbase and MetaMask.

To order to protect their private data from being leaked, some users attempt to uninstall crypto wallet apps or reset data on their Android platforms. These methods completely remove the files in the internal storage of the apps. Since this topic is outside the scope of this research, analysis of the evidence generated and deleted by a crypto wallet app itself is not discussed in this chapter.

To reiterate, mobile crypto wallet apps make it very convenient for users to conduct financial transactions, but exactly what data is stored on mobile devices and uploaded to servers is unknown. Indeed, forensic studies of crypto wallet apps on Android platforms are practically nonexistent.

3 Motivating Example

Several malicious crypto wallet apps have been implemented to steal user funds. Fake wallets distributed on Chinese websites and advertised on the Telegram channel in 56 Facebook groups led to a ban on cryptocurrency exchanges and the suspension of new user registrations in Mainland China. In January 2022, Google Play Store removed 13 malicious applications that impersonated the legitimate Jaxx Liberty Wallet app [28].

In 2021, Hu et al. [16] reported that BitcoinJ [3], a widely-used Bitcoin client library, had a vulnerability that leaked Bitcoin addresses of mobile crypto wallet apps. Hu and colleagues also discovered that crypto wallet apps using BitcoinJ continuously downloaded client transactions without raising alerts or notifications.

A study of the Android library by Shi et al. [23] identified a third-party advertisement library named `iscom.yrkfgo.assxqx4` that is used by several crypto wallet apps. Shi and colleagues discovered that location information was generated and accessed by the advertisement library. Figure 1 shows the code of method `getLastKnownLocation` in the `iscom.yrkfgo.assxqx4` library. When the GPS location of a device changes, the crypto wallet app receives the new

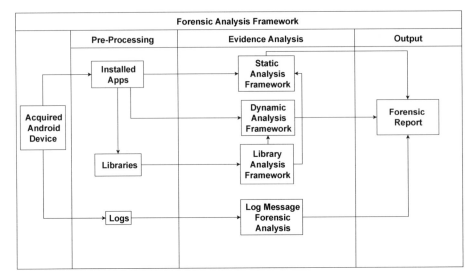

Fig. 2. Forensic analysis method.

GPS location. Method `getLastKnownLocation` then proceeds to write the GPS location to the system log.

4   Methodology

Figure 2 provides an overview of the forensic analysis method for Android crypto wallet apps. The method incorporates two phases, evidence collection and evidence analysis. A significant improvement is the inclusion of logging system message collection which is not considered by other forensic analysis methods for crypto wallet apps [20]. Since the messages in the logging system are volatile data, they are collected after operating crypto wallet apps using an automated testing script. This is followed by the logical extraction of the filesystem and the examination and validation of the extracted evidence.

4.1   Log Message Forensic Analysis

Log messages assist app developers by providing debugging information such as the line numbers of code where errors occurred. Each log message has a system timestamp, message level, message tag, process identifier and message body.

The message tag and message body are provided by API arguments whereas timestamps and process identifiers are generated by the system. The message level, which is used to filter messages, is determined by the invoked API, which is the only way that an app can access the logging system. For example, the DEBUG level is assigned to the message written by Log.d(String tag, String msg) and the INFO level is tagged to the message written by Log.i(String `tag, String msg)`. Since a log message always has a timestamp associated with it, a log message containing a network URL can be treated as a browsing history record. Log messages containing latitude and longitude data can be used to reconstruct user movements. Therefore, log messages must be parsed when performing forensic analysis on crypto wallet apps in order to understand user activity.

The Android operating system allocates four memory buffers, main, radio, events and system, to implement the logging system. Each buffer is assigned to store messages for different purposes. For example, any message logged by official APIs, such as `Log.d(String tag, String msg)`, is stored in the main buffer in the kernel-level implementation. Although certain Android operating system versions set the buffer size to 64 KB, the size may be reconfigured by users in the developer mode. When a buffer is full, the oldest message is overwritten. The Android Debug Bridge (ADB) interface is used to communicate between a host computer and mobile device to retrieve log messages. After the connection is set up, the command `#adb logcat` is issued to retrieve log messages.

In the experiment, the command `#adb logcat -b main -b radio -b events -b system -v time » /path_to_dump_file` was executed to obtain log messages. This command retrieves the log messages from all four log buffers, appends timestamps to the messages and stores them at the specified destination.

There are two advantages to considering log messages during the forensic analysis of crypto wallet apps. First, the logging system can be accessed without root permission, enabling forensic practitioners to extract log messages immediately after a device is obtained. Second, even if the device user intentionally deletes data such as previous transactions, the log messages are not affected. These benefits improve the chances of obtaining digital evidence for forensic analysis.

4.2   Filesystem Forensic Analysis

Filesystem forensic analysis focuses on the artifacts stored in an Android filesystem. The target of filesystem forensic analysis is to identify the locations of evidence that can help understand recent user activity. Filesystem data is obtained using logical and/or physical extraction. Logical extraction performs file copy operations recursively to collect data whereas physical extraction images every block of the filesystem. The forensic analysis method engages a logical extraction technique for evidence acquisition. This is because the recovery of deleted files on an Android platform is challenging and beyond the scope of this research. Additionally, logical extraction is faster than physical extraction, which has to image the entire storage media.

The Android filesystem is divided into internal and external storage. After an app is installed on a device, the Android operating system assigns its internal storage at /data/data/<package name>/ where <package name> is the unique identifier of the Android app. For example, the package name of the Coinbase app is com.coinbase.android. The app is only allowed to access its own directory in internal storage without applying for permission. Unlike internal storage, external storage designated as /sdcard/ is mounted to be publicly-available to all apps.

Since it is not known *a priori* which files contain evidence, data collection must cover internal as well as external storage. Unlike external storage that is accessed without permission, root permission is required to access files in internal storage. Therefore, before extracting evidence from internal storage, a forensic practitioner has to ensure that the device is unlocked and rooted. However, unlocking a device with factory reset protection may cause a system reset and corrupt the evidence. To address this problem, data collection must leverage SRSRoot [21] to safely root the Android device without flashing it.

Rooting an Android device provides complete access to the internal storage. Logical extraction is then performed using #adb pull to set up a connection that sends the extracted files from the device to the host computer. To locate file that may contain evidence, taint analysis is employed to track data flows from source methods to sink methods. When files do not store data in plaintext format, tools such as SQLite browser and hexdump may be used to parse SQLite database files and binary files, respectively.

5 Experimental Evaluation

This section evaluates the application of the proposed forensic analysis method on crypto wallet apps. Case studies are presented to cover the common types of evidence identified in a large-scale analysis of crypto wallet apps. The analysis results are intended to assist forensic practitioners in extracting evidence in real-world scenarios.

The experimental evaluation environment included a workstation running the Ubuntu Linux 18.04 LTS operating system. Two Android devices were employed, a Google Pixel 2 running an Android Oreo 8.1 emulator and a Google Pixel 1 running Marshmallow 6.0.

A total of 253 crypto wallet apps were obtained from 46 Android app markets. Log message forensic analysis and taint analysis were applied to the internal filesystem of each app to create forensic reports. Since some apps were large and required considerable time to be analyzed completely, an eight-hour limit was set for each app. Most of the apps were analyzed within the eight-hour limit.

5.1 Log Message Analysis Results

In the log analysis experiments, the latest versions of each crypto wallet app was downloaded and installed on an Android device. The logging system was reset and cleared before installation. After running the automated testing script written in Monkey [11] for eight hours, the log messages were dumped to a file.

Figure 3 shows a portion of a log message containing location information. The information includes the latitude and longitude along with an appended timestamp. The timestamped location can be used to reconstruct user activity.

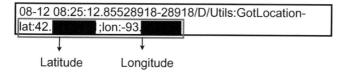

08-12 08:25:12.85528918-28918/D/Utils:GotLocation-
lat:42.█████ ;lon:-93.█████

Latitude   Longitude

Fig. 3. Location information in a log message.

Extracting log messages is simple because root permission is not required for access. This result demonstrates that log messages constitute useful evidence obtained during the forensic analysis of crypto wallet apps.

8-12 10:23:12.231 21437 21437 I chromium: [INFO: CONSOLE (1)] " ", source: https://www.google.com

8-12 10:23:12.231 21437 21437 I chromium [INFO: CONSOLE(1)] " ", https://www.google.com/maps
@42.████-93.████,15z

8-12 10:23:12.231 21437 21437 I chromium: [INFO: CONSOLE (1)] '*, Waiting for response,
source: https://www.google.com/

8-12 10:23:12.231 21437 21437 I chromium: [INFO: CONSOLE (1)1 ** Battery Power Supply logging
Daemon start, source: https://www.google.com/

8-12 10:23:12.231 21437 21437 I chromium: [INFO: CONSOLE(1)] '*, Could not open 'system/etc/user,
source: https://www.google.com

8-12 10:23:12.231 21437 21437 I chromium: [INFO: CONSOLE (1)] **, ERROR: could not read
system/etc/user. conf
source: https://www.google.com/

8-12 10:23:12.231 21437 21437 I chromium: [INFO:CONSOLE (1)] '* source: https://www.google.com

Fig. 4. Log messages from the Bread Wallet app.

Other types of evidence stored in log messages include visited URLs, IP addresses and timestamps. Research was conducted to examine why visited URLs are written to the logging system. Tracing back from the message tag chromium in Figure 4 revealed that the log messages came from the Android WebKit API. Specifically, the WebChromeClient in the WebKit API writes a message to the Android logging system when the callback method onConsoleMessage(...) is invoked by a console message received from the visited website server. If the webpage has JavaScript code such as console.log(String) where the argument is the message body, a console message is sent. When the browser app on the client device receives the console message, the message body and source website of the message are written to the logging system of the device. This mechanism provides valuable evidence about user browsing history.

5.2   Filesystem Analysis Results

Forensic artifacts are also stored in the filesystem. The large-scale evaluation revealed that more than half of the real-world crypto wallet apps generate and access evidentiary data, and save the data in internal storage.

Table 1. Forensic analysis report for the com.crypto.multiwallet app.

App Package	Downloads	Evidence Type	Evidence Log	Evidence File Paths File Paths
com.crypto.multiwallet	50K	Timestamp	*	/data/user/0/com.crypto.multiwallet/shared_prefs /data/user/0/com.crypto.multiwallet/databases/Journal-centeringStoreDatabase.db
		Visited URL	*	
		Cookie		/data/app_webview/Cookies.db
		Location	*	/data/user/0/com.crypto.multiwallet/databases/Journal-centeringStoreDatabase.db

*: Information exists in the log.

Table: loc

#	TIME	LATITUDE	LONGITUDE	ACCURATE
Filter	Filter	Filter	Filter	Filter
1	1	1666744372	42.04717	-93.631913	3737316582
2	2	1666744412	42.03078	-93.64614	3737316582
3	3	1666744456	42.04717	-93.64614	3737316582
4	4	1666744474	42.04717	-93.64614	3737316582
5	5	1666744558	42.04717	-93.64614	3737316582
6	6	1666744725	42.04717	-93.64614	3737316582
7	7	1666745092	42.04717	-93.64614	3737316582
8	8	1666745172	42.04717	-93.64614	3737316582
9	9	1666745265	42.04717	-93.64614	3737316582
10	10	1666745471	42.04717	-93.64614	3737316582
11	11	1666745613	42.04717	-93.64614	3737316582
12	12	1666745624	42.04717	-93.64614	3737316582
13	13	1666745843	42.04717	-93.64614	3737316582
14	14	1666745843	42.04717	-93.64614	3737316582

Fig. 5. Location information in the com.crypto.multiwallet app database.

A case study involving the com.crypto.multiwallet app was used to gain insights into the general files that contain evidentiary data. Table 1 shows the forensic analysis report for the app. Forensic artifacts are stored in three files in the filesystem. Note that the file paths are under the app's internal storage directory: data/data/com.crypto.multiwallet/.

Figure 5 shows the locations and timestamps parsed from the SQLite database file StoreDatabase.db located at /databases/Journal/. The database file records user location information every 60 minutes.

Figure 6 shows that the cookie database located in the WebView directory /app_webview/ contains user browsing history. WebView is a significant component of the Android WebKit API. A cookie is a simple key-value data pair received from a website and stored by the web browser. Each cookie record is associated with a website URL. Therefore, the browsing history can be obtained by associating the URL with its last accessed timestamp. Since the content is designed by the website developer, it might contain other private data that enables the website to provide user-oriented services. For example, as shown in Figure 6, google.com saves the device's geo-data and country code in rows 12 and 36. By parsing geo-location information from the cookies, forensic practitioners can also track users.

Fig. 6. Visited URLs in app_webview/Cookies.db of com.crypto.multiwallet app.

Fig. 7. App ID data in `device_info.db` of com.crypto.multiwallet app.

Figure 7 shows that the `device_info.db` database located at /data/data/LocalStorage/ contains app ID data and timestamps. The app ID is the package name (unique Android app identifier) and the timestamp records the time that the app was last accessed. This information provides insights about the user's mobile device activity. Three apps stored data in the `device_info.db` database: TikTok (com.zhiliaoapp.musically), Snapchat (com.snapchat.android) and Outlook (com.microsoft.office.outlook).

5.3   Large-Scale Forensic Analysis Results

The large-scale forensic analysis focused on 253 real-world crypto wallet apps. The apps were collected from 46 app markets in the U.S. and abroad. The logging system was reset and the internal storage wiped before installing each app. Following app installation, the app was exercised for up to eight hours using the Monkey automated testing script. Next, the app was closed and forensic analyses of the log messages and extracted files were performed. Finally, the forensic artifacts pertaining to the app were published in a report.

The experiments revealed that 212 of the 253 crypto wallet apps stored evidentiary data in the logging system and/or the local filesystem. Sixty-seven of the 212 apps had user location information in their internal storage. One hundred and thirty-five apps periodically recorded device timestamps and stored them in the logging system or filesystem. Fifty-four apps recorded user SMS text messages and 124 apps recorded visited URLs and stored them in log messages or in the database. Especially interesting was that 37 apps stored other kinds of evidentiary data such as call logs and account information.

Table 2. Forensic analysis results for the 253 Android crypto wallet apps.

Evidence Type	Apps	Evidence File Paths	
		Static	Dynamic
Location	67	42	2
Time	135	97	12
Text Input	54	16	1
Visited URL	124	132	52
Other Evidentiary Data	122	40	7

Table 2 summarizes the forensic analysis results for each type of evidentiary data. Among the 17 types of extracted evidentiary data, time data is the most common and 49.6% of crypto wallet apps store this data in their local filesystems. File paths are characterized as dynamic if they include the patterns <timestamp>, <UUID>, <android version> or <intent>; otherwise, they are characterized as static. The results demonstrate that Android crypto wallet apps use static file paths more often (75.5%) than dynamic file paths (24.5%).

Table 3. Credit card information stored by the com.breadwallet app.

```
<string name = "6SHYZH": billingAddress: billingCity>
<string name = "6SHYZH": billingAddress: billingState>
<string name = "6SHYZH": billingAddress: billingCountry>
<string name = "6SHYZH": billingAddress: billingLine1>
<string name = "6SHYZH": billingAddress: billingLine2>
<string name = "6SHYZH": billingAddress: billingZipCode>
...
...
...
<string name = "08APZS": creditCard: shortDescription>
<string name = "08APZS": creditCard: last4>
<string name = "08APZS": creditCard: expirationDate>
<string name = "08APZS": creditCard: CVC>
```

The analysis also revealed that the com.breadwallet app stores credit card information in an XML document. The information includes the full billing address, credit card number, card verification number, issuing bank and expiration date; however, the cardholder's name was not recorded. Table 3 summarizes the credit card information stored by the com.breadwallet app.

The analysis also revealed that a local database file potentially stores credit card information. However, manual verification found that the database contained no records even when credit cards were added to the app for testing. It is possible that credit card data is kept in the cloud and only saved to the local database under conditions that were not met during the testing. More research is needed to determine the triggers that store credit card information in the local database.

It is challenging to evaluate the forensic analysis results for crypto wallet apps without the ground truth. As a result, best-effort manual verification was conducted. In the manual verification, 20 apps were randomly selected from the dataset. The apps were installed in turn on a real device and were exercised by Monkey, which generated pseudo-random streams of user events, such as clicks, touches and many system-level events. All the apps were tested for up to eight hours and all the files generated by the apps were examined manually. A total of 821 files created by the apps were discovered and forensic analysis revealed that 37 of them contained evidentiary data.

In the manual verification, a forensic analysis result was designated as a false positive if the file did not contain the type of evidentiary data reported. Taking Table 1 as an example, if the manual examination of file `shared_prefs` located at data/user/0/com.crypto.multiwallet/ did not contain timestamp evidence, the file was marked as a false positive. Similarly, if unreported evidentiary data was found in a file, then the file was marked as a false negative. The manual verification results revealed that the forensic analysis method yielded an average precision of 93% and average recall of 91% over all the types of evidentiary data.

Overall, the large-scale evaluation results demonstrate the effectiveness of the forensic analysis method on crypto wallet apps. Log messages and app filesystems are significant evidence containers and digital forensic practitioners can apply the forensic analysis method to find the evidence.

6   Related Work

This section discusses related work on forensic analysis of logging systems and taint analysis.

6.1   Logging System Analysis

While several research efforts have focused on the forensic analysis of Android apps, they largely ignore logging system analysis. Satrya et al. [22] have conducted live and offline forensic analyses of three popular social messenger apps, but they were unable to identify evidentiary data during live analysis compared with offline analysis. Baggili et al. [2] describe a forensic method for Android smartwatches that collects log messages of system events to extract evidence. However, unlike the automated method described in this chapter, they manually parsed and analyzed log messages.

Recent studies [14, 15, 17] mention the importance of considering Android logging systems in mobile device forensics by treating logging as an evidentiary data sink API. However, these studies did not perform logging system analyses or develop any analysis tools. A notable exception is the work by Cheng et al. [6], which developed LogExtractor, a tool that integrates fine-grained taint analysis with automaton-based string analysis to analyze complicated string-expression constructions such as `StringBuffer` and `Arrays.toString()` in Android log messages.

Two other approaches, OmegaLog [13] and UIScope [27], attempt to identify the root causes of Android events by analyzing and correlating log messages. UIScope discovers the root causes by monitoring and correlating user interaction events with system events. OmegaLog analyzes log message patterns offline by symbolically executing C/C++ binary programs and then adopts an online approach to identify the root causes from log message patterns.

6.2 Taint Analysis

Program analysis is applied heavily in forensic analyses of Android applications. Taint analysis is used to retrieve data flows between source APIs and sink APIs. If the logging system APIs are included in the sink list, taint analysis can determine whether a tainted variable is eventually written to a log message. Previous Android taint analysis efforts that cover information flows to logging systems include EviHunter [5], CHEX [19], FlowDroid [1], AmanDroid [26], IccTA [18] and DroidSafe [12]. These approaches provide coarse-grained answers on whether certain kinds of forensic artifacts are written to logging systems.

The EviHunter [5] static analysis tool leverages Soot [25] and FlowDroid [1] to construct call graphs and entry points and identify the types of sensitive data and file paths to which data is written. Flowdroid [1] is the first flow-sensitive taint analysis approach that considers the Android application life-cycle and user interface widgets. CHEX [19], which is built on top of Wala [9], first parses app code and constructs app-splits. Next, it creates a data flow summary for each app-split utilizing the Wala data flow engine to detect component hijacking on Android platforms. DroidSafe [12] models an Android framework and adopts a flow-insensitive points-to-analysis algorithm to handle all possible run-time event orderings.

7   Discussion

Bitcoin and other cryptocurrencies offer anonymizing features that are heavily used in illicit activities. The anonymity of cryptocurrency accounts has made them attractive to criminals on the dark web, the portion of the Internet accessible through special software that makes forensic analyses very challenging. Tracing illegal transactions, especially those associated with ransomware payments, requires anonymity breaches. The use of multiple wallets and Bitcoin further obfuscates the identification process. A Bitcoin mixer is a service that combines Bitcoin from different sources and separates them into multiple client wallets in exchange for a mixing fee. The proposed forensic analysis method for Android cryptocurrency wallet apps has the ability to detect such mixing services.

One limitation of the proposed forensic analysis method is the best-effort manual verification. A total of 253 real-world Android crypto wallet apps were used in the evaluation, but due to the effort involved, only 20 apps could be feasibly used to verify the results with ground truth. Also, only plaintext results could be verified. For example, when GPS coordinates are encrypted, hashed or encoded before being written to the logging system, their presence in log entries could not be determined and they were designated as false positives. Additionally, the manual verification may have under-approximated the false negative rate due to the best-effort approach employed. But of course, it was infeasible to achieve 100% code coverage of 253 Android apps.

8   Conclusions

This chapter has presented the results of a large-scale forensic investigation of evidence generated by 253 Android cryptocurrency wallet apps. The method involves application and framework analyses that examine evidentiary data located in app logging systems and filesystems. Location information, timestamps and other types of forensic artifacts are extracted from the cryptocurrency wallet apps. The manual verification of forensic analysis method yields an average precision of 93% and average recall of 91% over all the types of evidentiary data considered. The forensic analysis method is expected to be a valuable asset to digital forensic practitioners because cryptocurrency wallet apps are heavily used in illegal activities.

Acknowledgment This research was partially supported by the National Institute of Standards and Technology (NIST) CSAFE under Cooperative Agreement no. 70NANB20H019, by the National Science Foundation under Grant nos. CNS 1619201, CNS 1730275, DEB 1924178 and ECCS 2030249, and by the Boeing Company.

References

1. S. Arzt, S. Rasthofer, C. Fritz, E. Bodden, A. Bartel, J. Klein, Y. Le Traon, D. Octeau and P. McDaniel, FlowDroid: Precise context, flow, field, object-sensitive and lifecycle-aware taint analysis for Android apps, *ACM SIGPLAN Notices*, vol. 49(6), pp. 259–269, 2014.
2. I. Baggili, J. Oduro, K. Anthony, F. Breitinger and G. McGee, Watch what you wear: Preliminary forensic analysis of smart watches, *Proceedings of the Tenth International Conference on Availability, Reliability and Security*, pp. 303–311, 2015.
3. bitcoinj, A library for working with Bitcoin, GitHub (github.com/bitcoinj/bitcoinj), 2023.

4. S. Calzavara, I. Grishchenko and M. Maffei, HornDroid: Practical and sound static analysis of Android applications by SMT solving, *Proceedings of the IEEE European Symposium on Security and Privacy*, pp. 47–62, 2016.

5. C. Cheng, C. Shi, N. Gong and Y. Guan, EviHunter: Identifying digital evidence in the permanent storage of Android devices via static analysis, *Proceedings of the ACM SIGSAC Conference on Computer and Communications Security*, pp. 1338–1350, 2018.

6. C. Cheng, C. Shi, N. Gong and Y. Guan, LogExtractor: Extracting digital evidence from Android log messages via string and taint analysis, *Forensic Science International: Digital Investigation*, vol. 37, article no. 301193, 2021.

7. Cision, Mobile wallet market share is projected to reach USD 750.3 billion by 2028: Zion Market Research, Chicago, Illinois (`www.prnewswire.com/news-releases/mobile-wallet-market-share-is-projected-to-reach-usd-750-3-billion-by-2028-zion-market-research-301477413.html`), February 8, 2022.

8. FinancesOnline, Number of blockchain wallet users 2022/2023: Breakdowns, timelines and predictions, Boston, Massachusetts (`financesonline.com/number-of-blockchain-wallet-users/#:~:text=As%20of%20February%202021%2C%20there a%20%24928.50%20billion%20market%20cap`), 2021.

9. S. Fink, J. Dolby and F. Tip, Wala – Static Analysis Capabilities for Java Bytecode and Related Languages, IBM Research, Yorktown Heights, New York (`researcher.watson.ibm.com/researcher/view_page.php?id=7238`), 2012.

10. Gartner, Gartner Annual Worldwide PC, Mobile Device Market Share Report, 2013, Stamford, Connecticut, 2014.

11. Google Developers, UI/Application Exerciser Monkey, Mountain View, California (`developer.android.com/studio/test/other-testing-tools/monkey`), 2022.

12. M. Gordon, D. Kim, J. Perkins, L. Gilham, N. Nguyen and M. Rinard, Information flow analysis of Android applications in DroidSafe, *Proceedings of the Twenty-Second Annual Network and Distributed System Security Symposium*, 2015.

13. W. Hassanand, M. Noureddine, P. Datta and A. Bates, OmegaLog: High-fidelity attack investigation via transparent multi-layer log analysis, *Proceedings of the Twenty-Seventh Annual Network and Distributed System Security Symposium*, 2020.

14. N. Htun and M. Thwin, Proposed workable process flow with analysis framework for Android forensics in cyber-crime investigations, *International Journal of Engineering and Science*, vol. 6(1), pp. 82–92, 2017.

15. N. Htun, M. Thwin and C. San, Evidence data collection with ANDROSICS tool for Android forensics, *Proceedings of the Tenth International Conference on Information Technology and Electrical Engineering*, pp. 353–358, 2018.

16. Y. Hu, S. Wang, G. Tu, L. Xiao, T. Xie, X. Lei and C. Li, Security threats from Bitcoin wallet smartphone applications: Vulnerabilities, attacks and countermeasures, *Proceedings of the Eleventh ACM Conference on Data and Application Security and Privacy*, pp. 89–100, 2021.

17. P. Khandelwal, D. Sahu and D. Tomar, Scrutinizing evidence in Android phones, *International Journal of Computer Science and Information Technology*, vol. 5(2), pp. 2528–2533, 2014.

18. L. Li, A. Bartel, T. Bissyande, J. Klein, Y. Le Traon, S. Arzt, S. Rasthofer, E. Bodden, D. Octeau and P. McDaniel, IccTA: Detecting inter-component privacy leaks in Android apps, *Proceedings of the Thirty-Seventh IEEE/ACM International Conference on Software Engineering*, pp. 280–291, 2015.

19. L. Lu, Z. Li, Z. Wu, W. Lee and G. Jiang, CHEX: Statically vetting Android apps for component hijacking vulnerabilities, *Proceedings of the ACM Conference on Computer and Communications Security*, pp. 229–240, 2012.

20. M. Mirza, A. Ozer and U. Karabiyik, Mobile cyber forensic investigations of Web3 wallets on Android and iOS, *Applied Sciences*, vol. 12(21), article no. 11180, 2022.

21. OfflineModAPK, SRSRoot Apk latest 2022 for Android SRSRoot (`offlinemodapk.com/srsroot-apk`), March 27, 2022.

22. G. Satrya, P. Daely and S. Shin, Android forensics analysis: Private chat on social messenger, *Proceedings of the Eighth International Conference on Ubiquitous and Future Networks*, pp. 430–435, 2016.

23. C. Shi, C. Cheng and Y. Guan, LibDroid: Summarizing information flow of Android native libraries via static analysis, *Forensic Science International: Digital Investigation*, vol. 42(S), article no. 301405, 2022.

24. Statista, Number of Bitcoin block explorer Blockchain.com wallet users worldwide from November 2011 to November 17, 2022, Hamburg, Germany (`www.statista.com/statistics/647374/worldwide-blockchain-wallet-users`), March 8, 2023.

25. R. Vallee-Rai, P. Co, E. Gagnon, L. Hendren, P. Lam and V. Sundaresan, Soot – A Java bytecode optimization framework, *Proceedings of the Conference of the Centre for Advanced Studies on Collaborative Research*, 1999.

26. F. Wei, S. Roy, X. Ou and Robby, Amandroid: A precise and general inter-component data flow analysis framework for security vetting of Android apps, *ACM Transactions on Privacy and Security*, vol. 21(3), article no. 14, 2018.

27. R. Yang, S. Ma, H. Xu, X. Zhang and Y. Chen, UIScope: Accurate, instrumentation-free and visible attack investigation for GUI applications, *Proceedings of the Twenty-Seventh Annual Network and Distributed System Security Symposium*, 2020.

28. M. Young, 13 apps removed after researchers uncover Trojan crypto wallet scheme, *Cointelegraph*, New York (`cointelegraph.com/news/13-apps-removed-after-researchers-uncover-trojan-crypto-wallet-scheme`), March 30, 2022.

An Anti-Fuzzing Approach for Android Apps

Chris Chao-Chun Cheng, Li Lin, Chen Shi, and Yong Guan

Iowa State University, Ames, Iowa, USA
guan@iastate.edu

Abstract. Extracting evidence pertaining to mobile apps is a key task in mobile device forensics. Since mobile apps can generate more than 19,000 files on a single device, it is time consuming and error prone to manually inspect all the files. Fuzzing tools that programmatically produce interactions with mobile apps are helpful when paired with sandbox environments to study their runtime forensic behavior and summarize patterns of evidentiary data in forensic investigations. However, the ability of fuzzing tools to improve the efficiency of mobile app forensic analyses has not been investigated.

This chapter describes AFuzzShield, an Android app shield that protects apps from being exercised by fuzzers. By analyzing the runtime information of mobile app interaction traces, AFuzzShield prevents real-world apps from being exercised by fuzzers and minimizes the overhead on human usage. A statistical model is employed to distinguish between fuzzer and human patterns; this eliminates the need to perform graphical user interface injections and ensures compatibility with apps with touchable/clickable graphical user interfaces. AFuzzShield verifies mobile app program coverage in situations where apps engage anti-fuzzing technologies. Specifically, it was applied to apps in AndroTest, a popular benchmark app dataset for testing fuzzers. The experimental results demonstrate that applying AFuzzShield significantly impacts mobile app program coverage in terms of reduced evidentiary data patterns.

Keywords: Android Apps · Evidentiary Data · Forensic Analysis · Anti-Fuzzing

1 Introduction

As of March 2023, around 2.67 million Android apps were available to the public [31]. Whereas a manual examination by a forensic practitioner can cover most usage scenarios of an individual app to understand the evidentiary data generated at runtime, the manual approach does not scale to handle the thousands of files generated by the numerous apps residing on a typical mobile device [5]. Automated fuzzing tools that programmatically generate interactions with Android apps provide an alternative. In fact, Android app fuzzers have been applied in security/privacy leakage analyses [12, 33] as well as in forensic analyses [38].

Android app fuzzers are categorized according to how they generate interaction events, namely, random-based [13, 22, 40], model-based [1, 3, 6, 16, 39] and

© IFIP International Federation for Information Processing 2023
Published by Springer Nature Switzerland AG 2023
G. Peterson and S. Shenoi (Eds.): DigitalForensics 2023, IFIP AICT 687, pp. 37–53, 2023.
https://doi.org/10.1007/978-3-031-42991-0_3

systematic [2, 3, 5, 23, 34]. Their common goal is to improve app code coverage in a limited time frame. However, while these fuzzers provide key insights on driving and running apps efficiently, they can be leveraged to discover app vulnerabilities and launch the corresponding attacks. To combat abuses, researchers have proposed anti-analysis techniques for Android devices [10, 17, 24, 26, 35]. The general idea is to perform software checks on certain system parameters to detect the sandbox environments in which fuzzers and dynamic analyzers are usually deployed. But the anti-analysis techniques can be disabled by automatically removing the conditional statements that check system parameters to detect sandbox environments [28].

At this time, no study has systematically analyzed how anti-fuzzing techniques impact the mobile app program coverage achieved by fuzzers. As a result, it is not possible to assess the reliability of using fuzzers to generate mobile app evidentiary data patterns in sandbox environments. Diao et al. [10] detect programming patterns in order to block the use of fuzzing tools. However, their approach, which is implemented and evaluated only for a proof-of-concept app, may hinder app functions by overlapping with the original graphical user interface (GUI) layouts, reducing its value as a real-world anti-fuzzing solution. Fuzzification [18], an anti-fuzzing tool, is preferred by developers. It profiles the frequencies of program paths visited by fuzzers and injects timing delays in less-frequently-used program paths to slow down the program while minimizing the impacts to normal use. However, due to Fuzzification's distinct environment, user behaviors and Linux command-line interface, it is unable to analyze the impacts of adopting Android app anti-fuzzing approaches to hinder forensic analyses.

An Android app anti-fuzzing technique must meet two requirements. First, it should introduce minimal overhead to real-world app users without inducing app malfunctions. Second, it should hinder fuzzers from exercising apps when they are triggered. Due to the lack of tools that meet these requirements, this research has developed AFuzzShield, an app shield that protects apps from being exercised by fuzzers. AFuzzShield is employed to analyze the reliability of Android app fuzzers that could be leveraged by forensic practitioners to generate evidentiary data patterns of mobile apps. AFuzzShield dynamically collects usage patterns such as clicks and swipes, and determines if the interaction events are triggered by human users or fuzzers. By injecting timing delays into app programs when fuzzer patterns are identified, AFuzzShield hinders fuzzer testing and prevents fuzzers from exercising apps. AFuzzShield also has the ability to profile fuzzer usage based entirely on runtime information. Since sandbox detection is unreliable and overwriting a GUI may negatively impact the original app functions, runtime pattern identification is more stable and less likely to crash the app.

This chapter presents several programming patterns for identifying existing fuzzers and demonstrates how the patterns are exploited in anti-fuzzing solutions. Experimental results involving more than 68 real-world apps in AndroTest [41] demonstrate that evidentiary data extraction from mobile apps using fuzzers is not reliable because fuzzing can be detected and mitigated.

2   Android App Fuzzing

Fuzzing is a software testing technique that automatically generates and injects inputs into software, helping detect vulnerabilities in tested programs more efficiently than human testers. Fuzzing tools that programmatically produce interactions with mobile apps such as tapping and swiping are useful when paired with sandbox environments to study their runtime forensic behavior and summarize patterns of evidentiary data. Android app fuzzers such as TaintDroid [12] and others [33, 38] have been used very effectively for dynamic program analysis, including generating evidentiary data and determining app vulnerabilities.

Android app fuzzers are categorized according to how they generate user interaction events. Random-based fuzzers [13, 22, 40] cover as many program branches as possible by randomly generating input events that trigger the app functions being called. Monkey [13], a fully-automated random-based fuzzer, randomly generates user interaction events such as swipes and clicks according to the configured probabilities, pushes them into the event queue and executes them as required.

Model-based fuzzers, unlike random-based fuzzers, require knowledge of runtime user interaction events that prevents them from generating redundant input events. During app runtime, a model-based fuzzer constructs GUI models by parsing the runtime information into a user interaction hierarchy that enables the fuzzer to employ a path finding algorithm to produce maximum code coverage with minimal inputs.

Systematic fuzzers typically instrument apps under test using program analysis techniques. By thoroughly analyzing the input events required to cover portions of an app program, a systematic fuzzer gains complete knowledge about the appropriate events needed for app testing. For example, after instrumenting an app, when certain activity transitions require a user to click a button twice, a systematic fuzzer can do so without attempting other useless combinations of inputs.

3   Methodology

AFuzzShield is a pattern-based anti-fuzzing solution. Unlike other approaches that extract system characteristics to detect sandbox environments [10, 17, 24, 26, 35] or modify the original GUI layouts of apps [10], AFuzzShield identifies fuzzers using their programming patterns. This section describes the AFuzzShield design framework, discusses the pattern differences between fuzzers and human users, and presents the AFuzzShield anti-fuzzing solution.

3.1   AFuzzShield Overview

Figure 1 presents an overview of AFuzzShield. AFuzzShield is designed as a third-party library for use in app development, where users instrument AFuzzShield

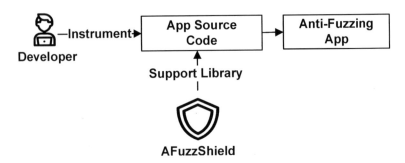

Fig. 1. AFuzzShield overview.

APIs in their implemented GUI callback methods. During app execution, AFuzzShield monitors the interaction traces and dynamically-adjusted pattern-based timing delays that correlate with the likelihood of fuzzer usage. This reduces the app code coverage using the same amount of time as when the app is exercised by fuzzers.

3.2 App Fuzzer Patterns

This section discusses the patterns of Monkey and other fuzzers.

Monkey Monkey [13] is a popular random-based, open-source fuzzer with fingerprinting features. Investigation of Monkey's source code revealed that its click and swipe event implementations are adequate to identify Monkey. Since clicks and swipes are fundamental GUI object operations, simply excluding them in Monkey's options results in significant coverage loss during software testing. Therefore, AFuzzShield can exploit the click and swipe patterns of Monkey to detect the use of fuzzers.

Three utility methods enable Monkey to implement randomness on top of uniform distributions:

- **randomPoint:** This method returns coordinates (x, y) where x is picked randomly from zero to the device width and y is picked randomly from zero to the device height.
- **randomVector:** This method returns a set of random values in the range –25 to 25 pixels.
- **randomWalk:** This method, upon being given a set of coordinates (x, y), randomly modifies their values in the range –25 to 25, but casts the results within the boundaries of the device display.

The three utility methods yield the following patterns for click and swipe events:

- **Click**: A click event comprises two consecutive touch events. The first touch event receives coordinates from `randomPoint` and the second touch event receives coordinates from `randomWalk` applied to the first set of coordinates.

– **Swipe**: A swipe event is extended from a click event by randomly adding one to nine movements between the first and second touch events of the click event. Each movement is the result of calling `randomWalk` with the previous set of coordinates, i.e., it moves randomly –25 to 25 pixels along the x and y axes, respectively.

The stability of the click and swipe events in fuzz testing enables AFuzzShield to use them as programming patterns that identify Monkey.

Other Fuzzers A stable feature of Android fuzzing tools is the set of coordinates corresponding to their generated click events. Specifically, investigations revealed that all existing open-source fuzzers [1–3, 6, 7, 11, 14, 16, 20, 22, 32] click the centers of GUI objects regardless of their exploration strategies.

Consider, for example, A3E [3], which relies on Robotium [29] to interact with an app being tested. When A3E picks an exploration strategy, it instructs Robotium to click the target GUI object. Robotium then computes the center of the target object on the screen and clicks the target. When computing the centers of odd lengths, some fuzzers like Robotium that do not round values yield different center coordinates from fuzzers that round values. To address the different implementations when one side of a GUI object has an even length, AFuzzShield picks the nearest point with an integer value as the center.

It is surprising that fuzzers have such explicit artificial patterns. The likely reason is that they click the centers of objects to avoid clicking the wrong targets when the object sizes are small. One exception is APE [14], which enables users to choose between Monkey's strategy or clicking the centers of objects using its designed strategy. However, this exception does not impact AFuzzShield because it considers both patterns.

3.3   Real-World Human Patterns

This research employed the Rico [9] dataset to identify the differences between fuzzer and human patterns in user interactions. The Rico dataset contains more than 9,300 app GUI layouts and human interaction traces generated by 11 real users. The human interaction traces include 52,456 effective click event coordinates and 13,377 swipe event traces.

Human patterns were learned by mapping click and swipe event coordinates to the corresponding topmost GUI object and normalizing the coordinates by transforming them linearly to a standard 2×2 square. Interestingly, the heatmap in Figure 2 reveals that the hottest area with the most click events is not near the center of a button. Clearly, human patterns do not follow common normal or uniform distributions. In fact, Figure 3 shows that, even when the two-dimensional plot is reduced to a one-dimensional plot for each coordinate, the normalized human clicking data does not have a clear bell shape. This means that very special human click patterns must be considered to combat fuzzing tools.

The swipe events generated by Monkey contained no more than nine consecutive movements and the scale of movement in any direction was bound by

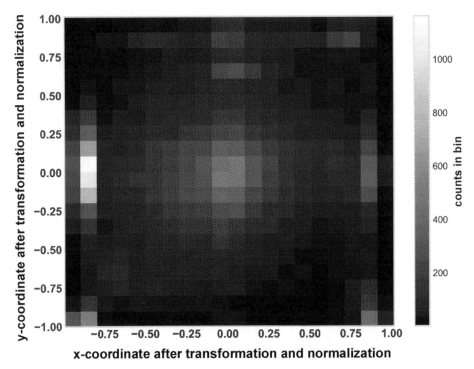

Fig. 2. Heatmap distributions of normalized human click coordinates on buttons.

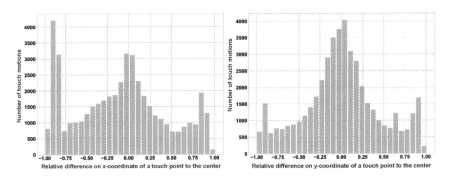

Fig. 3. Normalized click coordinate histograms (left: x-axis, right: y-axis).

25 pixels. However, only 56.67% of the Rico dataset traces were determined to have less than ten movements. Additionally, among the 373,635 movements in 13,377 real-world swipe events, just 55,187 (14.77%) along the x-axis or y-axis were determined to have scales larger than 25 pixels. Since the Rico dataset

contains such large numbers of outliers from Monkey's model, it is reasonable to designate outlier swipe events as being produced by human users.

3.4   Differentiating Fuzzer and Human Patterns

All the model-based fuzzers investigated clicked the exact centers of buttons in the interaction traces, which were explicitly different from human interaction patterns. In the Rico dataset, only eight out of thousands of human click events touched the button centers. Even when the ranges were extended to two pixels from the centers, the amount of human click events was less than 300. In fact, the probability of a human user touching the center of a GUI object is less than $300/46,694 = 0.6\%$ and the probability of a human user touching the center n times is $(\frac{0.6}{100})^n$, which is extremely small when $n \geq 3$. Therefore, if the center of a button is clicked consecutively more than three times, it is safe to assume that the events were created by a fuzzer instead of a human user.

Based on the Monkey patterns discussed above, human patterns can be distinguished from Monkey patterns using the Chi-square test to test the independence of click regions from click event data. The Chi-square test is selected because the Rico data indicates a human preference or bias towards click regions whereas Monkey views all click regions the same.

After experiments and analysis, it was decided to divide an entire normalized button GUI into three regions with equivalent rectangle areas and compare the difference between the expected frequency to the observed frequency in order to set up a hypothesis for testing. Specifically, the null hypothesis H_0 is that the events are produced by the Monkey fuzzer in that the click data has a uniform distribution on the two-dimensional plane. The alternative hypothesis H_1 is that the data does not have a uniform distribution.

For all the GUIs in a single app, if there are n touches, the theoretical frequency for a partition is $\frac{n}{3}$. Let k_1, k_2 and k_3 be the numbers of touches in the three regions. Then, under the null hypothesis H_0, if the statistic:

$$V = \frac{3}{n} \sum_{i=1}^{3} (k_i - \frac{n}{3})^2$$

is viewed as a random variable v, then v follows a Chi-square distribution with a degree of freedom of two (i.e., $v \sim \chi_2^2$). The corresponding p-value for this hypothesis test is computed as:

$$p = Prob(v \geq V)$$

where v has a χ_2^2 distribution. It is well known that p-values weight evidence against the null hypothesis. Therefore, the smaller the p-value, the stronger the evidence to reject H_0.

4   Evaluation

AFuzzShield was evaluated in a virtual machine environment created by AndroTest [41], a widely-adapted sandbox with 68 open-source real-world apps for experimenting with Android app fuzzers [5, 11, 20, 25, 32]. Attempts made to debug and fix AndroTest's scripts for PUMA [16], A3E [3], Dynodroid [22], ACTEve [2] and GUIRipper [1] (PADAG) were successful. However, it was not possible to fix and run the script for SwiftHand [6].

The deployment of AFuzzShield required the manual identification and instrumentation of 632 user interaction callback methods in millions of lines of app code, after which the output Android Package Kit (APK) file was built. The impacts of real-world human user experiences were evaluated using the public Rico dataset [9]. Simulations were employed to evaluate AFuzzShield performance against human users, who received minimal impacts. Monkey and PADAG were executed on the original apps as well as on the apps with AFuzzShield deployed. Each fuzzer was executed for an hour and the line coverage results were collected using EMMA [30] every five minutes. Note that AndroTest employs a one-hour experiment time and five-minute data collection intervals. The same parameters were used to consistently reproduce the experimental environment.

4.1   Real-World App Performance

This section discusses the performance of AFuzzShield on real-world apps with human users and with Monkey and other fuzzers.

Human User Evaluation While it would be best to employ human user click coordinates on the evaluated apps, difficulty in obtaining institutional review board approval for human subjects during the research window forced the use of data from the Rico dataset. Therefore, the statistics discussed above were applied to random samples from the Rico dataset of sizes 18, 24, 30, 60 and 90 with 100 times random experiments without replacements, following which the p-values were computed.

Table 1 summarizes the Chi-square test results for the Rico data where, by convention, the significance level threshold for rejecting H_0 is set to $p \leq 0.05$. Note that identification using the p-values of the Chi-square test with more than 60 click events yields a low false negative rate (FNR), i.e., the error rate of misclassifying human users as Monkey. However, in practice, many more click events are required to achieve sufficient power for a significance level of 0.05. Therefore, to enhance classifier performance in real-world scenarios, especially those with lower numbers of clicks, a much larger p-value, such as $p < 0.1$, would indicate that the events are more likely to have been created by a fuzzing program.

Although the larger number of click events improves the false negative rate, it deteriorates fuzzer performance as more program paths are covered. Based on the evaluation results, in order to balance user experience while protecting apps from being exercised by fuzzers, a three-stage timing delay was injected into each app source function similar to the Fuzzification approach [18] of hindering fuzzers. Specifically, the runtime number of click event thresholds N_0, N_1, N_2 of 24, 30, 60, respectively, and P_0, P_1, P_2 of 0.05, 0.05, 0.1, respectively, were

Table 1. Performance of the Chi-square test as a classifier of human clicks.

Humans Clicks	FNR (Reject if $p < 0.05$)	FNR (Reject if $p < 0.1$)	Max p-Value
18	58%	40%	0.1573
24	38%	26%	0.1024
30	25%	20%	0.7400
60	2%	0%	0.1572
90	0%	0%	0.0160

applied in the three-stage timing delays. When N_i event data was collected, the computed p-value was compared against P_i to determine whether the injected timing delay should be updated. In the evaluation, timing delays of $T_0 = 0.2\,$s, $T_1 = 1\,$s and $T_2 = T_{max} = 5\,$s were employed for the three stages.

Existing Fuzzer Evaluation The experiments for evaluating AFuzzShield performance with existing fuzzers was designed based on their runtime patterns. The evaluation covered a random-based fuzzer (Monkey) and model-based fuzzers (PADAG). In addition to PADAG, open-source code of the other fuzzers was examined to confirm that they shared the same programming patterns observed in PADAG.

- **Monkey Evaluation:** A preliminary test was performed for one hour to obtain background knowledge about how much runtime information AFuzzShield obtained when deploying Monkey on an app. Because AFuzzShield relies only on app runtime information to evade fuzzer performance and the statistical model requires the number of click events to be higher than 60, apps that could not satisfy the requirement were filtered from the Monkey evaluation. For the remaining apps, line coverages upon running Monkey on them with and without AFuzzShield were compared in the evaluation.

  Table 2 shows the aforementioned preliminary results and results with AFuzzShield for 20 real-world apps. Note that Inst. denotes the number of instrumented user interfaces, Recv. denotes the number of events received per hour, LC_0 denotes the line coverage without AFuzzShield, LC_A denotes the line coverage with AFuzzShield, Delta denotes the absolute change of line coverage and R. Delta denotes the relative reduced line coverage.

  The results reveal that AFuzzShield effectively evades the performance of Monkey for 14 of the 20 real-world apps (highlighted in the table) and the best case demonstrates a reduction of line coverage from 59.85% to 43.41%. Although three apps have zero evasion and three apps have slightly elevated line coverages, AFuzzShield still protects most of the apps from being exercised by Monkey.

  Upon parsing the evaluation results, it was discovered that the more complex the app design, such as the number of user interface buttons, the more likely

Table 2. Monkey evaluation results.

App	Inst.	Recv.	LC_0	LC_A	Delta	R. Delta
A2DP Volume	17	158	42.44%	39.92%	**2.52%**	**5.94%**
AnyMemo	82	133	26.39%	22.56%	**3.83%**	**14.51%**
Baterrydog	5	107	62.47%	62.47%	0.00%	0.00%
BookCatalogue	68	147	33.39%	27.69%	**5.70%**	**17.07%**
Battery Circle	6	176	72.99%	73.92%	–0.93%	–1.27%
Alarm Clock	9	140	71.14%	66.97%	**4.16%**	**5.85%**
aCal	44	77	21.84%	16.15%	**5.69%**	**26.05%**
Yahtzee	8	64	59.97%	52.23%	**7.74%**	**12.91%**
CountdownTimer	4	198	71.14%	75.85%	–4.71%	–6.62%
Dialer2	15	546	37.71%	34.86%	**2.86%**	**7.58%**
MunchLife	4	215	72.45%	72.45%	0.00%	0.00%
MyExpenses	19	188	47.96%	40.52%	**7.44%**	**15.51%**
LearnMusicNotes	8	537	59.85%	43.41%	**16.44%**	**27.47%**
passwordmanager	17	123	9.00%	8.22%	**0.78%**	**8.67%**
RandomMusicPlay	6	347	78.19%	77.72%	**0.48%**	**0.61%**
SoundBoard	2	82	46.81%	46.81%	0.00%	0.00%
SyncMyPix	15	125	21.57%	21.87%	–0.30%	–1.39%
TippyTipper	20	64	82.05%	79.01%	**3.04%**	**3.71%**
WeightChart	3	127	52.52%	51.11%	**1.41%**	**2.68%**
WhoHasMyStuff	8	111	74.13%	69.43%	**4.71%**	**6.35%**

that anti-fuzzing techniques reduce app program coverage, contributing to the reduced reliability of Android app fuzzers in generating evidentiary data. Since AFuzzShield requires runtime data to determine whether or not operations are due to fuzzers, if an app is designed in a straightforward manner and has very few branches or event handlers to be triggered, it is highly likely that fuzzers would have explored many programs in the app before being effectively evaded by AFuzzShield. For example, Table 2 shows that apps receiving non-positive impacts from AFuzzShield have only six instrumented GUI objects on average compared with apps effectively protected by AFuzzShield that have more than 20 instrumented GUI objects on average.

- **Other Fuzzer Evaluation:** PADAG was deployed on over 68 apps from AndroTest with and without AFuzzShield during the performance evaluation. Tables 3 and 4 show the PADAG evaluation results – the highlighted results indicate exercising apps for which fuzzers were detected successfully by AFuzzShield. Note that no available GUI objects to monitor were discovered in 19 out of 68 apps, 22 apps with clickable GUIs received no click events and three apps crashed after launching. These app evaluation results were classified as ineffective because AFuzzShield exhibited limitations in applying its knowledge to protect the apps from fuzzing.

The results in Tables 3 and 4 reveal that, in the best case, AFuzzShield reduced 35.33% of app code coverage on average, down from the original

Table 3. PADAG evaluation results.

App Name	Inst.	LoS	LC_0	LC_A	Delta	R. Delta
aCal	44	45,161	9.62%	4.08%	**5.55%**	**57.69%**
Manpages	1	385	43.39%	48.85%	−5.47%	−12.61%
Wordpress	42	10,100	2.30%	1.45%	**0.85%**	**36.96%**
Translate	3	799	25.10%	20.35%	**4.74%**	**18.88%**
LearnMusicNotes	8	1,114	23.38%	17.60%	**5.79%**	**24.76%**
Jamendo	12	4,430	6.13%	6.12%	**0.01%**	**0.16%**
TippyTipper	20	2,623	31.33%	10.21%	**21.12%**	**67.41%**
SyncMyPix	15	10,431	9.91%	5.58%	**4.34%**	**43.79%**
BookCatalogue	68	27,235	3.64%	3.87%	−0.22%	−6.04%
AnyMemo	82	25,824	5.79%	4.81%	**0.98%**	**16.93%**
Dialer2	15	2,057	27.78%	21.74%	**6.05%**	**21.78%**
Divide&Conquer	2	814	42.25%	37.46%	**4.79%**	**11.34%**
QuickSettings	2	2,934	22.35%	23.65%	−1.29%	−5.77%
AndroidomaticK	6	1,307	24.89%	18.18%	**6.72%**	**27.00%**
K-9Mail	41	22,208	3.92%	3.97%	−0.05%	−1.28%
Blokish	1	93	29.54%	29.71%	−0.17%	−0.58%
MyExpenses	19	8,058	21.08%	16.36%	**4.72%**	**22.39%**
A2DP Volume	17	7,040	17.17%	10.27%	**6.90%**	**40.19%**
AardDictionary	4	2,197	14.67%	9.13%	**5.53%**	**37.70%**
RandomMusicPlay	6	1,053	32.88%	21.39%	**11.48%**	**34.91%**
Multi SNS	9	828	24.60%	9.68%	**14.92%**	**60.65%**
Ringdroid	6	2,928	4.12%	4.04%	**0.08%**	**1.94%**
Yahtzee	8	1,349	19.19%	5.95%	**13.24%**	**68.99%**
Baterrydog	5	985	20.51%	9.64%	**10.87%**	**53.00%**
SoundBoard	2	99	30.75%	26.62%	**4.13%**	**13.43%**
Nectroid	5	2,536	24.35%	20.85%	**3.49%**	**14.33%**
Alarm Clock	9	5,765	22.59%	19.95%	**2.64%**	**11.69%**
HotDeath	8	3,902	11.12%	9.42%	**1.70%**	**15.29%**
World Clock	4	1,242	53.03%	17.69%	**35.33%**	**66.62%**
AnyCut	3	436	29.50%	29.67%	−0.17%	−0.58%
MunchLife	4	506	39.80%	30.02%	**9.78%**	**24.57%**
aGrep	6	928	2.88%	11.16%	−8.28%	−287.5%
Mileage	13	4,628	12.88%	11.74%	**1.13%**	**8.77%**
LolcatBuilder	5	646	13.74%	11.16%	**2.58%**	**18.78%**
ImportContacts	2	1139	19.84%	16.43%	**3.41%**	**17.16%**
Battery Circle	6	739	46.51%	44.43%	**2.09%**	**4.49%**
WhoHasMyStuff	8	1,555	37.78%	30.29%	**7.48%**	**19.80%**
Photostream	4	1,375	10.26%	9.83%	**0.43%**	**4.19%**
SpriteMethodTest	1	1,018	15.14%	14.76%	**0.38%**	**2.51%**
PasswordMakerPro	4	1,535	25.17%	17.09%	**8.09%**	**53.33%**
myLock	3	885	17.21%	17.95%	−0.74%	−4.30%
aagtl	4	11,724	8.36%	8.01%	**0.35%**	**4.19%**

Table 4. PADAG evaluation results (continued).

App Name	Inst.	LoS	LC_0	LC_A	Delta	R. Delta
FileExplorer	1	126	35.59%	37.58%	−2.00%	−5.62%
LockPatternGen	2	669	37.09%	29.42%	**7.66%**	**20.65%**
CountdownTimer	4	1,415	43.90%	19.80%	**24.09%**	**54.87%**
HNDroid	1	1,038	5.22%	5.17%	**0.05%**	**0.96%**
WeightChart	3	23,67	18.92%	18.05%	**0.87%**	**4.60%**
MiniNoteViewer	21	3,673	11.49%	2.29%	**9.20%**	**80.07%**
passwordmanager	17	38,104	3.46%	0.70%	**2.76%**	**79.77%**

fuzzing result of 53.03%. More than half of the apps were effectively protected by AFuzzShield from being exercised by PADAG. While AFuzzShield effectively protects most apps, there are four instances where app fuzzing results became slightly better when AFuzzShield was deployed. Investigations of the results revealed the reason for the anomaly. Specifically, Dynodroid and GuiRipper restarted the Android emulator after running each trace and erased AFuzzShield intermediate data (i.e., logging traces and accumulated statistics) stored on the SD card. AFuzzShield's re-monitoring and re-computing the patterns contributed to the performance deterioration.

4.2 Discussion

While AFuzzShield enables analyses of the reliability of Android app fuzzers in generating app evidentiary data at runtime, certain technical limitations exist in the underlying technique. First, AFuzzShield performance depends on the original GUI layout design. If an app GUI layout is too simple and does not have enough GUI elements that can help AFuzzShield monitor runtime interaction patterns, AFuzzShield cannot effectively reduce fuzzer performance. Second, AFuzzShield does not consider situations where the entire device storage is frequently restored during runtime, resulting in performance deterioration. To address this issue, future research will attempt to force AFuzzShield to sync with a network to permanently store runtime data.

Another limitation comes from the best-effort matching of apps and human data in the evaluations. Without an appropriate dataset containing real-world apps with source code and corresponding human user interaction traces, it was possible only to derive the statistic model from Rico's relative interaction user interface data and apply the model to the AndroTest apps. This limitation could be addressed if the apps used to create the Rico dataset were open-source to support AFuzzShield deployment or data pertaining to human user traces could be collected for AndroTest apps.

5   Related Work

Conventional Android app testing is event-driven and GUI-based, which is different from the scope of this research. Therefore, the related work discussion focuses on Android app fuzzing techniques.

5.1   Android App Fuzzing Techniques

AndroTest [41] compares and summarizes existing Android fuzzing studies prior to 2016. Fuzzers are categorized into three groups by their exploration strategies, random-based [13, 22, 40], model-based [1, 3, 6, 16, 39] and systematic [2, 3, 5, 23, 34]. Even fuzzers with similar exploration strategies have their own minimization algorithms that reduce running time while maximizing code coverage. Sapienz [25] stands out from other fuzzers in that it combines the three exploration strategies and proposes to exploit a genetic algorithm to minimize test sequences. DetReduce [7] incorporates a minimization algorithm that reduces the Android GUI testing suites generated by existing fuzzers. APE [14] creates its initial GUI model using runtime information that produces finer granularity models than Stoat [32]. TimeMachine [11], which outperforms Sapienz and Stoat, records and explores GUI state via virtual machine snapshots instead of the traditional GUI models. In order to improve fuzzing performance, VET [37] attempts to detect and drive fuzzer user interaction automation to avoid tarpits such as looping in login and cancel buttons. In contrast, TOLLER [36] extracts user interaction information by accessing app runtime memory instead of depending on Android system services.

5.2   Android App Anti-Analysis Techniques

Existing anti-analysis techniques do not specifically protect Android apps from fuzzers; instead, they generally attempt to evade program analysis tools deployed on Android apps. Lim et al. [21] divide anti-analysis techniques as static or dynamic. Static approaches include obfuscation [15], repacking app code [19] and verifying the integrity of executable files [4]. While static approaches are designed to protect apps at the code level, dynamic techniques focus on detecting sandbox environments (e.g. Android emulators) on which most fuzzers depend. Specifically, dynamic approaches fingerprint the data patterns of sandbox artifacts and match them at runtime. Most approaches [10, 17, 24, 26, 35] distinguish sandbox environments by checking device identifiers. Other characteristics include the cumulative distribution function of intervals between sensor events [26], system file content [17], consistent Android versions [24], frames per second [35] and swiping trajectories [10].

The work of Diao et al. [10] is the closest to AFuzzShield. It leverages several interesting ideas beyond system profiling, including swiping trajectories, phishing activity and invisible user interaction traps, to distinguish human users from fuzzers. However, some of these ideas are difficult to implement with real-world apps because they require sufficient user data such as swiping trajectories or they may introduce malfunctions in the original apps due to invisible user interactions. A key difference between the work of Diao and colleagues and AFuzzShield is the targeting and evaluation scales that are unique to AFuzzShield. Additionally, AFuzzShield is actually implemented on real-world apps and evaluated against existing Android app fuzzers.

Costamagna et al. [8] determine sandbox environments via usage profiles such as contact list information and installed apps instead of system profiles. However, usage profiles in a sandbox environment are usually empty or are constructed randomly, which are distinct from user device profiles. To address these issues in dynamic approaches, Harvester [28] automatically replaces every conditional constraint related to system characteristics with a Boolean value controlled by the user space and, therefore, covers the protected program statements. AFuzzShield stands out from existing approaches in that it fingerprints the patterns of Android app fuzzers instead of sandbox environments.

6   Conclusions

Android app fuzzers can reduce the manual effort required in mobile device forensics by improving the efficiency of generating mobile app evidentiary data in runtime by exercising apps. However, research has not investigated the reliability and app program coverage when anti-fuzzing techniques are employed. The AFuzzShield anti-fuzzing solution presented in this chapter helps understand the impacts of anti-fuzzing techniques on app programs. Statistical differences identified by comparing the programming patterns shared by Android app fuzzers and the interaction traces collected from human users were leveraged for this purpose. The evaluation results demonstrate that 70% of the real-world apps in AndroTest can be hindered successfully by anti-fuzzing techniques. Additionally, the more complex the app GUI, the lower the program coverage obtained by a fuzzer.

Future research will focus on extending AFuzzShield to cover more reliability analysis cases of fuzzers by employing a larger app database than AndroTest that contains more complex GUI designs that are closer to real-world apps as well as more real-world human user interaction traces corresponding to the archived apps.

Acknowledgment This research was partially supported by the National Institute of Standards and Technology (NIST) CSAFE under Cooperative Agreement no. 70NANB20H019, by the National Science Foundation under Grant nos. CNS 1527579, CNS 1619201, CNS 1730275, DEB 1924178 and ECCS 2030249, and by the Boeing Company.

References

1. D. Amalfitano, A. Fasolino, P. Tramontana, S. De Carmine and A. Memon, Using GUI ripping for automated testing of Android applications, *Proceedings of*

the *Twenty-Seventh IEEE/ACM International Conference on Automated Software Engineering*, pp. 258–261, 2012.

2. S. Anand, M. Naik, M. Harrold and H. Yang, Automated concolic testing of smartphone apps, *Proceedings of the Twentieth ACM SIGSOFT International Symposium on the Foundations of Software*, article no. 59, 2012.

3. T. Azim and I. Neamtiu, Targeted and depth-first exploration for systematic testing of Android apps, *Proceedings of the ACM SIGPLAN International Conference on Object-Oriented Programming Systems, Languages and Applications*, pp. 641–660, 2013.

4. K. Chen, Y. Zhang and P. Liu, Leveraging information asymmetry to transform Android apps into self-defending code against repackaging attacks, *IEEE Transactions on Mobile Computing*, vol. 17(8), pp. 1879–1893, 2018.

5. C. Cheng, C. Shi, N. Gong and Y. Guan, EviHunter: Identifying digital evidence in the permanent storage of Android devices via static analysis, *Proceedings of the ACM SIGSAC Conference on Computer and Communications Security*, pp. 1338–1350, 2018.

6. W. Choi, G. Necula and K. Sen, Guided GUI testing of Android apps with minimal restart and approximate learning, *Proceedings of the ACM SIGPLAN International Conference on Object-Oriented Programming Systems, Languages and Applications*, pp. 623–640, 2013.

7. W. Choi, K. Sen, G. Necula and W. Wang, DetReduce: Minimizing Android GUI test suites for regression testing, *Proceedings of the Fortieth IEEE/ACM International Conference on Software Engineering*, pp. 445–455, 2018.

8. V. Costamagna, C. Zheng and H. Huang, Identifying and evading Android sandbox through usage-profile based fingerprints, *Proceedings of the First Workshop on Radical and Experiential Security*, pp. 17–23, 2018.

9. B. Deka, Z. Huang, C. Franzen, J. Hibschman, D. Afergan, Y. Li, J. Nichols and R. Kumar, Rico: A mobile app dataset for building data-driven design applications, *Proceedings of the Thirtieth Annual ACM Symposium on User Interface Software and Technology*, pp. 845–854, 2017.

10. W. Diao, X. Liu, Z. Li and K. Zhang, Evading Android runtime analysis through detecting programmed interactions, *Proceedings of the Ninth ACM Conference on Security and Privacy in Wireless and Mobile Networks*, pp. 159–164, 2016.

11. Z. Dong, M. Bohme, L. Cojocaru and A. Roychoudhury, Time-travel testing of Android apps, *Proceedings of the Forty-Second IEEE/ACM International Conference on Software Engineering*, pp. 481–492, 2020.

12. W. Enck, P. Gilbert, S. Han, V. Tendulkar, B. Chun, L. Cox, J. Jung, P. McDaniel and A. Sheth, TaintDroid: An information-flow tracking system for realtime privacy monitoring of smartphones, *ACM Transactions on Computer Systems*, vol. 32(3), article no. 5, 2014.

13. Google Developers, UI/Application Exerciser Monkey, Mountain View, California (developer.android.com/studio/test/other-testing-tools/monkey), 2022.

14. T. Gu, C. Sun, X. Ma, C. Cao, C. Xu, Y. Yao, Q. Zhang, J. Lu and Z. Su, Practical GUI testing of Android applications via model abstraction and refinement, *Proceedings of the Forty-First IEEE/ACM International Conference on Software Engineering*, pp. 269–280, 2019.

15. Guardsquare, ProGuard: The industry-leading Java optimizer for Android apps, Leuven, Belgium (www.guardsquare.com/proguard), 2023.

16. S. Hao, B. Liu, S. Nath, W. Halfond and R. Govindan, PUMA: Programmable UI-automation for large-scale dynamic analysis of mobile apps, *Proceedings of the*

Twelfth Annual International Conference on Mobile Systems, Applications and Services, pp. 204–217, 2014.

17. Y. Jing, Z. Zhao, G. Ahn and H. Hu, Morpheus: Automatically generating heuristics to detect Android emulators, *Proceedings of the Thirtieth Annual Computer Security Applications Conference*, pp. 216–225, 2014.

18. J. Jung, H. Hu, D. Solodukhin, D. Pagan, K. Lee and T. Kim, Fuzzification: Antifuzzing techniques, *Proceedings of the Twenty-Eighth USENIX Security Symposium*, pp. 1913–1930, 2019.

19. L. Li, D. Li, T. Bissyande, J. Klein, Y. Le Traon, D. Lo and L. Cavallaro, Understanding Android app piggybacking: A systematic study of malicious code grafting, *IEEE Transactions on Information Forensics and Security*, vol. 12(6), pp. 1269–1284, 2017.

20. Y. Li, Z. Yang, Y. Guo and X. Chen, Humanoid: A deep-learning-based approach to automated black-box Android app testing, *Proceedings of the Thirty-Fourth IEEE/ACM International Conference on Automated Software Engineering*, pp. 1070–1073, 2019.

21. J. Lim, Y. Shin, S. Lee, K. Kim and J. Yi, Survey of dynamic anti-analysis schemes for mobile malware, *Journal of Wireless Mobile Networks, Ubiquitous Computing and Dependable Applications*, vol. 9(3), pp. 39–49, 2018.

22. A. Machiry, R. Tahiliani and M. Naik, Dynodroid: An input generation system for Android apps, *Proceedings of the Ninth Joint Meeting on Foundations of Software Engineering*, pp. 224–234, 2013.

23. R. Mahmood, N. Mirzaei and S. Malek, EvoDroid: Segmented evolutionary testing of Android apps, *Proceedings of the Twenty-Second ACM SIGSOFT International Symposium on Foundations of Software Engineering*, pp. 599–609, 2014.

24. D. Maier, M. Protsenko and T. Muller, A game of droid and mouse: The threat of split-personality malware on Android, *Computers and Security*, vol. 54, pp. 2–15, 2015.

25. K. Mao, M. Harman and Y. Jia, Sapienz: Multi-objective automated testing for Android applications, *Proceedings of the Twenty-Fifth International Symposium on Software Testing and Analysis*, pp. 94–105, 2016.

26. T. Petsas, G. Voyatzis, E. Athanasopoulos, M. Polychronakis and S. Ioannidis, Rage against the virtual machine: Hindering dynamic analysis of Android malware, *Proceedings of the Seventh European Workshop on System Security*, 2014.

27. J. Qin, H. Zhang, S. Wang, Z. Geng and T. Chen, Acteve++: An improved Android application automatic tester based on Acteve, *IEEE Access*, vol. 7, pp. 31358–31363, 2019.

28. S. Rasthofer, S. Arzt, M. Miltenberger and E. Bodden, Harvesting runtime values in Android applications that feature anti-analysis techniques, *Proceedings of the Twenty-Third Annual Network and Distributed System Security Symposium*, 2016.

29. Robotiumtech, Robotium: User scenario testing for Android, GitHub (`github.com/RobotiumTech/robotium`), 2023.

30. V. Roubtsov, EMMA: A Free Java Code Coverage Tool (`emma.sourceforge.net`), 2006.

31. Statista, Number of available applications in the Google Play Store from December 2009 to March 2023, Hamburg, Germany (`bit.ly/30fsg6W`), 2022.

32. T. Su, G. Meng, Y. Chen, K. Wu, W. Yang, Y. Yao, G. Pu, Y. Liu and Z. Su, Guided stochastic model based GUI testing of Android apps, *Proceedings of the Eleventh Joint Meeting on Foundations of Software Engineering*, pp. 245–256, 2017.

33. M. Sun, T. Wei and J. Lui, TaintART: A practical multi-level information flow tracking system for Android RunTime, *Proceedings of the ACM SIGSAC Conference on Computer and Communications Security*, pp. 331–342, 2016.
34. H. van der Merwe, B. van der Merwe and W. Visser, Verifying Android applications using Java PathFinder, *ACM SIGSOFT Software Engineering Notes*, vol. 37(6), 2012.
35. T. Vidas and N. Christin, Evading Android runtime analysis via sandbox detection, *Proceedings of the Ninth ACM Symposium on Information, Computer and Communications Security*, pp. 447–456, 2014.
36. W. Wang, W. Lam and T. Xie, An infrastructure approach to improving effectiveness of Android UI testing tools, *Proceedings of the Thirtieth ACM SIGSOFT International Symposium on Software Testing and Analysis*, pp. 165–176, 2021.
37. W. Wang, W. Yang, T. Xu and T. Xie, VET: Identifying and avoiding UI exploration tarpits, *Proceedings of the Twenth-Ninth ACM Joint Meeting on European Software Engineering Conference and Symposium on the Foundations of Software Engineering*, pp. 83–94, 2021.
38. Z. Xu, C. Shi, C. Cheng, N. Gong and Y. Guan, A dynamic taint analysis tool for Android app forensics, *Proceedings of the IEEE Security and Privacy Workshops*, pp. 160–169, 2018.
39. W. Yang, M. Prasad and T. Xie, A grey-box approach for automated GUI model generation of mobile applications, *Proceedings of the International Conference on Fundamental Approaches to Software Engineering*, pp. 250–265, 2013.
40. H. Ye, S. Cheng, L. Zhang and F. Jiang, DroidFuzzer: Fuzzing Android apps with intent-filter tag, *Proceedings of International Conference on Advances in Mobile Computing and Multimedia*, pp. 68–74, 2013.
41. X. Zeng, D. Li, W. Zheng, F. Xia, Y. Deng, W. Lam, W. Yang, T. Xie, Automated test input generation for Android: Are we really there yet in an industrial case? *Proceedings of the Twenty-Fourth ACM SIGSOFT International Symposium on Foundations of Software Engineering*, pp. 987–992, 2016.

Nintendo 3DS Forensic Examination Tools

Konstantinos Xynos[1], Huw Read[2], Iain Sutherland[3], Matthew Bovee[2], and Trang Do[2]

[1] Cyber Security Consultant, Stuttgart, Germany
[2] Norwich University, Northfield, Vermont, USA
hread@norwich.edu
[3] Noroff University College, Kristiansand, Norway

Abstract. This chapter describes a suite of digital forensic examination tools for the Nintendo 3DS series of game consoles. The Nintendo 3DS is a handheld game console with capabilities that include video recording, photography, web browsing and network communications. Originally released in 2011, the consoles remain popular, with almost 76 million units sold. Since the consoles can enable illegal activities, they are potential containers of evidence in criminal investigations. Previous research has highlighted the artifacts found on Nintendo 3DS and other similar devices. However, this chapter expands the body of research focused on automating artifact extraction and validation. The extraction and validation efforts would be of interest to forensic practitioners as well as researchers focusing on small-scale embedded devices.

Keywords: Nintendo 3DS · Game Console · Forensic Examination · Forensic Tools

1 Introduction

The Nintendo 3DS is an eighth-generation handheld game console and the immediate predecessor to the Nintendo Switch. Several Nintendo 3DS variants have been released during its production run from 2011 to 2020. The model releases from oldest to most recent are: 3DS, 3DS XL, 2DS, New 3DS, New 3DS XL and New 2DS XL [27]. As of March 2021 almost 76 million Nintendo 3DS consoles have been sold [26, 30]. This figure accounts for 14% of all Nintendo handheld console sales to date.

From a software perspective, 3DS consoles may be categorized as those with the designation "New" and those without the designation (original). Subtle differences exist in the file formats of applications on the two categories of consoles. For example, the modding community has demonstrated differences in the web browser file structure [3]. These and other variations are examined later in this chapter.

Although Nintendo has stopped producing 3DS consoles, the devices continue to be popular. A robust second-hand market exists for "retro" game systems, especially fully-functional old consoles. Searches at online enterprises specializing

© IFIP International Federation for Information Processing 2023
Published by Springer Nature Switzerland AG 2023
G. Peterson and S. Shenoi (Eds.): DigitalForensics 2023, IFIP AICT 687, pp. 55–70, 2023.
https://doi.org/10.1007/978-3-031-42991-0_4

in used game consoles show that these systems are plentiful. For example, on November 1, 2022, more than 6,500 units were on sale on eBay and approximately 10,000 Nintendo 3DS auctions, some for multiple units, were completed during the previous month.

The nature of Nintendo 3DS devices and their popularity imply that possibilities exist for misuse, which renders them evidentiary sources in digital forensic investigations. In addition to copyright violations, game consoles and their online environments have been the focus of other investigations. In 2019, the FBI sought information from Sony about communications involving a PlayStation user in a drug-related investigation [7]. Mainstream media such as BBC News have highlighted how games can be used to promote extremism [23]. Urquhart [37] describes how game consoles feature prominently in police investigations.

The previous-generation Nintendo DS has featured in a number of criminal cases. In 2020, evidence of physical abuse of a minor obtained from a Nintendo DS was relevant in the prosecution of a U.S. Army soldier, who received a life sentence [12, 29]. Holmes [18] highlighted a case where a Nintendo DS camera was used for voyeurism. BBC News [6] reported a case where a Nintendo DS was used to access child abuse material. Sutherland et al. [34] examined the criminal use of game consoles in the United Kingdom and noted that older consoles still featured in police investigations.

These and other incidents highlight the risk of purchasing used game consoles such as Nintendo DS/3DS because the devices may have been used for criminal purposes and could contain illegal material. Another issue is that older, discontinued and unsupported devices may have vulnerabilities that will never be patched, potentially leading to exposures of personally-identifiable information. However, because of its continued popularity, Nintendo has continued to release system updates for the Nintendo 3DS. The latest update (version 11.16.0.49U) was released in September 2022 [28], two years after 3DS production ended.

The Nintendo 3DS has been the subject of research seeking to identify forensic artifacts and provide guidance for manual evidence extraction and analysis [31, 32]. However, the research has certain limitations. Although a 3DS NAND dump is easily mounted as a FAT16 filesystem on a forensic workstation, existing forensic tools are not designed to decode Nintendo 3DS file types. Additionally, manual file and string carving approaches [31] require significant amounts of effort to extract artifacts from NAND images. This research addresses the limitations by generating datasets containing Nintendo 3DS artifacts that support empirical analyses. These datasets facilitated the development and validation of a suite of automated forensic tools for extracting and analyzing evidence in Nintendo 3DS console images.

2   Previous Research

Previous research has progressed along two paths. The first research path covers first-look methodology development approaches that focus on creating methodologies for manually extracting forensically-important artifacts. For example,

Turnbull [36] conducted a first look of the Nintendo Wii. Xynos et al. [39] provided "suggested basic guidelines" for analyzing Xbox 360 devices. Conrad et al. [9] presented an evidence recovery procedure for the Sony PlayStation 3. Moore et al. [24] described a "preliminary forensic analysis" of the Microsoft Xbox One game console. Davies et al. [11] conducted a first look at the Sony PlayStation 4. Read et al. [32] developed a live forensic acquisition methodology for Nintendo 3DS consoles.

The second research path covers forensic tool development and/or reverse engineering, often after exploits that permit greater filesystem access have been released. Such exploits stemming from greater access often lead to the development of advanced forensic methodologies and tools. For example, Pessolano et al. [31] presented a forensic analysis of the Nintendo 3DS filesystem that leveraged exploits identified by Scires et al. [33]. Commercial forensic tool vendors such as Cellebrite laud such exploit disclosures because they can help law enforcement. Referring to the checkm8/checkra1n exploit [8], Cellebrite [22] stated: "Every now and then, there is a breakthrough that surfaces to help the good guys in the forensic community."

The last official firmware update for the Nintendo 3DS was released on September 12, 2022 [28]. However none of the updates released by Nintendo since 2018, when Scires et al. [33] publicly documented a boot ROM exploit, have addressed the vulnerability. Because the 3DS system has been discontinued, it is unlikely the vulnerability will never be patched. The Scires et al. [33] exploit is leveraged in this research to create a forensic dump of a 3DS NAND chip (verified by hashes) and to extract the decryption key required to convert the dump to a viable FAT16 image. Given this image, software such as FTK from Exterro (formerly AccessData) can be used to carve the filesystem, extract artifacts from container files and perform keyword searches. Similarly, Barr-Smith et al. [5] leveraged the Fusée Gelée exploit [35] that enabled the analysis of Nintendo Switch NAND dumps and the creation of modules for Autopsy, the popular open-source digital forensic tool.

Forensic analysis and tool development efforts for game consoles have largely been conducted in academia instead of in commercial settings. However, commercial examples do exist. An example is Magnet Forensics Internet Evidence Finder v6.3 [21] that includes tools for Microsoft Xbox 360 analysis. Nevertheless, an extensive literature survey reveals that no open-source or commercial methods or tools are available for Nintendo 3DS devices. Thus, the research described in this chapter stands out in that it addresses the extraction of large portions of the binary data on 3DS devices and its presentation in human-readable reports.

3   Toolset Workflow

A Nintendo 3DS console has two key storage components, a NAND memory chip (i.e., eMMC) mounted on a circuit board with up to 2 GB storage capacity (1 GB for the 2DS) and a removable SD or microSD card depending on the model of the console. Read et al. [32] noted that the SD/microSD card can be removed

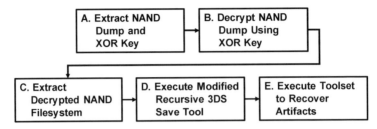

Fig. 1. Toolset workflow.

and analyzed using existing forensic tools. Therefore, the focus of this paper is on evidence contained in the internal NAND memory chip.

Pessolano et al. [31] developed a method for extracting and decrypting NAND chip content in a forensically-sound manner. It is worth noting that successive extractions can be obtained more quickly than the initial extraction. Specifically, the console has a unique encryption key (XORpad file) that is static, and does not change even if the console is formatted. Therefore, after the initial extraction obtains the XORpad key, subsequent extractions only need to extract the NAND content. Pessolano et al. [31] also employed file carving to identify where artifacts are located in a decrypted NAND filesystem. The artifacts tend to reside in containers with DISA and DIFF formats [2]. It is necessary to extract the raw files from their containers before further analysis. The toolset presented in this chapter first extracts files from their DISA/DIFF containers, after which data is extracted from the files.

Figure 1 shows the toolset workflow. Steps A and B correspond to the extraction and decryption procedures documented in [31]. Step C requires a forensic practitioner to load the FAT16 filesystem in the decrypted NAND image on a forensic workstation. Exterro FTK Imager [13] is employed to mount the image. Step D employs a modified version of the 3DS Save Tool [38] with a recursive function that enables all the DISA and DIFF containers to be extracted at once. In Step E, the forensic practitioner specifies the tools to be used for extraction and, by extension, the artifacts to be extracted. The complete list of tools and the artifacts they extract are presented later in Tables 1 and 2.

4   Artifact Generation

Validation, which is an essential step when developing digital forensic tools, requires appropriate datasets. Several forensic datasets have been developed for tool validation. Prominent datasets include the Computer Forensics Reference Data Set (CFReDS) [25], Artefact Genome Project (AGP) [17] and Digital Corpora [16].

A search for forensic images related to game consoles using CFReDS resulted in two hits, one from an Xbox 360 (hosted by Digital Corpora) and the other from a PlayStation 3 (actually a capture of the then-supported Linux/Other OS feature instead of the game console filesystem). The AGP dataset did not contain any game console extractions. Regrettably, no publicly-available Nintendo 3DS datasets were found to support the toolset validation efforts.

The two alternatives were to procure used 3DS consoles and extract their data to create a validation dataset or to create a synthetic dataset from scratch. Employing used consoles was problematic because there would be no guarantees on the quality and quantity of data they contained. Manual analysis would also be required to confirm the presence of artifacts expected to be found by digital forensic tools. Additionally, the used consoles could contain personally-identifiable information that would require additional safeguards.

The alternative promoted by Garfinkel [15] – using "artificially-constructed or fake data" – was selected in this research. Barr-Smith et al. [5] used a similar approach to develop tools for the Nintendo Switch. Specifically, they employed one new device and two used devices to "provide test data for tool development and evaluation."

A brand-new Nintendo 3DS XL console was procured to create the toolset validation dataset. Artifacts were generated by using the console functions in a controlled manner and meticulously documenting the actions (with timestamps) performed on the console. This led to the creation of a log of all system interactions that could be referenced later to validate that the toolset extracted artifacts correctly. While the process of documenting artifacts was relatively straightforward, decisions had to be made about the artifacts to generate. Fortunately, previous 3DS forensics research conducted by the authors of this chapter [31, 32] provided insights into the artifacts of forensic significance that are accepted by the scientific community. This was bolstered by the collective work of the 3DBrew contributors [1] that provided useful opportunities for exploration.

Generating artifacts on a real system is not without risk; errors can alter the expected results and can lead to extensive tool debugging when the tool was not at fault. Drawing from work with virtualized environments where system snapshots taken earlier are restored at a later stage, Pessolano et al. [31] recommended that initial data captures be restored to confirm the validation results. Therefore, multiple snapshots were taken of the test 3DS console after groups of related artifacts were introduced. For example, web browsing, web history and bookmarks would be considered to be a group of related artifacts.

Figure 2 shows the detailed information required when generating artifacts. The left-hand side of the figure shows samples of successive extractions with indications of their content. The top right-hand side of the figure shows an excerpt from a log generated for the mydata structure showing, to the minute, the actions taken on the device. The bottom right-hand side of the figure shows the data retrieved by the forensic tool. Artifact generation involved 16 distinct extractions, each of which was verified forensically using SHA256. The 16 extractions, along with detailed logs of the actions, artifacts and their timestamps, constituted the artificially-generated dataset used for toolset validation.

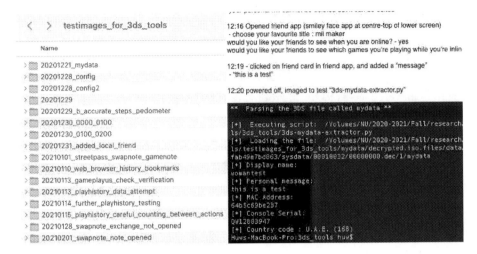

Fig. 2. Detailed information required during artifact generation.

5   Forensic Tool Development

Command-line tools were implemented as Python scripts. The individual tools were developed using publicly-available information about the binary file formats found at 3DBrew [1] along with additional structures that were identified during tool development. The Python scripts leveraged the defined data structures to interpret the extracted data. The information about the Nintendo 3DS filesystem provided at 3DBrew served as an excellent resource for tool development, especially information pertaining to filesystems, file formats and diverse metadata. However, as the materials posted at 3DBrew do not appear to have been peer reviewed, it would be improper to take them at face value. Therefore, regardless of source, all the forensics tools described in this work underwent a thorough validation process described in Section 6.

Publicly-available information and a verifiable testing process were used to deserialize binary data describing the data structures and obtain the relevant information. Figure 3 shows information obtained about the Wi-Fi settings. The top of the figure shows a portion of the network data structure. The bottom of the figure shows that the structure was reused in three blocks. Figure 8 later in this chapter shows the resulting extraction.

The toolset created in this research comprises 16 tools (scripts) that automate the extraction and reporting of artifacts in Nintendo 3DS consoles. The tools can be executed together to batch-process evidence extractions. Tables 1 and 2 describe the tools and the artifacts they recover. Each tool accepts as input the path of the file to be processed. The script processes the binary data and extracts information that is correctly defined in the data structures and presents it in human-readable form.

The tools are designed to be verbose in that they parse and extract more information than is presented. For example, many of the artifacts listed in Ta-

```
network_struct = Struct(
    "is_network_set" / Flag,
    "use_network_struct" / Flag,
    "network_struct_number" / Int16ul,
    Padding(1),
    "SSID" / Bytes(32),
    "SSID_length" / Int8ul,
    "AP_crypt_type" / Bytes(1),
    Padding(2),
    "passphrase" / Bytes(64),
    "PBKDF2_passphrase_SSID" / Bytes(32)
)

wifi_struct = Struct(
    "unknown1" / Bytes(2),
    "crc" / Int8ul,
    "network_block_01" / network_struct,
    Padding(32),
    "network_block_02" / network_struct,
    Padding(524),
    "network_block_03" / network_struct,
    "dhcp" / Flag,
    "dns" / Flag,
```

Fig. 3. Extracted Wi-Fi settings information.

bles 1 and 2 have accompanying metadata that is extracted. Only summary details of the artifacts are presented to enhance readability and adhere to the space constraints.

Figure 4 demonstrates the process of launching the toolset. Although each tool may be executed individually, all the tools are collectively incorporated in a single front-end application named 3ds-one-script-to-rule-them-all.py. Upon invoking the help function (-help), a list of individual tools and their corresponding artifacts with their filesystem locations are displayed. Figure 4 also shows that the same scripts are executed for localizations of the same data. For example, gameplay(us/eu) is stored in different locations, but the binary format is the same.

6   Toolset Validation

Figure 5 shows toolset validation workflow. In the iterative workflow, the five steps are repeated for each tool in the toolset until all the tools are validated.

- **Step A. Restore Extraction to 3DS:** This step has been demonstrated to be forensically sound by Pessolano et al. [31] who restored a NAND dump extraction, reimaged and compared hashes to the previous image and found the two hashes to be identical. Pessolano and colleagues noted the date and time had to be set correctly on the console after restoring an extraction. For example, the pedometer did not display the step counts until the date process was corrected (Figure 6).

Table 1. Summary of artifacts recovered by tools.

Tool	Description	Artifacts Recovered
account-extractor	Prints out the principal ID and information related to online authentication	Local friend code, NEX password, principal ID, principal ID HMAC
config-extractor	Extracts parental settings, (including PIN set by parent, email and the secret), Wi-Fi settings, username, birthday, state and coordinates	Parental controls, Wi-Fi settings, cleartext password, username, birthday, state, coordinates
cookies-and-bookmarks-extractor	Extracts bookmark and cookie information	Bookmarks (description, URL default), creation time, cookie information
mii-extractor	Extracts Mii character information, Mii name, author name, system ID and MAC address where it was created, descriptive Mii information	Mii entry number, Mii name, Mii author name, Mii ID, system ID, MAC address, Mii birthday, Mii gender
mydata-extractor	Extracts information from mydata file, serial number, display name, personal message	Serial number, display name, Mii data (similar to mii-extractor), personal message
amiibo-parser	Parses amiibo (not on a 3DS device) data extracted from a tag and presents the owner(s), date changes and amiibo settings	Amiibo owner, second owner, setup date, last write date, write counter, game ID, model number
blocklist-extractor	Extracts usernames blocked by console owner	Blocked usernames
exbanner-extractor	Extracts messages stored in exbanner files	Texture names, messages
friendlist-extractor	Extracts a list of friends, including display name and personal message, Mii data section and details about the friend entries	Friend display name, personal message, Mii data (similar to mii-extractor), friend details (country, area, language, platform)
gamecoin-extractor	Parses gamecoint.dat file, extracts the number of play coins, last update date	Total coins, coins on date, step count for new coin, step count for last coin

Table 2. Summary of artifacts recovered by tools (continued).

Tool	Description	Artifacts Recovered
gamernote-process-external-memo-folder	Recursively processes folder where gamernotes are stored, references gamernote-process-external file	Shim to recursively process gamernotes
gamernote-process-external	There are 16 gamernotes, unused ones appear as white images	Images and thumbnails in PNG format
gameplay-extractor	Shows game title ID and total played, times played, when title was first and last played	Game title ID, total played, times played, first played, last played
pedometer-extractor	Shows number of steps registered by console and timestamps	Hourly, daily, monthly, yearly step counts, timestamps, last update
playhistory-extractor	Extracts play history, including title ID, possibly title name	Title ID, title name
streetpass-cec-extractor	Extracts StreetPass containers, inbox and outbox messages	StreetPass messages, send method, message state, send/forward count

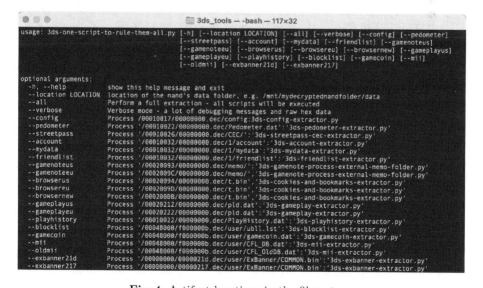

Fig. 4. Artifact locations in the filesystem.

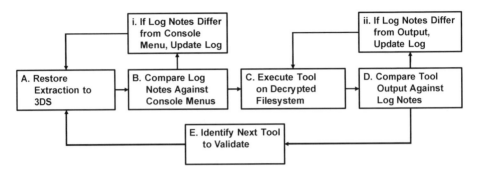

Fig. 5. Toolset validation workflow.

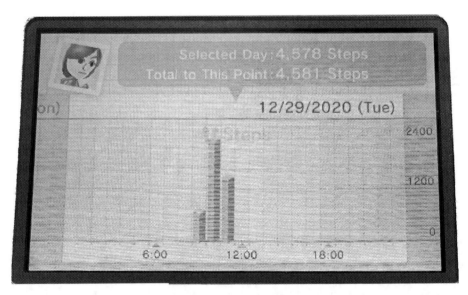

Fig. 6. Live analysis to minimize errors in log notes.

- **Step B. Compare Log Notes Against Console Menus:** Live analysis is performed on the running console to identify errors (Figure 6). The native 3DS operating system applications are used to interpret data, following which on-screen values are compared against the log notes.
  - *(i) If Log Notes Differ from Console Menu, Update Log:* If the log notes differ from a console menu, the log notes are updated to reflect what was shown on the console. The same image is restored to the 3DS device (Step A) and checked a second time (Step B). This ensures that the log notes are consistent with image content.
- **Step C. Execute Tool on Decrypted Filesystem:** This step is geared toward a particular tool. After filesystem extraction in the toolset workflow in Figure 1 is completed, the tool is executed taking care to provide the correct path/file as input (Figure 4).

13:40 - imaged sd card

22:09 steps - total to this point: 4581. 12/29/2020 - 4,578 (9am 10am 11am most active),
    12/28 - 3 (11:30ish?)
imaged - 29122020_b_accurate_steps_pedometer
observations in pedometer.dat
bytes[0-3]: unknown, always 01000000?
bytes[4:5] - total steps recorded so far (little endian)

```
                                3ds_tools — -bash — 95×27
** Parsing the 3DS file called pedometer.dat **

[+] Loading the file:  /Volumes/NU 1/2020-2021/Fall/research/nitendo3ds_study/tools/testimages
_for_3ds_tools/20201229_b_accurate_steps_pedometer/decrypted.iso.files/data/6994afbaa1ed5977a4c
2fab49e7bd863/sysdata/00010022/00000000.dec/Pedometer.dat
[+] File size is:  182288

Nintendo 3DS Pedometer analysis, with daily and monthly totals.
========================================================================

2020/12/28      1200    Steps: 3        Approx.:  2.29 metres, or 7.5 feet.
        Daily Total:3

2020/12/29      0900    Steps: 685      Approx.:  521.97 metres, or 1712.5 feet.
2020/12/29      1000    Steps: 2395     Approx.:  1824.99 metres, or 5987.5 feet.
2020/12/29      1100    Steps: 1495     Approx.:  1139.19 metres, or 3737.5 feet.
2020/12/29      2200    Steps: 3        Approx.:  2.29 metres, or 7.5 feet.
        Daily Total:4578

Monthly Total:4581


Grand Total: 4581
Pedometer last updated: Wed, 30 Dec 2020 03:10:47 GMT (Check local time)
========================================================================
```

Fig. 7. Successful comparison of tool output against log notes.

- **Step D. Compare Tool Output Against Log Notes:** Since the log
  entries are formally validated against the console (Step B), any difference
  between the tool output and log notes indicates misinterpretation by the
  tool that must be resolved. Figure 7 shows an example of a successful comparison. The top image shows the log notes and the bottom image shows the
  `pedometer-extractor` tool output, which exhibits consistent values.

  - *(ii) If Log Notes Differ from Output, Update Tool:* The application is
    updated to display the same information that appears on the console.
    Differences may occur due to programming errors (bugs), logical errors
    (from third parties) and/or formatting errors (e.g., 3DS timestamp is
    DD/MM/YYYY instead of MM/DD/YYYY [USA format]).

- **Step E. Identify Next Tool to Validated:** After a tool has been validated
  and its output is consistent with the log notes (and console, by association),
  the next tool is validated starting with Step A in the tool validation workflow.

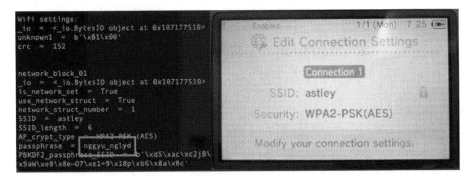

Fig. 8. Recoverable and unrecoverable plaintext Wi-Fi passphrase.

7   Observations

The Nintendo 3DS is a fairly complex device with a number of artifacts of significance in forensic investigations. Tables 1 and 2 present details about artifacts recovered by the tools. However, it is pertinent to make observations about five tools:

- **pedometer-extractor:** The pedometer data in the Activity Log application was decoded to reveal the number of steps recorded by the device on an hourly basis. Figure 7 shows the validation of the console details.
- **config-extractor:** A 3DS device stores a maximum of three Wi-Fi access points. Figure 8 shows that the Wi-Fi passphrase is recoverable as plaintext using the tool (left-hand side) but is not recoverable via the native 3DS graphical user interface (right-hand side).
- **cookies-and-bookmarks-extractor:** 3DBrew [3] reveals that 3DS devices with the moniker "New" (e.g., New Nintendo 2DS XL) store browser files in certain locations whereas 3DS devices without the moniker store browser files based on region. The tool identifies console type according to folder structure and file location (Figure 4) when extracting browser history and bookmarks, displaying URL, timestamp and cookie data.
- **mydata-extractor:** As shown in Figure 9, the tool extracts the console MAC address, serial number, personal message, etc. Although a sticker with the serial number is located on the rear of the console, the tool output provides an opportunity to identify the system should the sticker be removed or the printed serial number become illegible.
- **friendlist-extractor:** A fictitious friend profile was created on a formatted second 3DS device and the users on the first and second devices befriended each other. Figure 10 shows that the tool displays the creator's MAC address, providing a tangible link (and possibly, probable cause) between devices. The script also shows the friend's name, birthday and gender.

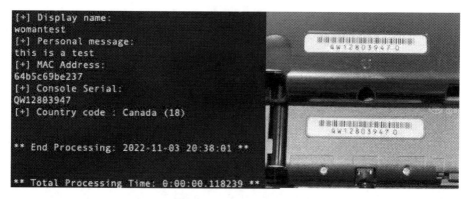

Fig. 9. Validation of console details.

Fig. 10. MAC address of Mii creator and Mii representation.

8   Toolset Evaluation

The focus of this work was to facilitate authorized forensic examinations of 3DS consoles. This has been accomplished by developing tools that expedite the extraction of many types of 3DS artifacts. Whereas previous work [31] provided access to seven types of 3DS artifacts, the toolset presented in this chapter almost doubles the available artifact types. Additionally, it acquires artifacts from binaries and provides the convenience of batch-processing 3DS device evidence extraction and consolidating the findings in a single report.

The toolset leverages an exploit identified by Scires et al. [33] that was reported in the public domain nearly five years ago [1–3, 31, 33]. The exploit could be leveraged to circumvent copyright protection in video games. Unfortunately, the most recent firmware update, released nearly four years after the exploit became public, does not address the vulnerability. The authors of this chapter neither imply that Scires and colleagues developed the exploit for nefarious purposes nor do they condone the use of the exploit for nefarious purposes. Nevertheless, should the vulnerability remain unpatched, it benefits authorized entities to leverage the exploit and toolset in official investigations.

The toolset is available only to law enforcement and other legitimate users by contacting the lead author of this chapter. However, caution is advised when using the toolset and its outputs. Variations in hardware releases in different countries have been noticed and may persist. Forensic practitioners should follow best practices [4, 14, 20], admissibility guidelines such as the Daubert standard [19] and/or criminal procedure rules and practice directions [10] to properly validate the toolset outputs. Tool errors or omissions should also be reported to the lead author.

Statistics and feedback on toolset usage in live investigations provide opportunities to advance the validation of the toolset. Unfortunately, the opportunities may be limited because the investigative community (law enforcement and intelligence agencies) are reluctant to share usage statistics and, in some cases, even mention that game consoles are being examined [34]. This situation presents challenges to the effective validation of this toolset and others like it.

9   Conclusions

The functionality and widespread use of game consoles renders them potentially valuable sources of evidence in forensics investigations. This is true for older consoles that are no longer manufactured, but are still popular in the second-hand market. Forensic research on these consoles tends to start as initial explorations of the consoles soon after they are released, followed by in-depth research into the extraction and analysis of forensic artifacts. This two-stage approach, focused on enabling access to console content and the subsequent forensic analysis and presentation of artifacts in human-readable form, can extend over several years, delaying the development of tools for conducting forensic investigations.

The Nintendo 3DS console is a discontinued, albeit still popular, game console. The bespoke Nintendo 3DS suite of tools developed in this research facilitates the expeditious extraction and analysis of artifacts from the NAND memory chip, the primary 3DS evidence repository. The diverse artifacts extracted include usernames, Mii (avatar) names, network SSIDs, passphrases and numerous dates and timestamps. The scripted tools have verbose outputs for debugging purposes and to assist in identifying variations between different 3DS models.

Toolset enhancements will include a module that enables options for verbose, summary and machine-readable outputs of key evidentiary items. Additionally, research will focus on understanding the variations in evidentiary items between devices with and without SD card memory.

Acknowledgment This research was supported by the National Science Foundation under Grant no. DGE 1754014.

References

1. 3DBrew, Flash Filesystem (www.3dbrew.org/wiki/Flash_Filesystem, February 7, 2017.

2. 3DBrew, DISA and DIFF (www.3dbrew.org/wiki/DISA_and_DIFF), January 2, 2020.

3. 3DBrew, Internet Browser (www.3dbrew.org/wiki/Internet_Browser), March 11, 2023.

4. A. Arshad, A. Jantan and O. Abiodun, Digital forensics: Review of issues in the scientific validation of digital evidence, *Journal of Information Processing Systems*, vol. 14(2), pp. 346–376, 2018.

5. F. Barr-Smith, T. Farrant, B. Leonard-Lagarde, D. Rigby, S. Rigby and F. Sibley-Calder, Dead man's switch: Forensic autopsy of the Nintendo Switch, *Digital Investigation*, vol. 36(S), article no. 301110, 2021.

6. BBC News, Special Olympics winner caught with abuse images for second time, August 30, 2021.

7. B. Brousil, Affidavit in Support of Search Warrant, Case No. 19SW-00364-JTM, United States District Court for the Western District of Missouri, Kansas City, Missouri (s3.documentcloud.org/documents/6565970/PlayStation-Seach-Warrant-Application.pdf), October 22, 2019.

8. checkra1n Developers, checkra1n: Jailbreak for iPhone 5s through iPhone X, iOS 12.0 and up (checkra.in), 2023.

9. S. Conrad, G. Dorn and P. Craiger, Forensic analysis of a PlayStation 3 console, in *Advanced in Digital Forensics VI*, K. Chow and S. Shenoi (Eds.), Springer, Berlin Heidelberg, Germany, pp. 65–76, 2010.

10. Criminal Procedure Rule Committee, Criminal Procedure Rules and Practice Directions 2020, Ministry of Justice, London, United Kingdom (www.gov.uk/guidance/rules-and-practice-directions-2020), 2020.

11. M. Davies, H. Read, K. Xynos and I. Sutherland, Forensic analysis of a Sony PlayStation 4: A first look, *Digital Investigation*, vol. 12(S1), pp. S81–S89, 2015.

12. C. Duncan, Fort Bragg soldier sexually abused adopted children for years, FBI says, *The News and Observer*, April 24, 2019.

13. Exterro, FTK Imager, Portland, Oregon (www.exterro.com/ftk-imager), 2023.

14. Forensic Science Regulator, Forensic Science Regulator Guidance: Method Validation in Digital Forensics, FSR-G-218, Issue 2, London, United Kingdom, 2020.

15. S. Garfinkel, Lessons learned writing digital forensics tools and managing a 30 TB digital evidence corpus, *Digital Investigation*, vol. 9(S), pp. S80–S89, 2012.

16. S. Garfinkel, P. Farrell, V. Roussev and G. Dinolt, Bringing science to digital forensics with standardized forensic corpora, *Digital Investigation*, vol. 6(S), pp. S2–S11, 2009.

17. C. Grajeda, L. Sanchez, I. Baggili, D. Clark and F. Breitinger, Experience constructing the Artifact Genome Project (AGP): Managing the domain's knowledge one artifact at a time, *Digital Investigation*, vol. 26(S), pp. S47–S58, 2018.

18. W. Holmes, Blackpool child rapist tries to use secret Nintendo DS camera to record people on toilet two months after release, *Blackpool Gazette*, February 20, 2020.

19. Legal Information Institute, Daubert Standard, Cornell Law School, Ithaca, New York (www.law.cornell.edu/wex/daubert_standard), 2022.

20. J. Lyle, B. Guttman, J. Butler, K. Sauerwein, C. Reed and C. Lloyd, Digital Investigation Techniques: A NIST Scientific Foundation Review, NISTIR 8354-Draft, National Institute of Standards and Technology, Gaithersburg, Maryland, 2022.

21. Magnet Forensics, Magnet Forensics releases Internet Evidence Finder v6.3, Waterloo, Canada (investors.magnetforensics.comr/news/press/news-details/2014/Magnet-Forensics-Releases-Internet-Evidence-Finder-v63/default.aspx), February 5, 2014.

22. H. Mahalik, S. Tal, G. Rutenberg and R. Arato, checkm8 and checkra1n – Full Filesystem Extractions for iOS Devices, Webinar, Petah Tikva, Israel (cellebrite.com/en/checkm8-and-checkra1n-full-filesystem-extractions-for-ios-devices), 2023.

23. C. Miller and S. Silva, Extremists using video-game chats to spread hate, *BBC News*, September 23, 2021.

24. J. Moore, I. Baggili, A. Marrington and A. Rodrigues, Preliminary forensic analysis of the Xbox One, *Digital Investigation*, vol. 11(S2), pp. S57–S65, 2014.

25. National Institute of Standards and Technology, Computer Forensic Reference Data Set Portal, Gaithersburg, Maryland (cfreds.nist.gov), 2023.

26. Nintendo, Dedicated Video Game Sales Units, Kyoto, Japan (www.nintendo.co.jp/ir/en/finance/hard_soft/index.html), December 31, 2022.

27. Nintendo, Nintendo 3DS Family, Windsor, United Kingdom (www.nintendo.co.uk/Hardware/Nintendo-3DS-Family/Nintendo-3DS-Family-94560.html), 2023.

28. Nintendo, System Menu Update History, Redmond, Washington (en-americas-support.nintendo.com/app/answers/detail/a_id/231/~/system-menu-update-history), 2023.

29. Office of Public Affairs, U.S. Department of Justice, U.S. Army soldier sentenced to life in prison for aggravated sexual assault, Washington, DC (www.justice.gov/opa/pr/us-army-soldier-sentenced-life-prison-aggravated-sexual-assault), July 8, 2020.

30. T. Owens, Unit sales of Nintendo's home consoles from 1997 to 2021 (in millions), Statista, New York (www.statista.com/statistics/227012/lifetime-unit-sales-of-nintendos-home-consoles), August 11, 2022.

31. G. Pessolano, H. Read, I. Sutherland and K. Xynos, Forensic analysis of the Nintendo 3DS NANO, *Digital Investigation*, vol. 29(S), pp. S61–S70, 2019.

32. H. Read, E. Thomas, I. Sutherland, K. Xynos and M. Burgess, A forensic methodology for analyzing Nintendo 3DS devices, in *Advances in Digital Forensics XII*, G. Peterson and S. Shenoi (Eds.), Springer, Cham, Switzerland, pp. 127–143. 2016.

33. M. Scires, M. Mears, D. Maloney, M. Norman, S. Tux and P. Munroe, Attacking the Nintendo 3DS boot ROMs, arXiv: 1802.00359v2 (arxiv.org/abs/1802.00359), 2018.

34. I. Sutherland, H. Read and K. Xynos, An analysis of the prevalence of game consoles in criminal investigations in the United Kingdom, *Proceedings of the Twenty-Frist European Conference on Cyber Warfare and Security*, pp. 289–295, 2022.

35. K. Temkin, FAQ: Fusée Gelée (www.ktemkin.com/faq-fusee-gelee), April 4, 2018.

36. B. Turnbull, Forensic investigation of the Nintendo Wii: A first glance, *Small Scale Digital Device Forensics Journal*, vol. 2(1), pp. 1–7, 2008.

37. L. Urquhart, U.S. police use game consoles in crime investigations, *Naked Security by Sophos*, January 26, 2012.

38. W. Wang, 3DS Save File Extraction Tools, GitHub (github.com/wwylele/3ds-save-tool), 2023.

39. K. Xynos, S. Harries, I. Sutherland, G. Davies and A. Blyth, Xbox 360: A digital forensic investigation of the hard disk drive, *Digital Investigation*, vol. 6(3-4), pp. 104–111, 2010.

Forensic Data Collection

Revealing Human Attacker Behaviors Using an Adaptive Internet of Things Honeypot Ecosystem

Armin Ziaie Tabari[1], Guojun Liu[2], Xinming Ou[2], and Anoop Singhal[3]

[1] OPSWAT, Tampa, Florida, USA
[2] University of South Florida, Tampa, Florida, USA
xou@usf.edu
[3] National Institute of Standards and Technology, Gaithersburg, Maryland, USA

Abstract. Honeypots have been used as decoy devices to understand the dynamics of threats on networks and their impacts. However, the questions of whether and how honeypots can elicit rich human attacker behaviors have not been investigated systematically. These capabilities are especially important for Internet of Things devices given the limited knowledge about attacker goals.

This chapter attempts to answer three questions. Can an Internet of Things honeypot that gradually adapts or increases its emulation sophistication elicit richer human attacker behaviors over time? Is it possible to engage human attackers using dynamically-adapting Internet of Things honeypots? Does the large amount of data captured by honeypots embody patterns that can enable security analysts to understand attacker intentions on Internet of Things devices?

To answer the questions, a new approach is presented for creating an adaptive honeypot ecosystem that gradually increases the sophistication of honeypot interactions with adversaries based on observed data. The approach is employed to design custom honeypots that mimic Internet of Things devices and an innovative data analytics method is applied to identify attacker behavior patterns and reveal attacker goals. The honeypots in the experiments actively observed real-world attacker behaviors and collected increasingly sophisticated attack data over more than three years. In the case of Internet of Things camera honeypots, human attack activities were observed after adapting the honeypots based on previous attacker behaviors. The data analytics results indicate that the vast majority of captured attack activities share significant similarities, and can be clustered to better understand the goals, patterns and trends of Internet of Things attacks in the wild.

Keywords: Honeypots · Internet of Things Devices · Human Attacker Behaviors

1 Introduction

The massive proliferation of Internet-connected devices raises serious security concerns. Many Internet of Things devices have simple vulnerabilities such as

© IFIP International Federation for Information Processing 2023
Published by Springer Nature Switzerland AG 2023
G. Peterson and S. Shenoi (Eds.): DigitalForensics 2023, IFIP AICT 687, pp. 73–90, 2023.
https://doi.org/10.1007/978-3-031-42991-0_5

default usernames and passwords, and open SSH and Telnet ports. Often, the devices are located in weak or insecure networks, such as home or public space networks. In fact, Internet of Things devices are subject to as many attacks as traditional computing systems, if not more.

New Internet of Things devices open up new attack entry points and expose their entire networks. According to a report by Symantec [20], 50,000 Internet of Things attacks were detected in 2017, an increase of 600% over 2016. Kaspersky reported that Internet of Things attacks more than doubled in the first six months of 2021 compared with the previous six-month period [19]. In addition, attackers demonstrated improved skills by launching sophisticated attacks such as VPNFilter [21], Wicked [11], UPnProxy [1], Hajime [7], and the Masuta [4] and Mirai [3] botnets.

Unfortunately, few systematic studies have focused on the nature or scope of Internet of Things attacks in the wild. At this time, most large-scale attacks on Internet of Things devices have involved distributed denial-of-service (DDoS) (e.g., Mirai attacks [3]). Understanding what attackers are doing with Internet of Things devices and their motives are of utmost importance.

Honeypots are real or emulated Internet-facing devices that are configured to attract attackers and attacks. Since they are not intended to serve any other purpose, any access to them is presumed to be malicious or anomalous. Researchers uncover new methods, tools and attacks by analyzing data such as network logs and downloaded files collected by honeypots. This enables the discovery of vulnerabilities and attack trends. Honeypots possess significant potential for improving security defenses based on the intelligence gathered, especially in organizations with limited resources.

Despite the long history of honeypots, relatively little research has focused on deploying and utilizing them for security defense. In particular, no systematic study has concentrated on increasing the sophistication of human attacker behaviors elicited by honeypots in order to maximize intelligence gathering. While it is often reported that honeypots in the wild collect huge amounts of data, limited research has attempted to investigate whether the data embodies patterns that could contribute to greater understanding of attacker behaviors.

This chapter attempts to answer three questions. Can an Internet of Things honeypot that gradually adapts or increases its emulation sophistication elicit richer human attacker behaviors over time? Is it possible to engage human attackers using dynamically-adapting Internet of Things honeypots? Does the large amount of data captured by honeypots embody patterns that can enable security analysts to understand attacker intentions on Internet of Things devices?

To answer these questions, an adaptive honeypot approach was employed in which the sophistication of emulated honeypot responses increased as data was analyzed to understand what the attackers were attempting to accomplish. Several facets of honeypots were flexibly composed to mimic a variety of Internet of Things devices. The adaptive Internet of Things honeypot ecosystem was deployed worldwide over a period of three years. Since the massive amount of collected data – more than 28 million hits – would inundate human analysts, a data clustering approach was designed to reveal attack patterns and trends in the data. The experimentation and data analytics suggest that an adaptive honeypot design can elicit richer human attacker behaviors over time. In particular, the experimentation reveals that human attackers can be effectively engaged by adaptive honeypots. The data analytics demonstrates that the huge amount of honeypot data embodies patterns that can be organized to advance the understanding of human attacker behaviors.

2   Related Work

The use of honeypots can be traced back in the research literature as early as 2000 [15]. Honeypots are categorized into two classes, low-interaction honeypots and high-interaction honeypots. Low-interaction honeypots emulate services such as SSH and HTTP whereas high-interaction honeypots provide real operating systems with many vulnerable services [15].

Luo et al. [14] designed an intelligent-interaction honeypot for Internet of Things devices. They also created a framework that automated honeypot responses to make honeypots more realistic and attract attackers.

Wang et al. [25] developed a hybrid Internet of Things honeypot framework that incorporated a low-interaction component with Telnet/ SSH services and high-interaction vulnerable Internet of Things devices. Vetterl and Clayton [24] employed firmware images to emulate customer premises equipment and Internet of Things devices, and run them as honeypots. Pa et al. [17] designed a combination of low-interaction honeypots and sandbox-based high-interaction honeypots. HoneyPLC [13] is a collection of high-interaction honeypots targeted at programmable logic controllers in industrial control systems.

Semic and Mrdovic [22] employed multi-component honeypots to investigate Telnet attacks by the Mirai botnet. Honeypots were designed to recruit and target attackers by exposing weak, generic passwords in the honeypot front-ends. Instead of using emulation files, the front-ends were programmed to generate responses to attacker inputs based on logic defined in the code.

Anirudh et al. [2] developed a honeypot model of a main server to shift denial-of-service (DoS) attacks on Internet of Things networks and improve Internet of Things device performance. Hanson et al. [10] extended the Internet of Things honeypot concept by developing a hybrid honeynet system that included virtual and real devices. The system used machine learning algorithms to analyze traffic and predict the next moves of attackers. Pauna et al. [18] proposed IRASSH-T for developing an Internet of Things honeypot that automatically adapts to new threats. To capture more information about target malware, IRISSH-T employs reinforcement learning algorithms to identify optimal rewards for self-adaptive honeypots that communicate with attackers. Lingenfelter et al. [12] captured data on Internet of Things botnets by simulating an Internet of Things system using three Cowrie SSH/Telnet honeypots. To handle as much traffic as possible, their system set the prefabricated command outputs to match those of actual Internet of Things devices and used sequence matching connections on ports.

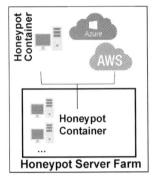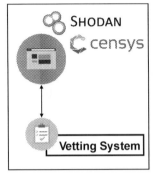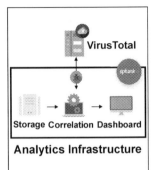

Fig. 1. Adaptive honeypot ecosystem.

Oza et al. [16] presented deception and authorization mechanisms for mitigating man-in-the-middle attacks. Other researchers have also utilized low-interaction honeypots and high-interaction honeypots either separately or together to study attacks on Internet of Things devices [5, 6, 8, 9, 26].

In comparison with the related work described above, this research has focused on eliciting richer attacker behaviors by adapting Internet of Things honeypots and using data analytics to understand the large amounts of data captured by the honeypots over more than three years.

3 Adaptive Honeypot Ecosystem

Figure 1 shows the adaptive Internet of Things honeypot ecosystem [23]. The ecosystem has three components. The first comprises honeypot server farms on premises and in the cloud that host honeypot instances that interact with attackers and collect data. The second is a vetting system, which ensures that attackers find it difficult to identify that the honeypot devices are in fact honeypots. The third component is an analytics infrastructure that is used to analyze the collected data to gain intelligence about attackers and attacker behaviors.

The adaptive honeypot ecosystem employed on-premises servers and cloud instances supported by Amazon Web Services and Microsoft Azure in multiple countries. Since Internet of Things devices have different specifications and configurations, each honeypot instance had to be designed and configured in a unique manner. In creating the ecosystem, off-the-shelf honeypot emulators were adapted and custom emulators were built from scratch.

A honeypot is valuable only as long as it remains undetected, i.e., attackers are unaware that it is a fake system. This is an inherently difficult task because honeypots – especially low-interaction ones – inevitably fail to demonstrate some observable features that only real systems can possess or present features that real systems never manifest. An important goal of the vetting system is to detect information leaks that would indicate a device is a honeypot and to mitigate the leaks promptly.

Table 1. Numbers of hits on various honeypot facets.

Honeypot	Uptime	Hits
HoneyShell	23 months	23,355,621
HoneyWindowsBox	7 months	1,618,906
HoneyCamera	25 months	3,667,029

The primary task of the data analytics infrastructure was to identify attacker interactions and understand attacker behaviors. This information was used to adapt the honeypots. The popular Splunk tool was employed to manage and analyze logs from honeypot devices in the ecosystem. Example analyses include identifying the username-password combinations used by attackers, examining attack locations, identifying the most and least frequent commands executed during attack sessions, scrutinizing downloaded files and sending them to the popular VirusTotal website, storing the results and checking attacker IP addresses using the DShield and AbuseIPDB systems.

4   Eliciting Rich Attacker Behaviors

The longer a honeypot can keep an attacker on the hook, the more useful is the information gained about the attacker's goals and tactics. Of course, the more interested an attacker becomes in a honeypot device, the more sophisticated the honeypot needs to be to fool the attacker that it is a real device. The effectiveness of this competition is measured by the number of useful insights gleaned given the amount of engineering effort expended. Therefore, the ecosystem was designed to incorporate a variety of honeypot devices that worked in concert with the vetting system and data analytics infrastructure to achieve a high return on investment.

The first research question was whether rich human attacker behaviors could be elicited by adapting the deployed honeypots based on the observed traffic. A multi-phase process was employed to continuously increase the complexity of the honeypot instances. In the first phase, honeypots were deployed to collect data. This data was analyzed to design adaptations for the next phase. During the second phase, the honeypots emulated responses according to the attackers' perceived goals. Multiple iterations were performed until the insights were deemed to be satisfactory.

Due to the rich interactions that Internet of Things devices have with their environments, an Internet of Things honeypot must be organized to allow a flexible combination of components that provide services such as SSH, Telnet and HTTP. Therefore, honeypot components called facets were constructed to emulate the various services provided by Internet of Things devices.

Table 1 presents the numbers of hits received by three honeypot facets, HoneyShell, HoneyWindowsBox and HoneyCamera, positioned in the adaptive honeypot ecosystem. A total number of 28,641,556 hits were captured by the honeypot ecosystem over more than three years. This section describes two of the facets, HoneyShell and HoneyCamera, how they were adapted to attract attackers, and the experimental results.

4.1   Adapting Shell Services

Many Internet of Things devices have shell services such as SSH and Telnet that allow remote logins. Since shell services constituted a major portion of the attack surface based on the collected data, a honeypot version of the shell services dubbed HoneyShell was created.

HoneyShell uses Cowrie honeypots to emulate vulnerable Internet of Things devices that support SSH (port 22) and Telnet (port 23). Cowrie can be configured to emulate different operating systems. HoneyShell was configured to emulate BusyBox, a command suite with Unix utilities that is commonly provided by Internet of Things devices. HoneyShell was adapted during the two phases as follows:

- **Phase 1:** An initial version of HoneyShell was deployed with minimal changes to the original Cowrie code. Data that would be useful in the next phase was collected and responses that might reveal the device as a honeypot were identified. Every possible username-password combination was accepted by HoneyShell during the first phase. Three HoneyShell instances were deployed in this phase, two on premises and one in the cloud (Singapore).
- **Phase 2:** Phase 2 was initiated on one of the two on-premises HoneyShells nine months after the first phase was initiated. The other on-premises HoneyShell kept running in its Phase 1 configuration for comparison purposes. In Phase 2, the top 30 username-password combinations of sessions that executed at least one command after logging in during Phase 1 were accepted as valid authentication credentials; login failure messages were displayed for all other username-password combinations.

  The environments provided to attackers were made more meaningful by incorporating new users and filesystems. Additional commands were implemented to attract more activity. Also, Phase 1 logs were analyzed for fingerprinting techniques used by attackers and efforts were made to ensure that the Phase 2 honeypot handled them properly. An example was emulating responses to the `file` command.

Does Adaptation Elicit Rich Behaviors? Figure 2 shows the numbers of hits received by the two on-premises HoneyShells and the Singapore cloud HoneyShell. The Phase 1 on-premises HoneyShell ran from January 2018 to November 2019. The Phase 2 on-premises HoneyShell ran from October 2018 to November 2019; it operated as a Phase 1 honeypot for the first nine months before moving to Phase 2 and ran in parallel with the Phase 1 honeypot. The two on-premises HoneyShell instances operated simultaneously (except for the first

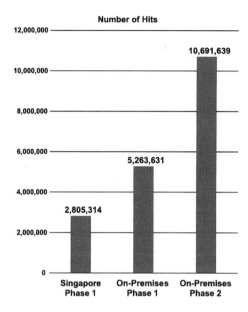

Fig. 2. Hits captured by HoneyShells in the two phases.

six months) at the same location with very similar public-facing IP addresses. This made it possible to examine the effects of adapting honeypot responses with as few confounding factors as possible. The Singapore HoneyShell, which ran as a Phase 1 honeypot in the cloud, was deployed from January 2018 to January 2019.

Several observations were made regarding the data collected by the two on-premises HoneyShell instances:

- **Hits:** The on-premises Phase 2 HoneyShell received many more hits than the on-premises Phase 1 HoneyShell. Specifically, the Phase 2 HoneyShell received 10 million hits over 13 months whereas its Phase 1 counterpart received five million hits in 23 months. It appears that the differences in the numbers of hits received were due to the different responses produced by the two honeypots. This is a strong indication that the adaptation implemented in the Phase 2 HoneyShell made it more interesting to attackers.

  At first glance, it is questionable that adaptation would increase the number of hits because hits occur before any interactions with a honeypot. However, individual hits may not be totally independent. Multiple hits are very likely to have come from the same attacker or group of attackers. It is likely that a device deemed to be fake by attackers would be blacklisted and ignored, resulting in few hits.

- **Sessions:** Many more sessions were established with the on-premises HoneyShell during Phase 2 compared with Phase 1. Specifically, there were 2,933,646 sessions in Phase 2 compared with 1,314,465 sessions in Phase 1.

This is another indicator that attackers were drawn to the adapted Phase 2 HoneyShell.

- **Successful Logins:** The on-premises Phase 2 HoneyShell had many more successful logins than the on-premises Phase 1 HoneyShell. The Phase 2 HoneyShell had 1,311,227 successful logins in 4,919,923 login attempts corresponding to a 27% success rate. In contrast, the Phase 1 HoneyShell had 409,771 successful logins in 2,279,376 login attempts, corresponding to a 18% success rate.

  The Phase 2 HoneyShell only accepted the top 30 username-password combinations whereas the Phase 1 HoneyShell accepted all username-password combinations. Despite its stringent password policy, the Phase 2 HoneyShell login success rate of 27% is much higher than the Phase 1 HoneyShell success rate of 18%. This indicates that the Phase 1 login attempts were more indiscriminate, using the wrong protocols and incorrect parameters that resulted in login failures. In contrast, Phase 2 login attempts were much more methodical – the 27% success rate is reasonable given that attackers had to correctly guess one of the 30 accepted username-password to succeed, which would involve multiple failed login attempts.

- **Commands:** Attackers executed various commands after logging into the Phase 1 and Phase 2 HoneyShells. The commands collected by the Phase 1 HoneyShell were dominated by scripted commands such as:

```
echo -e '\\x47\\x72\\x6f\\x70/' > //.nippon;
cat //.nippon;
rm -f //.nippon
```

```
uname -a;unset HISTORY HISTFILE HISTSAVE HISTZONE HISTORY HIS
TLOG WATCH;history -n;export HISTFILE=/dev/null;export HISTSI
ZE=0;export HISTFILESIZE=0;cd;mkdir .ssh;rm -rf .ssh/authoriz
ed_keys;touch .ssh/authorized_keys;echo 'ssh-rsa AAAAB3NzaC1y
c2EAAAABJQAAAQEAvN5GkpS25Z9eA2bARaXTVfVN2m/N5V5ddOTyVPftA3ljo
rQitmh1pyuZDty9oTWF+JOcOtGBvRaQ7NvZCaDC2q6QROiMOfq7zs+4b18WO8
UnaQcVVIBeEt3YPo8PXwVm5fR4wgoq9SZp29/2jFzOUmAOhiUyImh9/P7jFW
qpv3gSxZ8neq+4pSCUfE24OGiFBpJGkAE+wMmJcBXOWjFfjedcbBs1FO/C+x8
WY9bFkQ3NwwjVbh3c3mYy9zqdPhm6GI/heVAZUWSKHausOwb+Rem+eKhkrKv
oeteqJXEIrlLbHyRHn+12nN/qgG5kIcICv4TRD59GHMYZH3ILngyFJQ==' >>
.ssh/authorized_keys;cd
```

The first sample above was one of 1,128 occurrences produced by the Mirai botnet with 1,128 occurrences. In the second sample above, the attacker disabled shell history logging and attempted to plant an SSH public key on the server. The type of command and its large number of occurrences (562) indicate that the sample was likely due to an automated script.

In contrast, the commands collected by the Phase 2 HoneyShell comprised fewer scripted commands and commands from known botnets such as Mirai. In fact, many commands collected by the Phase 2 HoneyShell resembled human actions, such as the following three independent commands:

Table 2. Top ten username-password combinations captured by HoneyShells.

Username/Password	Occurrences
admin/1234	975,729
root/(empty)	167,869
admin/(empty)	82,018
0/(empty)	62,140
(empty)/root	52,780
1234/1234	50,305
admin/admin	39,349
admin/1234567890	12,444
root/admin	10,359

```
ls -la /var/run/gcc.pid
ifconfig
rm -rf /var/tmp/dota*
```

The Phase 1 HoneyShell had very few such commands. Clearly, the Phase 2 HoneyShell commands are more interesting and more of them are likely due to direct human actions than automated programs.

Analysis of the data collected by the on-premises Phase 1 HoneyShell and Phase 1 HoneyShell deployed in the Singapore cloud indicated they had similar characteristics in terms of command patterns. In fact, the vast majority of commands collected by the two Phase 1 HoneyShells appeared to be issued by automated programs.

HoneyShell Statistics Most of the logins used random username-password combinations, which indicates that automated scripts were used to guess the correct credentials. Table 2 shows the top ten username-password combinations used by attackers. The login data indicates that attackers preferentially targeted users with high privileges and weak passwords. However, other username-password combinations such as university-florida, root-university and university-student were used on the on-premises honeypot located at a university. This indicates that attackers were aware that the honeypot was located at a university and attempted to customize their attacks accordingly.

Only 314,112 (13%) unique sessions were detected with at least one successful honeypot command execution. This indicates that only a small proportion of the attacks proceeded to the next attack step. Also, the remaining (87%) attacks focused on discovering a correct username-password combination.

Table 3 provides information about the files captured by the HoneyShells. A total of 236 unique files were collected. In all, 46% of the downloaded files were collected by the on-premises university honeypots whereas the remaining 54% were collected by the Singapore cloud honeypot. VirusTotal flagged all the collected files as malicious.

Table 3. Downloaded files captured by HoneyShells.

Malicious File Campaign	Count
DoS/DDoS	59
IRCBot/Mirai	40
ShellDownloader	40
Backdoor	36
CoinMiner	31
Others	30

Denial-of-service and distributed-denial-of-service executables were the most common files. IRCBot/Mirai and ShellDownloader were the second most common files. This demonstrates that Mirai, which surfaced in 2016, is still an active botnet and continues to attempt to add more devices to its botnet. As expected, ShellDownloader attempted to download files in various formats that execute on operating system architectures such as x86, ARM, i686 and MIPS. Often, adversaries gained access in their first attempt and proceeded to run all the executable files. The Others category in Table 3 includes SSH scanner, mass scan and Domain Name System (DNS) poisoning executables.

Table 4. Top ten commands captured by the Phase 2 HoneyShell.

Command	Occurrences
/gisdfoewrsfdf	1,243
mount ;/gisdfoewrsfdf	1,240
/bin/busybox cp; /gisdfoewrsfdf'	1,240
cat /proc/cpuinfo | grep name | wc -l	1,024
sudo /bin/sh	819
ls -la /var/run/gcc.pid	765
uname -a	248
cat /proc/cpuinfo	204
/ip cloud print	165
ifconfig	162

In addition to placing files in the HoneyShells, attackers attempted to execute numerous commands. Table 4 shows the top ten commands captured by the Phase 2 HoneyShell along with their occurrences. The top three commands in the table were issued by the Mirai botnet.

4.2   Adapting Honeypots to Device Types

An Internet of Things camera (D-Link) was chosen for the honeypot emulation of an Internet of Things device. The first HoneyCamera instance was placed in the cloud infrastructure. Phase 1 data was used to identify the possible weaknesses of HoneyCamera. The collected data was used to adapt the HoneyCamera configuration in its Phase 2 implementation. The following paragraphs provide details about the two phases:

- **Phase 1:** Three HoneyCamera instances were deployed. Two instances, which were deployed in the cloud in Sydney and Paris, only had port 8080 open. The third instance deployed in the cloud in London only had port 80 open. The first two HoneyCamera instances emulated D-Link DCS-5020L cameras and the third instance emulated a D-Link DCS-5030L camera. The HoneyCamera instances were configured as interaction-based honeypots to collect as much data as possible. The vetting system identified the three HoneyCamera instances as real Internet of Things devices. Data collected during Phase 1 indicated that attackers were attempting to exploit known vulnerabilities in Internet of Things cameras.
- **Phase 2:** The data collected in Phase 1 revealed that attackers attempted to exploit six HoneyCamera vulnerabilities, the most common being authentication information leakage. These vulnerabilities were carefully studied and the corresponding responses were incorporated in the Phase 2 HoneyCamera instances. Additionally, the Internet of Things cameras were equipped with SSH/Telnet ports for remote configuration and diagnostics. In order to replicate these activities, the HoneyShell and HoneyCamera implementations were integrated and deployed as single instances in the on-premises and cloud (Tokyo) infrastructures. The integrated instances were able to identify attacker behavior involving Unix command-line and camera-specific commands.

Six Internet of Things camera devices were emulated as HoneyCamera instances. Attackers attempted to install several malicious files on the honeypots, mainly CoinMiner and Mirai variants. Analysis of the captured logs revealed that the honeypots attracted many attacks that specifically targeted Internet of Things cameras. The following are some example attacks:

- The first attack sought to brute force the camera credentials (`/?action=str eam/snapshot.cgi?user=[USERNAME]&pwd=[PASSWORD]&count=0`). The attackers attempted to obtain a correct username-password combination to access a video streaming service.
- The second attack sought to exploit the CVE-2018-9995 vulnerability to bypass camera credentials using a `Cookie: uid=admin` header and gain access to the camera (`/device.rsp?opt=user&cmd=list`).
- Table 5 shows additional types of attacks executed on the HoneyCamera instances. The data collected from the honeypots revealed that the targets included D-Link, Hikvision, Netwave, AIVI, IP and Foscam cameras.

Table 5. Attack types executed on HoneyCamera instances.

HoneyCamera Instance	Attack
DLINK Camera	CVE-2013-1599
Hikvision IP Camera	Bypass Authentication
Netwave IP Camera	Password Disclosure
AIVI Tech Camera	Command Injection
IP Camera	Shellshock
Foscam IP Camera	Bypass Authentication
All Instances	Malicious Activity

Does Adaptation Elicit Rich Behaviors? A vulnerability that attackers leveraged to target the HoneyCamera was identified in Phase 1. The vulnerability, Exploit-DB ID-38853, enabled the exploitation of the web interface login page to view the username and password.

The Phase 2 honeypot implemented the correct response to the vulnerability, revealing the username and password for the login page. The vulnerable page was instrumented so that an exploit attempt would reveal the username and password in an image on the HTML page, which a human could not distinguish from what would be presented by a real Internet of Things camera.

Log file analysis revealed that attacks originating from 29 IP addresses exploited the vulnerability and successfully logged into the HoneyCamera web console using the username and password displayed in the image. The pattern of attacker movements between web pages and the fact that the username and password were embedded in an image that could be read by humans (machine recognition would be extremely unlikely) indicate that the activities were performed by humans as opposed to automated programs.

4.3 Summary

The experiments involving the three Internet of Things honeypot facets, HoneyShell, HoneyWindowsBox and HoneyCamera, revealed a consistent pattern – more malicious traffic was seen when the honeypots were adapted based on the observed traffic to provide attackers with information they would want to see. In all the experiments, richer attacker behaviors were discerned, such as more logins and human-like commands in the HoneyShell instance and human attack activities in the HoneyCamera instances.

5 Data Analytics

The third research question sought to investigate if the data captured by honeypots embodies patterns that enable security analysts to understand the intentions of human attackers. Analysis of the data revealed that the honeypot instances collected huge amounts of attack activities, most of them belonging to a few categories. Also, activities in the same category had similarities. This inspired the application of an unsupervised clustering approach to gain insights into attacker activities before attempting to discern attacker intentions.

5.1 Clustering Captured Commands

This section describes the similarity metric used for clustering and the clustering approach.

Similarity Metric The deployed honeypots captured large numbers of commands of varying lengths in SSH login sessions. Cosine similarity was selected as the metric for determining the similarity between two commands. It measures the cosine of the angle between two vectors – in this case, command embeddings – in multidimensional space. Frequency-based embedding was employed, where each vector component represents the number of occurrences of a given word in the command text. A smaller angle means a higher similarity value.

The similarity between two vectors $\mathbf{A}$ and $\mathbf{B}$ is computed as:

$$\text{similarity}(\mathbf{A}, \mathbf{B}) = \frac{\mathbf{A} \cdot \mathbf{B}}{\|\mathbf{A}\|\|\mathbf{B}\|} = \frac{\sum_{i=1}^{n} A_i B_i}{\sqrt{\sum_{i=1}^{n} A_i^2} \sqrt{\sum_{i=1}^{n} B_i^2}}$$

where A_i and B_i are components of vectors $\mathbf{A}$ and $\mathbf{B}$, respectively.

Similarity values range from zero to one. A similarity value of zero means that the two vectors are orthogonal and have no similarity. The closer a similarity value is to one, the smaller the angle and the greater the match between the two vectors.

As an example, consider the two commands:

- **Command A:** `cat /proc/cpuinfo | grep name | cut -f2 -d: | uniq -c`
- **Command B:** `cat /proc/cpuinfo | grep name | head -n 1 | awk {print $4, $5, $6, $7, $8, $9;}`

Executing Commands A and B on a real device reveals that both commands provide similar information. However, the manner in which the two commands are parsed and represented can lead to very different cosine similarity results:

- **Case 1:** Assume that all the commands, command options, variables and positional parameters are included in the word vocabulary. The unique vocabulary for Commands A and B is:
  - `[awk, cat, cpuinfo, cut, f2, grep, head, print, proc, uniq, -n, -d, -c, 1, 4, 5, 6, 7, 8, 9]`
  The similarity value of Commands A and B is 0.3953.
- **Case 2:** Assume that all the commands and command options are included in the word vocabulary. However, command variables and positional parameters are not included in the word vocabulary. In this case, the unique vocabulary for Commands A and B is:

- [awk, cat, cpuinfo, cut, f2, grep, head, print, proc, uniq, -n, -d, -c]

The similarity value for Commands A and B is 0.5270.
- **Case 3:** Assume that only the commands are included in the word vocabulary. In this case, the unique vocabulary for Commands A and B is:
  - [awk, cat, cpuinfo, cut, grep, head, print, proc, uniq]

The similarity value for Commands A and B is 0.6249.

The example demonstrates that command options and variables possess low relevance with regard to command similarity. Further analysis of the data revealed that IP addresses and port numbers also have low relevance. Therefore, command options and variables were ignored and IP addresses and port numbers were replaced by dummy values in a data pre-processing step before computing the command similarity values.

Clustering Approach Five clustering approaches, k-means clustering, agglomerative hierarchical clustering, spectral clustering, density-based spatial clustering of applications with noise (DBSCAN) and Gaussian mixture model (GMM) clustering, were investigated to find a suitable model that fitted the data. Except for agglomerative hierarchical clustering and DBSCAN, all the other clustering approaches require the *a priori* specification of the number of clusters k. The silhouette coefficient method was employed to determine the cluster number k that would partition the commands into clearly distinguishable clusters.

The first set of experiments focused on the commands collected by the Singapore HoneyShell. After evaluating the five clustering approaches with their optimal k values, it was determined that GMM clustering with $k = 150$ partitioned the commands into the most meaningful clusters.

Following the same approach, the optimal cluster numbers k were computed for the larger on-premises data. The results revealed that GMM clustering with $k = 250$ produced the most meaningful command clusters in reasonable time. Next, the unique commands in each cluster were examined to determine if they could be merged into larger clusters based on similar activities. Ultimately, the 526 unique commands were grouped into 41 clusters.

The objectives behind each cluster were identified. Some commands had multiple subcommands and attackers executed them together in single composite commands. Such composite commands were clustered with other commands that shared some, but not all, characteristics. Thus, clusters were labeled with multiple objectives, but not every command in the clusters met all the cluster objectives. Interested readers are referred to www.arguslab.org/honeyshell_clusters.html for details about the clusters, including their objectives and constituent commands.

5.2   Clustering Results

To experiment with the clustering approach, all the commands executed by attackers were extracted from the Singapore HoneyShell logs and clustered. Fig-

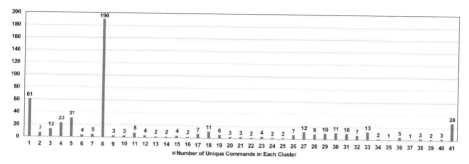

Fig. 3. Unique commands in each cluster (Singapore).

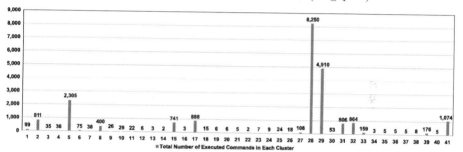

Fig. 4. Occurrences of commands in each cluster (Singapore).

ure 3 shows the distribution of the numbers of unique commands found in each cluster.

Figure 4 shows the occurrences of commands executed in each cluster corresponding to the Singapore HoneyShell logs. The vast majority of commands (79%) belong to just five clusters that contain 5, 17, 28, 29, 41 commands, respectively. Some of these clusters correspond to activities from the Mirai botnet and its variants. The others correspond to fingerprinting.

The same clustering experiments were performed on commands from the on-premises HoneyShell logs. Figure 5 shows the distribution of the numbers of unique commands found in each cluster. Figure 6 shows the occurrences of commands executed in each cluster.

6   Conclusions

The adaptive Internet of Things honeypot ecosystem presented in this chapter is a first step towards understanding human attacker behaviors targeting Internet of Things devices. Analysis of the data collected by the honeypot ecosystem over more than three years reveals that adversaries are actively looking for vulnerable Internet of Things devices to exploit. The results also demonstrate that adapting honeypot responses based on observed attacker activities elicits and captures increasingly sophisticated attacker behaviors, far exceeding the capabilities of a

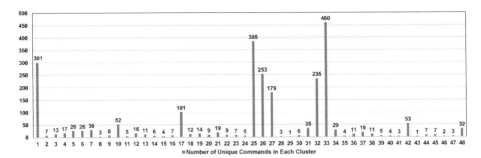

Fig. 5. Unique commands in each cluster (on premises).

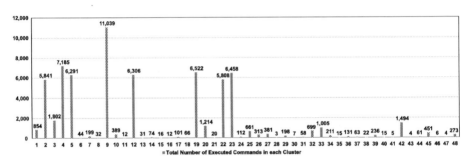

Fig. 6. Occurrences of commands in each cluster (on premises).

non-adaptive honeypot. Additionally, a clustering approach developed to understand the large number of attacker-executed commands captured by the Internet of Things honeypot ecosystem provides valuable insights into attacker intentions and modes of operation.

Commercial products are identified in this chapter in order to adequately specify certain procedures. In no case does such identification imply a recommendation or an endorsement by the National Institute of Standards and Technology, nor does it imply that the identified products are necessarily the best available for the purpose.

References

1. Akamai Technologies, UPnProxy: Blackhat Proxies via NAT Injections, Akamai White Paper, Cambridge, Massachusetts, 2018.
2. M. Anirudh, S. Thileeban and D. Nallathambi, Use of honeypots for mitigating DoS attacks targeted on IoT networks, *Proceedings of the International Conference on Computer, Communications and Signal Processing*, 2017.
3. M. Antonakakis, T. April, M. Bailey, M. Bernhard, E. Bursztein, J. Cochran, Z. Durumeric, J. Halderman, L. Invernizzi, M. Kallitsis, D. Kumar, C. Lever, Z. Ma, J. Mason, D. Menscher, C. Seaman, N. Sullivan, K. Thomas and Y. Zhou,

Understanding the Mirai botnet, *Proceedings of the Twenty-Sixth USENIX Security Symposium*, pp. 1093–1110, 2017.

4. A. Anubhav, Masuta: Satori creators' second botnet weaponizes a new router exploit, *NewSky Security*, January 23, 2018.

5. S. Chamotra, R. Sehgal, S. Ror and B. Singh, Honeypot deployment in broadband networks, *Proceedings of the International Conference on Information Systems Security*, pp. 479–488, 2016.

6. S. Dowling, M. Schukat and H. Melvin, A ZigBee honeypot to assess IoT cyberattack behavior, *Proceedings of the Twenty-Eighth Irish Signals and Systems Conference*, 2017.

7. S. Edwards and I. Profetis, Hajime: Analysis of a Decentralized Internet Worm for IoT Devices, Technical Report, Rapidity Networks, Boulder, Colorado, 2016.

8. J. Guarnizo, A. Tambe, S. Bhunia, M. Ochoa, N. Tippenhauer, A. Shabtai and Y. Elovici, SIPHON: Towards scalable high-interaction physical honeypots, *Proceedings of the Third ACM Workshop on Cyber-Physical System Security*, pp. 57–68, 2017.

9. M. Hakim, H. Aksu, A. Uluagac and K. Akkaya, U-PoT: A honeypot framework for UPnP-based IoT devices, *Proceedings of the Thirty-Seventh IEEE International Performance Computing and Communications Conference*, 2018.

10. P. Hanson, L. Truax and D. Saranchak, IoT honeynet for military deception and indications and warnings, in *Autonomous Systems: Sensors, Vehicles, Security and the Internet of Everything*, M. Dudzik and J. Ricklin (Eds.), International Society for Optics and Photonics (SPIE), Bellingham, Washington, pp. 106431A-1–106431A-11, 2018.

11. R. Joven and K. Yang, A wicked family of bots, *Fortinet Blog/ Threat Research*, May 17, 2018.

12. B. Lingenfelter, I. Vakilinia and S. Sengupta, Analyzing variations among IoT botnets using medium interaction honeypots, *Proceedings of the Tenth Annual Computing and Communications Workshop and Conference*, pp. 761–767, 2020.

13. E. Lopez-Morales, C. Rubio-Medrano, A. Doupe, Y. Shoshitaishvili, R. Wang, T. Bao and G. Ahn, *Proceedings of the ACM SIGSAC Conference on Computer and Communications Security*, pp. 279–291, 2020.

14. T. Luo, Z. Xu, X. Jin, Y. Jia and X. Ouyang, IoTCandyJar: Towards an intelligent-interaction honeypot for IoT devices, presented at *Black Hat USA*, 2017.

15. M. Nawrocki, M. Wahlisch, T. Schmidt, C. Keil and J. Schonfelder, A Survey of Honeypot Software and Data Analysis, arXiv: 1608.06249 (arxiv.org/abs/1608.06249), 2016.

16. A. Oza, G. Kumar, M. Khorajiya and V. Tiwari, Snaring cyber attacks on IoT devices with a honeynet, in *Computing and Network Sustainability*, S. Peng, N. Dey and M. Bundele (Eds.), Springer, Singapore, pp. 1–12, 2019.

17. Y. Pa, S. Suzuki, K. Yoshioka, T. Matsumoto, T. Kasama and C. Rossow, IoT-POT: Analyzing the rise of IoT compromises, *Proceedings of the Ninth USENIX Workshop on Offensive Technologies*, 2015.

18. A. Pauna, I. Bica, F. Pop and A. Castiglione, On the rewards of self-adaptive IoT honeypots, *Annals of Telecommunications*, vol. 74(7-8), pp. 501–515, 2019.

19. T. Seals, IoT attacks skyrocket, doubling in 6 months, *Threatpost*, September 6, 2021.

20. Security Response Team, ISTR 23: Insights into the cyber security threat landscape, *Symantec Enterprise Blogs/Threat Intelligence*, March 21, 2018.

21. Security Response Team, VPNFilter: New router malware with destructive capabilities, *Symantec Enterprise Blogs/Threat Intelligence*, May 23, 2018.

22. H. Semic and M. Sasa, IoT honeypot: A multi-component solution for handling manual and Mirai-based attacks, *Proceedings of the Twenty-Fifth Telecommunications Forum*, 2017.
23. A. Tabari, X. Ou and A. Singhal, What are Attackers After on IoT Devices? An Approach Based on a Multi-Phased Multi-Faceted IoT Honeypot Ecosystem and Data Clustering, arXiv: 2112.10974v1 (`arxiv.org/abs/2112.10974v1`), 2021.
24. A. Vetterl and R. Clayton, Honware: A virtual honeypot framework for capturing CPE and IoT zero days, *Proceedings of the APWG Symposium on Electronic Crime Research*, 2019.
25. B. Wang, Y. Dou, Y. Sang, Y. Zhang and J. Huang, IoTCMal: Towards a hybrid IoT honeypot for capturing and analyzing malware, *Proceedings of the IEEE International Conference on Communications*, 2020.
26. M. Wang, J. Santillan and F. Kuipers, ThingPot: An Interactive Internet-of-Things Honeypot, arXiv: 1807.04114 (`arxiv.org/abs/1807.04114`), 2018.

Towards Direct-Control Data Acquisition by Nano-Probing Non-Volatile Memory Cells

Shawn McKay[1], Nathan Hutchins[1], Steven Baskerville[2], and Sujeet Shenoi[1]

[1] University of Tulsa, Tulsa, Oklahoma, USA
sujeet@utulsa.edu
[2] U.S. Secret Service National Computer Forensics Institute Laboratory, Tulsa, Oklahoma, USA

Abstract. This chapter describes a data acquisition method for non-volatile memory that directly interfaces with the floating-gate transistors on a silicon die using nano-probes under a scanning electron microscope. The method involves chip preparation, memory cell reverse engineering, contact point identification and disinterring, following which nano-probes are positioned on control points on the die that are attached to the address, bit and ground lines associated with an individual memory cell. After the connections are established, a highly-sensitive sourcemeter applies voltage in a sweeping pattern to the address lines to enable current to flow between the bit and ground lines. The sourcemeter measures the minuscule current flow in the floating-gate transistor of the targeted memory cell to determine if it stores a zero or one. The research literature does not describe a data acquisition method that actively probes individual memory cells to read data.

Extensive experiments on ATmega328P microcontrollers demonstrate that the chip preparation, memory cell reverse engineering and contact point identification steps are successful. However, after the contact point disinterring step, it was difficult to verify that the contact points were fully exposed and free from contamination and damage. Indeed, the difficulty establishing consistent electrical connections between the nano-probe tips and address, bit and ground lines yielded non-ideal results. Nevertheless, the direct-control data acquisition method for non-volatile memory and the accompanying workflow that customizes a direct-control data acquisition method to a specific microcontroller or memory chip are technically sound.

Keywords: Non-Volatile Memory · Silicon Dies · Floating-Gate Transistors · Bit-Level Data Acquisition

1 Introduction

Evidence from electronic devices can be recovered non-invasively when the devices are functional and tools are available for data recovery. However, more invasive techniques are required when devices are damaged and non-repairable and/or tools are not available. In these scenarios, the device circuit boards are

© IFIP International Federation for Information Processing 2023
Published by Springer Nature Switzerland AG 2023
G. Peterson and S. Shenoi (Eds.): DigitalForensics 2023, IFIP AICT 687, pp. 91–122, 2023.
https://doi.org/10.1007/978-3-031-42991-0_6

exposed and reverse engineered to identify communications ports such as Universal Asynchronous Receiver-Transmitter (UART), Serial Peripheral Interface (SPI) [10] and Joint Test Action Group (JTAG) [14, 15, 17]. Following this, commercial or custom data manipulation/debugging tools [13, 15] are used to interact with the communications ports to extract data from microcontrollers and memory chips.

Device manufacturers often disable communications ports on circuit boards to protect data and intellectual property [7, 17]. In these instances, more invasive techniques are required because the communications connections only reside on the chips. Specifically, a chip is desoldered, and electrical connections are established between the communications pins on the underside of the chip and a data manipulation/debugging tool [13, 15] is employed for data acquisition. This invasive "chip-off" technique is also applied to extract evidence from electronic devices with damaged circuit boards, but whose microcontrollers and memory chips are intact. Rainwater [16] has demonstrated that it is also possible to expose the bond wires in a desoldered chip via laser ablation and ultrasonically weld tiny gold wires to the exposed bond wires on one side and a breakout board on the other side. Having established the connections between the chip and breakout board, a data manipulation/debugging tool [13, 15] can be employed to extract chip data.

Continuing their protection efforts, chip manufacturers may employ encryption [4, 5, 11] and lock bits [12] to thwart data recovery from desoldered chips. In such cases, data may be extracted using side-channel analysis, but the techniques are complex, tedious and have a low probability of success.

To address this problem, even more invasive techniques that expose the silicon dies of chips have been developed. One technique uses laser glitching to inject faults into a silicon die to defeat its data protection mechanism [3, 9]. A second technique, passive voltage contrast imaging [6], uses a scanning electron microscope to image the memory cells on a silicon die; the memory cell images are subsequently analyzed by image processing software to determine memory cell content. A third technique uses atomic force microscopy to measure the capacitance of memory cells on a silicon die to reveal the stored data [8]. Unfortunately, the laser glitching technique is highly unreliable because it uses brute force on the assumption that glitching will eventually defeat the memory protection mechanism and affect data recovery. The other two techniques require extremely precise preparation of silicon die samples and very high quality scanning electron/atomic force microscope images. The preparation of silicon die samples to the required tolerances often results in data loss due to memory circuit damage. Additionally, extremely sophisticated image processing algorithms are required to consistently distinguish between the zeros and ones stored in micron-scale memory cells.

This chapter describes a direct-control data acquisition method for non-volatile memory that directly interfaces with floating-gate transistors on a silicon die using nano-probes under a scanning electron microscope. The nano-probes are positioned on the die control points attached to the address, bit and ground lines associated with an individual memory cell. After the connections are established, a highly-sensitive sourcemeter applies voltage in a sweeping pattern (curve) to the address lines to enable current to flow between the bit and ground lines. The sourcemeter measures the minuscule current flow in the floating-gate transistor of the targeted memory cell to determine if the cell stores a zero or one. This strategy would defeat any data protection mechanism implemented for floating-gate transistors because, as long as transistors store bits, no protections could be positioned lower than the transistor level.

The principal contribution of this research is a comprehensive workflow for customizing the data acquisition method to a specific non-volatile microcontroller or memory chip. The workflow comprises the method development and method application phases. During the initial method development phase, a custom direct-control data acquisition method is developed for a specific chip. This phase involves five steps, chip preparation, memory cell reverse engineering, contact point identification and disinterring, data acquisition and data verification. The five steps are performed iteratively using sample chips until the custom direct-control data acquisition method is perfected. The custom direct-control data acquisition method is applied to the target chip containing evidentiary data during the final method application phase.

The direct-control data acquisition method is restricted to non-volatile memory because it is difficult to power volatile memory and/or refresh (rewrite) the stored data when its silicon die is inside a scanning electron microscope chamber. Although the proposed data acquisition method is designed to work on any type of non-volatile memory, the focus is on flash memory due to its ubiquitous use in modern electronic devices.

2   Background

Memory is a vital component of electronic devices. It stores programs and data needed for electronic devices to function and provides workspaces for devices to perform operations on data. Electronic devices would have minimal functionality without persistent memory. Standard devices with memory include cell phones, flash drives, personal computers and Internet of Things devices. Data is stored in memory as bits (zeros or ones). Each bit is stored in a single memory cell that is implemented using one or more transistors [19].

Memory hardware incorporates transistors that constitute the memory cells and circuitry that reads data from and writes data to the cells. The transistors that constitute the memory cells and logic reside in a silicon wafer and are interconnected via very-large-scale integration (VLSI). Memory resides in a standalone memory chip or is integrated with other logic circuitry in a microcontroller. Most electronic memory incorporates interconnected transistors that reside in integrated circuits.

Transistors are the building blocks of integrated circuits. Transistors function like light switches because they control current flow between two points. Depending on the transistor type, current flows or is blocked from flowing when

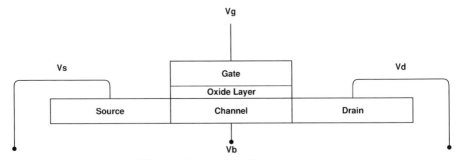

Fig. 1. Single field-effect transistor.

the transistor is not activated; the opposite is the case when the transistor is activated. Transistors are used in integrated circuits because they can be controlled electronically. Integrated circuit logic and memory cells incorporate various arrangements and interconnections of multiple transistors [18].

The two main types of transistors are bipolar junction transistors and field-effect transistors. Non-volatile memory typically incorporates field-effect transistors, so this research deals primarily with field-effect transistors.

Field-Effect Transistor A field-effect transistor has three connections, gate, drain and source. It is controlled by a voltage placed at the gate. A field-effect transistor does not leak current like a bipolar junction transistor, making it more energy efficient. Also, it has a much higher switching speed than a bipolar junction transistor. These characteristics render field-effect transistors well suited to implementing integrated circuits and memory cells.

Figure 1 shows a field-effect transistor with the source and drain on either side of a channel with the gate sitting above the channel. The oxide layer electrically isolates the gate from the channel. Depending on the type of field-effect transistor, two default situations are possible. In the n-channel type of transistor, the drain and source pins are electrically connected by default, enabling current to flow. In the p-channel type of transistor, the drain and source pins are electrically isolated by default, blocking current flow.

A field-effect transistor is activated by applying a voltage to the gate. The current flow through the channel is changed by adjusting the voltage Vg applied at the gate. Depending on the transistor type, activating the transistor allows current to flow between the source and drain or prevents current flow [18]. Ordinary field-effect transistors can be arranged in groups to store bits of data temporarily. However, an additional electrically-isolated gate, called a floating gate, is required to implement non-volatile memory.

Floating-Gate Transistor A floating-gate transistor is a field-effect transistor with an extra floating gate between the gate and channel. Although the floating gate is electrically isolated from the rest of the transistor, it causes the transistor

Table 1. Floating-gate transistor states.

Charged Floating Gate	Vg ≤ Vth	Vg > Vth
No	Off	On
Yes	Off	Off

to function differently depending on whether or not a charge is stored on the floating gate. If there is no charge on the floating gate, then the transistor works like a standard field-effect transistor. For example, in the case of an n-channel floating-gate transistor with no charge on the floating gate, a high voltage on the gate turns the transistor on, enabling current to flow between the source and drain. However, when the floating gate is charged in an n-channel enhancement-mode floating-gate transistor, a higher voltage at the gate is required to activate the transistor [2]. As a result, applying the same voltage at the gate of a charged floating-gate transistor will not activate the transistor, preventing current from flowing between the source and drain. Detecting the difference in the functionality of a floating-gate transistor with a charged floating gate and an uncharged floating gate enables data storage [20].

Table 1 shows the states of an n-channel enhancement-mode floating-gate field-effect transistor. How a transistor behaves when an activating voltage is applied depends on whether or not the floating gate is charged. A voltage greater than the threshold voltage Vth activates the transistor unless the floating gate is charged. Typically, n-channel enhancement-mode floating-gate field-effect transistors are used to implement electrically-erasable programmable read-only memory and flash memory.

Memory Operation Different types of memory are created using combinations of transistors and other electronic components. However, the methods for reading data from many types of memory are similar. A memory cell sits at the intersection of an address line and bit line. The address line connects to the gate of the transistor in the memory cell, controlling when the cell can manipulate the state of the bit line to which it is connected. The data contained in a memory cell is determined by observing the state of the bit line after the cell is activated.

Memory is either volatile or non-volatile. Volatile memory loses the data it stores with the loss of power whereas non-volatile memory retains the stored data with the loss of power.

Flash memory, an example of non-volatile memory, is employed in most devices that collect and store data, mainly due to its low cost to data capacity ratio compared with other types of non-volatile memory. The ability of flash memory to be programmed and erased electronically renders it a great candidate for storing user data such as photographs and videos that take up large amounts of space and are replaced frequently. Flash memory, currently the most commonly used non-volatile memory, is the focus of this research.

3   Direct-Control Data Acquisition Workflow

The direct-control data acquisition workflow has two phases, method development and method application. During the initial method development phase, a custom direct-control data acquisition method is developed for a specific chip. During the subsequent method application phase, the custom direct-control data acquisition method is applied to the target chip containing evidentiary data.

Specialized equipment and techniques are required to implement the workflow. In the research, a FALIT laser decapsulator was employed for bulk chip package removal. An Allied High Tech X-Prep high-precision mill was used to expose silicon dies and delayer the dies for viewing under an FEI dualbeam (i.e., integrated scanning electron microscope and focused ion beam). The focused ion beam was used for die layer disinterring, platinum contact point creation and nano-probe tip customization under the scanning electron microscope. The nano-probe tips were positioned on the contacts using a Zyvex nano-prober under the scanning electron microscope. A Keithley 6430 sub-femtoamp sourcemeter was employed to apply voltage to the address line contacts and measure current flow across the floating-gate transistor (between the bit and ground lines) to read the bit stored in the targeted memory cell.

3.1   Method Development Phase

This phase creates a chip-specific process for data acquisition utilizing sample chips that are identical to the target chip containing evidentiary data. Figure 2 shows the five steps in the method development workflow: (i) chip preparation, (ii) memory cell reverse engineering, (iii) contact point identification and disinterring, (iv) data acquisition and (v) data verification.

Step 1: Chip Preparation In this initial step, known data is written to identical sample chips and their silicon dies are exposed. Multiple equipment options exist to perform data population and chip decapsulation. Different chips require modifications to the process, including the amounts of material removed, equipment used and order in which the equipment is used. Numerous chip preparation process variations were attempted in this research, so the process described in this section is a general workflow for developing a custom chip decapsulation process for a new memory device. Detailed notes should be taken during chip preparation because the perfected method is repeated on the target chip during the method application phase.

The four tasks in the chip preparation step are known data population, laser etching, nitric acid etching, and milling and polishing:

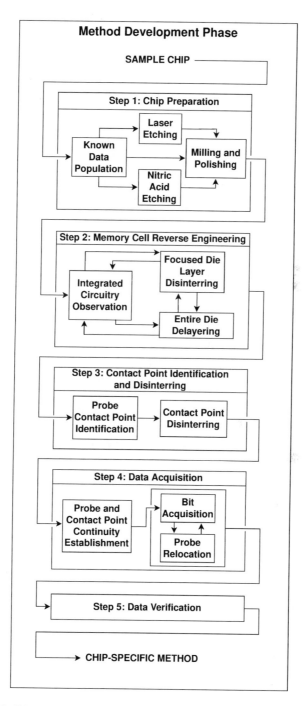

Fig. 2. Direct-control data acquisition method development phase.

- **Known Data Population:** Writing known data to the sample chips helps verify that the direct-control data acquisition attempt is successful and the method development phase can be terminated. Specifically, one chip is programmed with repeating patterns of the hex value 0xFFFF (binary 1111 1111 1111 1111) and the other chip is programmed with repeating patterns of the hex value 0xFAC0 (binary 1111 1010 1100 0000). The two data patterns help verify that the acquired data is correct without having to read large numbers of bits from the chips.

- **Laser Etching (Optional):** Laser etching is primarily used for chip preparation. Chips prepared for observation under a scanning electron microscope are "topside-prepped," meaning that the topsides of the dies are exposed. To reduce the amount of encapsulating material removed by a chip mill or polisher, a laser etcher is used on the backside of the chips to remove as much extraneous material as possible.

  A laser etcher removes plastic but does not damage metal. Because a copper lead frame protects the backside of a die, a laser etcher can be used to safely remove all the backside plastic down to the copper without damaging the die. In addition, the laser can be rastered over the entire chip package, even past the edges of the lead frame, to remove all the plastic material surrounding the die. Laser etching can be continued after the lead frame is exposed to remove material surrounding the die. After the surrounding material is thinned with the laser, it can be removed easily, leaving an area the size of the die for continued preparation with a high-precision mill or chip polisher.

- **Nitric Acid Etching (Optional):** Nitric acid etching is used to expose a bare die for further chip preparation. Nitric acid removes the plastic surrounding a die without damaging the die circuitry. Because nitric acid etching is a chemical process, the die is not accidentally scratched or damaged during decapsulation. Starting the die polishing process with a high-precision mill or polisher with a pristine, fully decapsulated die allows for precise leveling and even material removal across the die surface.

- **Milling and Polishing:** Milling and polishing are employed to remove bulk encapsulation material from a chip package that has not been etched using a laser or nitric acid. Milling and polishing may also be used to remove residual material after the optional laser and nitric acid etching tasks.

  The goal of chip milling and polishing is to expose die circuitry without damaging the die. An Allied High Tech X-Prep high-precision mill was primarily used for topside decapsulation of integrated circuits. Therefore, a typical process for topside chip decapsulation using an X-Prep high-precision mill is described in this chapter. An X-Prep high-precision mill can also be used for bulk material removal and chip polishing. The mill comes with several milling and polishing tips for the two processes.

  The four tasks involved in chip decapsulation and polishing using an X-Prep high-precision mill are chip mounting and leveling, bulk material removal, die leveling and die polishing:

- *Chip Mounting and Leveling:* A chip is mounted securely in an X-Prep high-precision mill before any encapsulation material is removed. A flat glass plate is used to hold the chip. The glass plate is heated and crystalline wax is applied to the plate. The chip is pressed into the crystalline wax before heating is terminated. After it has cooled, the glass plate with the chip is secured in an aluminum mount before it is placed in the X-Prep high-precision mill.

  The aluminum mount holding the chip is placed in the X-Prep mill and the chip is leveled using a ruby probe tip positioned on the head of the mill. The ruby tip is a perfect sphere, which increases the precision of the automated leveling process.

  The X-Prep mill levels the chip using three points provided by the user. The three points correspond to three corners of the encapsulation material. The X-Prep mill then levels to the surface of the encapsulation material. The ruby tip is periodically placed on each of the three locations, and the height differences are computed. Adjustments are made to the mount based on the height differences. This process is repeated until the chip is leveled within the specified tolerance (0.5 μm in this research).

- *Bulk Encapsulation Material Removal:* Encapsulation material must be removed after leveling the chip in the X-Prep mill. For bulk encapsulation material removal, a milling tip is positioned on the milling head of the X-Prep mill. The encapsulation material thickness above the die may not be known when decapsulating a new chip. In this case, x-ray images are taken of the sides of the die, and measurements of the resulting images are used to determine the thickness of the encapsulation above the die. Another method for estimating the thickness of encapsulating material above a die is to measure the distance from the top of the encapsulation to the top of the metal leads of the chip. This method is not as precise as measuring the thickness using x-ray images, so less material should be removed than the measured thickness to prevent damage to the chip. The first goal of chip decapsulation is to mill down to the bond wires of the chip. Since bond wires typically rise above a die, the wires can be used as landmarks to get close to the die. The milling tip must always be a safe distance from the die. If the milling tip makes contact with the die, the die could be damaged permanently. Until the exact thickness of the material above the die is known, removing less material than the estimated thickness is recommended. Small amounts of material can be removed repeatedly, but removing too much material at one time can result in permanent die damage.

  A die is close to the surface when the bond wires become visible. A milling tip can still be used, but only 5 μm to 10 μm of encapsulation should be removed until the die is visible under the plastic material covering.

- *Die Leveling:* After the die is visible under the plastic material, it is re-leveled based on the thickness of the plastic remaining above the die. Edges of the die that appear to have thicker layers of plastic above them are lower than the other edges. In such a situation, if milling is continued without die leveling, the high edges of the die could be damaged by the milling tip before the lower edges of the die are exposed.

- *Die Polishing:* After the die is leveled, the X-Prep high-precision mill mounted with a polishing tip is used to remove smaller amounts of material. This creates a smoother surface for observation and does not damage the die as quickly as a milling tip. Guides included with X-Prep mills provide guidance on the appropriate polishing pads, diamond paste and machine parameters for various chip polishing scenarios [1].

Step 2: Memory Cell Reverse Engineering After a sample chip is prepped for observation under a scanning electron microscope, individual memory cells are reverse engineered to locate the gates, drains and sources of the floating-gate transistors in the memory cells. The three tasks involved in memory cell reverse engineering are integrated circuit observation, focused die layer disinterring and entire die delayering:

- **Integrated Circuit Observation:** The internal circuitry of an integrated circuit must be viewed under a scanning electron microscope because the features are too small to be seen using a light microscope. Memory circuitry is often easy to identify in an integrated circuit because it is laid out as long, straight lines in a grid pattern. In fact, memory circuitry usually has a rectangular shape and stands out from the other circuitry.

  Memory cells are located at the intersections of address and bit lines. However, because a scanning electron microscope can only view the top layer of circuitry, layers of the die must be removed to expose the lower layers. This is accomplished by cutting into the die with a focused ion beam or using chip milling and polishing equipment.
- **Focused Die Layer Disinterring:** After locating the memory circuitry on a die via a scanning electron microscope, a focused ion beam is used to make edits to the circuitry and disinter individual memory cells for reverse engineering. A focused ion beam shoots ions at a target in a rastering pattern. The large ions ablate material from the surface, cutting through and/or removing the material.

  Because memory comprises numerous identical memory cells, various types of focused ion beam cuts are executed on memory circuitry to reverse engineer memory cells. This enables the memory cells to be observed from multiple angles to create a model of the memory layout and individual memory cell structures.

  Rectangular and cross-sectional focused ion beam cuts were employed:

  - *Rectangular Cuts:* Rectangular focused ion beam cuts are executed to remove surface material and de-layer portions of a die to expose small areas of interest on the die.
  - *Cross-Sectional Cuts:* Cross-sectional focused ion beam cuts are rectangular, but are cut in a stair-step pattern. Such a cut is typically executed

to view the wall created by the deepest portion of the cut from the side. In addition to providing side-views of the areas of interest, cross-sectional cuts also make it possible to simultaneously observe multiple layers of memory circuitry. Because memory comprises a large array of identical memory cells, a long cross-sectional cut can be made so that each step of the stair-step pattern shows a different integrated circuit layer. Changing the depths of cross-sectional cuts changes the depths of the stair steps. Cross-sectional cuts may be cut side-by-side to different depths, accelerating the reverse engineering process by showing how multiple layers connect in a single image.

- *Entire Die Delayering:* Additional delayering of an entire die can be performed as needed during chip characterization. For example, after a layer of the die is observed and mapped, the layer can be removed to reveal the next layer of the die.

Step 3: Contact Point Identification and Disinterring After locating the gate, drain and source of the floating-gate transistor in a memory cell, potential nano-probe contact points are located and disinterred. The contact points depend on the locations of the targeted memory cells and the limitations of the equipment used in the data acquisition method. After the nano-probe contact points are identified, they may be disinterred using a focused ion beam.

The contact point identification and disinterring step involves two tasks, probe contact point identification and contact point disinterring:

- **Probe Contact Point Identification:** A floating-gate transistor in non-volatile memory has three connectors, gate, drain and source. Current flow through the source and drain is controlled by a voltage applied at the gate. Electrical connections must be made to the three transistor contact points for data acquisition because they control the functionality of the memory cell transistors. However, direct connections do not have to be made to the transistors. Instead, connections may be made to the lines attached to the transistor connections. This provides flexibility with regard to the wires that need to be exposed to uncover contact points for the nano-probes.
- **Contact Point Disinterring:** Having identified the nano-probe contact points, a focused ion beam is used to expose the contact points needed to establish electrical connections. Edits utilizing a focused ion beam must not damage the memory cells and the connections vital to memory cell functionality.

Focused ion beam edits can separate memory circuitry from other connected circuitry. In some cases, the other circuitry may actively pull wires down to ground, preventing manual line control. To address this problem, the circuitry is detached from unnecessary circuitry using a focused ion beam.

Figure 3 shows the results of focused ion beam edits intended to disinter nano-probe contact points. The 45 μm square has exposed contact points along all four edges. The test square is separated from the surrounding circuitry by deep trenches cut by the focused ion beam. The vertical wires are

Fig. 3. Nano-probe contact points exposed by focused ion bean editing.

address (gate) and activation lines. The horizontal lines are bit lines (drain) and ground (source) lines. The horizontal lines run under the vertical lines. Only the edges of the horizontal lines are exposed to preserve the vertical lines needed to evaluate the direct-control data acquisition method on specific areas of memory.

Step 4: Data Acquisition Data acquisition is performed by positioning nano-probes on the exposed contact points and activating the memory cells. Data is read one bit at a time and the probes are repositioned between reads.

The three tasks in the data acquisition step are probe and contact point continuity establishment, bit acquisition and probe relocation:

- **Probe and Contact Point Continuity Establishment:** Nano-probes are positioned on the exposed contact points to manually control memory cells. However, the probe tips are very fragile. When a probe is landed on a contact point, vibrations caused by positioning other probes can damage the landed tip. Therefore, all the probes must be positioned as close as possible to the contact points without touching the points before any probes are landed. This minimizes probe movement after the probe tips are landed, preventing the tips from being damaged.

  Landing a probe involves moving the probe tip downward until a slight flex is seen in the probe tip. After the probe is landed, the next probe is brought into view by altering the beam-shift of the scanning electron microscope. This changes the area viewed by the scanning electron microscope without moving the stage, preventing damage to the landed nano-probes.

After all the probes are positioned on their contact points, the scanning electron microscope is turned off because it interferes with the measurement equipment used for bit acquisition.

- **Bit Acquisition:** The threshold voltage of a floating-gate transistor indicates whether or not a charge is stored on the floating-gate, corresponding to a one or a zero, respectively. The threshold voltage is measured by performing a voltage sweep on the control gate and simultaneously measuring the current through the source and drain. Current flow is restricted until the transistor is activated. The voltage at the control gate when current starts to flow between the source and drain reveals the threshold voltage of the floating-gate transistor, which also reveals the bit value stored in the memory cell.
- **Probe Relocation:** After data is read from a memory cell, the nano-probes are relocated to read the next memory cell. One or more probes may have to be moved between reads depending on the arrangement of cells. For example, if the targeted memory cells are controlled by the same address line, only the probe positioned on the bit line has to be moved to the next bit line. However, if a different address line activates the next memory cell, all four probes have to be relocated to the control points of the new memory cell.

Step 5: Data Verification The data acquired from the sample chip is verified by comparing it against the known data written to the chip in Step 1. This ensures that the correct nano-probe contact points are identified and the data acquisition method is successful. If the data recovered from the sample chip does not match the known data, additional reverse engineering of the memory circuitry must be performed to identify the correct nano-probe contact points. If the data recovered from the sample device matches the known data, the method development phase for the chip of interest is complete and the method application phase can proceed to acquire data from the target chip.

3.2   Method Application Phase

This phase applies the chip-specific method perfected in the method development phase to acquire data from the target chip. Figure 4 shows the three steps in the method development phase: (i) chip preparation, (ii) contact point disinterring and (iii) data acquisition.

Step 1: Chip Preparation The chip-specific preparation method developed in Step 1 of the method development phase is applied to prepare the target chip for observation under a scanning electron microscope. However, because chips have variations, the amount of material to be removed from the target chip to expose its die may not be exactly the same as that for the sample chips. Therefore, less material than the measured thickness should be removed from the target device to prevent damage to the die. After the bulk encapsulation is removed, the die is exposed using a polishing tip in the X-Prep high-precision mill following the integrated circuit polishing guidelines provided by Allied High Tech [1].

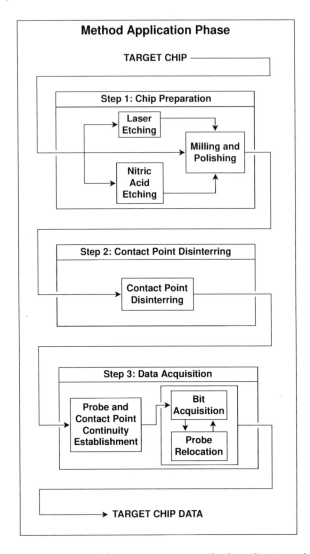

Fig. 4. Direct-control data acquisition method application phase.

Step 2: Contact Point Disinterring After the target chip die is exposed, the nano-probe contact points identified in Step 3 of the method development phase are exposed using a focused ion beam. Because the target chip contains data of interest, it is vital to disinter only the contact points to prevent damage to the surrounding circuitry. If the focused ion beam is aimed at areas other than the nano-probe contact points, damage may occur to the memory cells and circuitry that supports data retrieval, resulting in data destruction. Therefore, it is important to proceed cautiously and remove small amounts of material at a time.

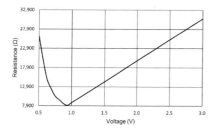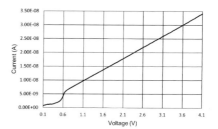

Fig. 5. Ideal voltage-resistance (left) and voltage-current (right) curves.

Step 3: Data Acquisition The same tasks applied to the sample chip die in Step 4 of the method development phase are repeated on the target chip die to acquire data. The nano-probes are positioned on the exposed contact points and data is read one bit at a time. The nano-probes are relocated between reads as necessary and the process is repeated until the data from the target die is acquired.

4 Experiments and Results

After extensive preliminary experimentation, a number of experiments were conducted to evaluate the application of the direct-control data acquisition method on ATmega328P microcontrollers. The first baseline experiment was conducted to validate the software, hardware and electrical connections used in subsequent experiments. Following the baseline experiment, 12 data acquisition experiments were conducted. The experiments incorporated modifications to address the limitations encountered in previous experiments. All the experiments adhered to the direct-control data acquisition workflow described in Section 3.

4.1 Baseline Experiment

The baseline experiment tested the connectivity between the Keithley sourcemeter and nano-probes, and validated the Python script used to control the sourcemeter. This was accomplished by connecting the sourcemeter cables to a standalone through-hole transistor that simulated connections to the ATmega328P microcontroller memory cells in the experiments. The Python script instructed the sourcemeter to sweep the voltage at the gate and drain of the through-hole transistor while simultaneously taking measurements. This was done twice to generate the ideal voltage-resistance and voltage-current curves.

Figure 5 (left-hand side) shows the ideal voltage-resistance curve for the through-hole transistor. The curve initially shows high resistance because the transistor was inactive and shows low resistance when the transistor was activated. This voltage-resistance curve is expected when a non-volatile memory cell of an ATmega328P microcontroller is probed during a direct-control data acquisition experiment.

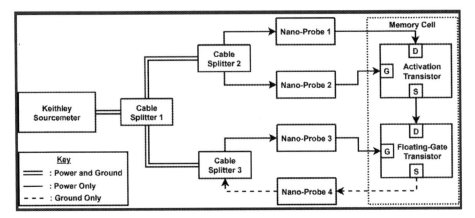

Fig. 6. Experimental setup.

Figure 5 (right-hand side) shows the voltage-current curve with the current initially limited because the through-hole transistor was inactive; the current was constrained by the in-circuit resistor when the transistor was activated. This voltage-current curve is expected when a non-volatile memory cell of an ATmega328P microcontroller is probed during a direct-control data acquisition experiment.

4.2   Data Acquisition Experiments

Twelve direct-control data acquisition experiments are presented in this section. Each experiment incorporated modifications to address the limitations encountered in the previous experiments. The experiments sought to address four principal challenges: discovering three-dimensional memory cell profiles, establishing probe/contact point continuity, adding electrical safeties and improving electrical grounding.

Experimental Setup Figure 6 shows the initial experimental setup with four nano-probes for evaluating the direct-control data acquisition method. In the setup, nano-probe 1 for the bit line and nano-probe 2 for the control gate on the activation transistor are connected to cable splitter 2; nano-probe 3 for the control gate on the floating-gate transistor and nano-probe 4 for ground are connected to cable splitter 3. Nano-probes 1, 2 and 3 are connected to the positive signal from the Keithley sourcemeter whereas nano-probe 4 is connected to ground.

Discovering Memory Cell Profiles The first set of experiments sought to map the three-dimensional structure of individual memory cells. The shape and placement of memory cells dictate the locations of disinterred contact points for

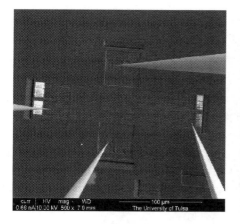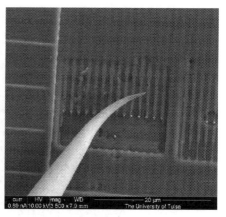

Fig. 7. Focused ion beam edits and nano-probe damage (Experiment 2).

nano-probe placement. The four experiments attempted to shape the layout of
the uncovered test area on the silicon die:

- **Experiment 1:** This experiment executed focused ion beam edits to expose
  contact points for the nano-probes. The layer containing the control gates
  and floating-gate transistors (address lines) was kept intact and deep cuts
  were made on both sides of the address lines to expose the bit and ground
  lines.

  The experiment was unsuccessful because the focused ion beam edits severed
  the connections to the tungsten plugs connecting the address lines to the
  transistors in the layers below. The address lines stretch across the memory
  circuitry, but only periodically extend down to the layers containing the
  transistors.

- **Experiment 2:** To address the failure in Experiment 1, the second experiment executed focused ion beam edits to expose the nano-probe contact
  points while retaining the tungsten plugs connecting the address lines in the
  top layer to the transistors in the lower layers. This was accomplished by
  keeping the area containing the tungsten plugs clear of edits and making
  deep cuts on both sides of the address lines to expose the bit and ground
  lines. The deep cuts, which exposed the bit and ground lines, were aligned
  with each other to maximize the number of bit lines that could be accessed
  without additional focused ion beam edits.

  Figure 7 (left-hand side) shows the result after disinterring the nano-probe
  contact points. The horizontal lines are the address lines and the vertical
  lines running under the address lines are the bit and ground lines.

  Experiment 2 was unsuccessful because the area containing the disinterred
  nano-probe contact points was too large to be viewed by the scanning electron microscope without adjusting the position of the stage. Figure 7 (right-
  hand side) shows a landed nano-probe tip that was damaged due to stage

Fig. 8. Focused ion beam edits (Experiment 3).

movement. The landed nano-probe was damaged when the stage was adjusted to view and position the second nano-probe.

- **Experiment 3:** This experiment executed focused ion beam edits to expose the nano-probe contact points while addressing the problems encountered in the previous two experiments. The region containing the disinterred nano-probe contact points was reduced to a $45\,\mu$m $\times$ $45\,\mu$m square to enable all the contact points to be viewed under the scanning electron microscope without moving the stage. The square region was centered on the tungsten plugs connecting the upper address line layer to the lower transistor layers to prevent them from being damaged by the focused ion beam.

  Figure 8 shows an attempt at disinterring the nano-probe contact points within the $45\,\mu$m $\times$ $45\,\mu$m square. The vertical lines are the address lines and the horizontal lines running under the address lines are the bit and ground lines.

  The experiment was unsuccessful because it was difficult to land nano-probes on different layers of the silicon die. Since the bit and ground lines are located in lower layers of the die than the address lines, the nano-probes on all three types of lines were not simultaneously in focus under the scanning electron microscope. Additionally, the tiny areas for landing nano-probes on the lower layer increased the risk of running the nano-probe tips into the elevated address line layer.

- **Experiment 4:** This experiment executed focused ion beam edits to ablate the top layer containing the address lines to address the problems encountered in Experiment 3. Because the tungsten plugs connect the upper address line layer to the lower transistor layers, suitable contact points for address lines are available in the same layer as the bit and ground lines since the layer

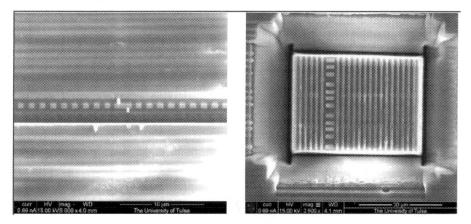

Fig. 9. Burrowed address line and focused ion beam edits (Experiment 4).

containing the bit lines and ground lines is located between the address line and transistor layers. Removing the upper address line layer enables nano-probe contact points for the three types of lines to be located in the same layer so that they are simultaneously in focus under the scanning electron microscope. Additionally, having all the nano-probe contact points in the same layer provides ample space for positioning the probes.

Figure 9 (left-hand side) shows a side view of the connection between the upper address line layer and lower transistor layer as an address line burrows through the layer containing the bit and ground lines. Because the address line burrows through the bit and ground line layer, the upper address line layer can be removed while making a suitable contact point available for the address line.

Figure 9 (right-hand side) shows the ion beam edit results. All the contact points are located in the same layer and are simultaneously in focus under the scanning electron microscope.

In Experiment 4, four nano-probes, two for an address line and one each for bit and ground lines, were landed successfully. Following this, voltage-current measurements were attempted using the Keithley sourcemeter. However, no measurements were made because, although the nano-probes were landed successfully, adequate electrical connections were not established between the nano-probes and contact points.

Establishing Probe/Contact Point Continuity Good electrical connections provide the best possibility of successful memory cell read operations. Therefore, the second set of experiments focused on establishing nano-probe and contact point continuity. The four experiments in the set sought to define the process used in later experiments for uncovering contact points, depositing platinum to improve electrical connections and modifying nano-probes:

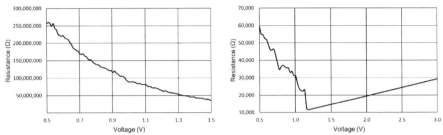

Fig. 10. Sample voltage-resistance curves (Experiment 6).

- **Experiment 5:** Experiment 5 executed ion beam edits that produced stair-step cuts to expose the bit and ground lines. Additionally, the focused ion beam was used to deposit platinum on the exposed nano-probe contact points. Platinum deposition on the contact points increases the likelihood of establishing adequate electrical connections between the nano-probes and contact points, and provides elevated surfaces for landing nano-probes. However, the close proximity of the platinum deposited on the bit and ground lines in this experiment made it difficult to position a nano-probe on a single bit or ground line without it touching an adjacent bit or ground line. As a result, the Keithley sourcemeter did not provide any measurements.
- **Experiment 6:** Experiment 6 executed ion beam edits that produced stair-step cuts to expose the bit and ground lines. Also, it sought to address the problem of nano-probes connecting to multiple bit lines by depositing platinum in an offset, alternating pattern.

  Figure 10 shows sample voltage-resistance curves obtained in Experiment 6. The curve on the left-hand side shows a steady decrease in resistance with no incline after reaching its lowest resistance measurement. This sample curve differs from the ideal curve in Figure 5 (left-hand side), which invalidated the measurements.

  A later experiment yielded the curve on the right-hand side that resembles the ideal voltage-resistance curve in Figure 5 (left-hand side). However, the positive result could not be reproduced in subsequent measurements.

  The poor and non-reproducible results indicate weak and/or improper electrical connections. Further investigation of the equipment revealed that the wiring of the fourth nano-probe was frayed and it was not electrically connected to the external port on the scanning electron microscope. As a result, the contact point of the damaged nano-probe was not pulled to ground during Experiment 6.
- **Experiment 7:** Experiment 7 executed ion beam edits that produced stair-step cuts to expose the bit and ground lines and sought to address the problem of nano-probes connecting to multiple bit lines by depositing platinum in an offset, alternating pattern. To establish better electrical connections, the vertical spacings between platinum deposits on the bit and ground lines, and the size of the platinum deposit on the ground line were increased from Experiment 6.

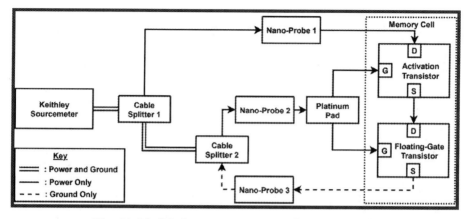

Fig. 11. Modified experimental setup (Experiment 7).

Due to the damage to the fourth nano-probe, the two address line contact points were electrically connected via platinum deposition to enable experimentation using the three operational nano-probes. This required the modification of the experimental setup in which splitters isolated the signals so that nano-probes 1 through 3 were connected to the positive signal coming from the Keithley sourcemeter while nano-probe 4 was connected to ground. Figure 11 shows the modified experimental setup using the three operational nano-probes. A platinum pad electrically connects (pairs) the control gates of the two memory cell transistors. In the modified setup, nano-probe 1 for the bit line is connected to cable splitter 1 and nano-probes 2 and 3 for the two paired address lines and ground lines are connected to cable splitter 2. Nano-probes 1 and 2 are connected to the positive signal coming from the Keithley sourcemeter while nano-probe 3 is connected to ground.

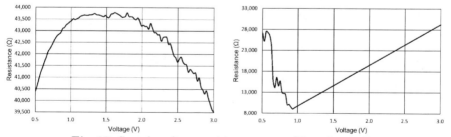

Fig. 12. Sample voltage-resistance curves (Experiment 7).

Figure 12 shows the voltage-resistance curves obtained in Experiment 7. The curve on the left-hand side does not match the ideal voltage-resistance curve in Figure 5 (left-hand side) and was not reproducible. The curve on the right-hand side resembles the ideal voltage-resistance curve, but it was also not reproducible.

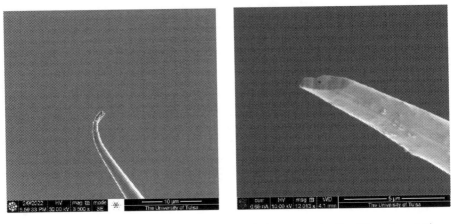

Fig. 13. Damaged nano-probe tip and modified nano-probe tip (Experiment 8).

– **Experiment 8:** This experiment was conducted in the same way as Experiment 7, except that the nano-probe tips were modified to improve the electrical connections with the platinum contact points. This was accomplished by using the focused ion beam to excise the tips of damaged nano-probes. Since the tip of a nano-probe is tapered, excising a damaged tip yields a larger contact area for the new probe tip and enhances the mechanical strength of the probe tip.

Figure 13 shows a damaged probe tip (left-hand side) and the probe tip (right-hand side) created from the damaged tip using the focused ion beam.

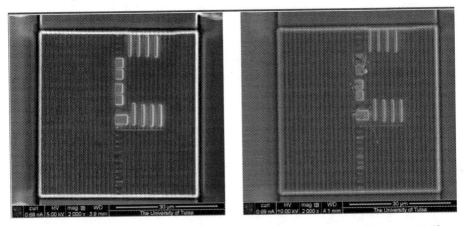

Fig. 14. Focused ion beam edits and damaged memory circuitry (Experiment 8).

Figure 14 (left-hand side) shows the attempt at disinterring nano-probe contact points in Experiment 8 (same as in Experiment 7). Unfortunately, as

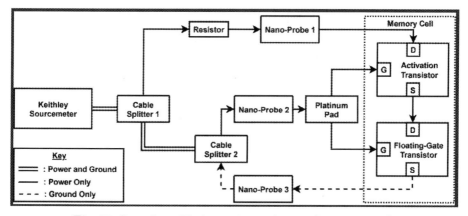

Fig. 15. Second modified experimental setup (Experiment 9).

seen in Figure 14 (right-hand side), the larger nano-probe tips induced high current flows that damaged the memory circuitry. However, Experiment 8 verified that the platinum deposits were helping establish better connections between the nano-probe tips and contact points.

Adding Electrical Safeties The third set of experiments added electrical safeties to protect memory cell transistors and nano-probes from damage caused by excessive current throughput, and to prevent false data reads by eliminating floating address lines:

– **Experiment 9:** This experiment was conducted in the same way as Experiment 8, but with two changes. First, a modified nano-probe tip was used for the ground line because, unlike the address and bit lines, it is possible to create a larger platinum pad for the ground line to accommodate a modified nano-probe tip. Second, four $30\,\text{M}\Omega$ resistors in series were added inline to the cable supplying current to the memory cell drain to prevent current from damaging memory circuitry as in Experiment 8.
  Figure 15 shows the second modified experimental setup using the three operational nano-probes. The modified experimental setup has the same configuration as the previous experimental setup in Figure 11, but with an added resistor between cable splitter 1 and nano-probe 1 to limit the current flow that damaged the memory circuitry in Experiment 8.
  Voltage-resistance measurements were attempted through Experiment 7 before switching to voltage-current measurements for the remaining experiments. The voltage-resistance curve was used because the point at which the transistor is activated should be the lowest resistance measurement on the curve and easily discernible. However, since a chip reads data by measuring current flow, the experiments were modified to mimic the chip functionality. Therefore, voltage-current measurements instead of voltage-resistance measurements were made in Experiment 9 and subsequent experiments.

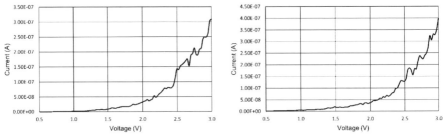

Fig. 16. Sample voltage-current curves (Experiment 9).

Figure 16 shows sample voltage-current curves obtained in Experiment 9. The curves on the left- and right-hand sides, obtained from different memory cells, look similar. However, neither curve resembles the ideal voltage-current curve in Figure 5 (right-hand side), invalidating the measurements.

– **Experiment 10:** Most of the voltage-current curves obtained in Experiment 9 resembled each other, potentially indicating that multiple memory cells were activated by nano-probing the floating address lines instead of single memory cells. Experiment 10 sought to remedy this situation by depositing a large platinum pad over the address lines that were not being probed as well as the ground line, connecting all the unused address lines to ground.

   Figure 17 shows the focused ion beam edits, which include the large platinum pad that prevents multiple memory cell activations due to floating address lines.

   Unfortunately, satisfactory voltage-current curves were not obtained. Further investigation revealed that the platinum deposits and/or electrical connections made to the memory circuitry were inadequate to address the problems.

Improving Electrical Grounding The fourth set of experiments improved the electrical grounding of the silicon substrate on the chip. Transistors require the substrate that they sit on to be controlled. In the case of the transistors encountered in the experiments, the substrate has to be grounded for the transistors to function properly. Therefore, two experiments were performed to improve the continuity between the silicon substrate of the target chip and electrical ground:

– **Experiment 11:** This experiment attempted a completely different approach to address the inadequate electrical connections, including the silicon substrate being biased (grounded) incorrectly. In particular, Experiment 11 executed the same focused ion beam edits as Experiment 9, but incorporated two key modifications. The first modification sought to address the problems induced by platinum splatter on adjacent circuitry during platinum pad deposition via focused ion beam ablation. The splatter created a thin layer of platinum that shorted the nano-probe contact points, affecting the measured current flow.

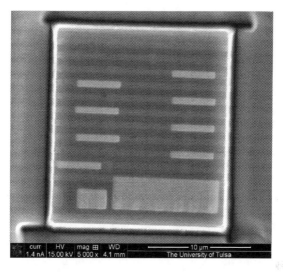

Fig. 17. Focused ion beam edits (Experiment 10).

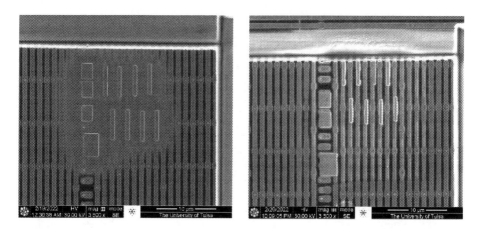

Fig. 18. Memory circuitry before and after spatter removal (Experiment 11).

Figure 18 (left-hand side) shows the memory circuitry covered with platinum spatter after platinum pad deposition. Figure 19 (right-hand side) shows the same memory circuitry after the focused ion beam ablated the platinum spatter.

The second modification focused on the silicon substrate bias problem. The die substrate is often considered to be the fourth transistor component apart from the source, drain and gate. The substrate is rarely documented because substrate biasing is typically handled by the chip and is not user-controlled. However, a transistor will not activate without a properly-biased silicon sub-

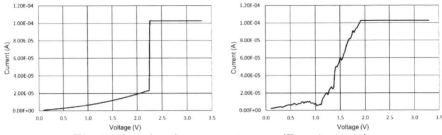

Fig. 19. Sample voltage-current curves (Experiment 11).

strate. In fact, the silicon substrate in the previous experiments may not have biased correctly because, after a die is removed from its package, the substrate may not be pulled to ground. Experiment 11 sought to address the bias problem by placing the lead frame of a chip being read directly on the scanning electron microscope sample holder instead of on a non-conductive crystalline wax support.

The exposed lead frame on the bottom of the chip was placed in direct contact with the sample holder, grounding the lead frame to the scanning electron microscope stage. The lead frame is electrically connected to the silicon substrate on some devices. In the case of electrically-connected lead frames and substrates, grounding the lead frame also grounds the silicon substrate.

Figure 19 shows sample voltage-current curves obtained in Experiment 11. The two curves resemble the ideal voltage-current curve in Figure 5 (right-hand side). However, the maximum current measurements in the two experimental curves greatly exceed the theoretical current maximum of 27.5 nA for a 3.3 V differential applied to a 120 MΩ resistor. If the current measurements are accurate, they would imply that the current traveled from the address line to ground and not through the memory cell transistors. The experimental curves also indicate that grounding the lead frame did not ground the silicon substrate, which prevented the memory cell transistors from activating.

- **Experiment 12:** This experiment executed the same ion beam edits as Experiment 9. Platinum spatter ablation was performed as in Experiment 11, but the silicon substrate bias correction technique was not applied because a new method for prepping sample chips was employed. Specifically, the sample chips were prepped to leave their bond wires and chip leads intact to facilitate the grounding of the silicon substrate. Solder was utilized to ensure good electrical connections between the chip leads and copper tape. This modification sought to enable the utilization of the chip circuitry to ground the silicon substrate through the external chip leads as intended in the chip design.

Figure 20 shows the voltage-current curves obtained in Experiment 12. The majority of the measurements made in Experiment 12 resembled the left-hand side voltage-current curve, which shows a steady increase in current as the voltage is raised. However, these voltage-current curves do not re-

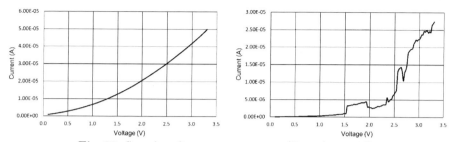

Fig. 20. Sample voltage-current curves (Experiment 12).

semble the ideal voltage-current curve in Figure 5 (right-hand side). The right-hand side voltage-current curve in Figure 20 loosely follows the ideal voltage-current curve until the voltage reaches about 2 V, followed by a sudden drop and sporadic increase in current flow. The drop in current at approximately 2 V typically indicates that the probe tip lost contact with the platinum pad. Attempts to repeat the measurements and obtain a similar curve were unsuccessful. As in the previous experiments, the readings were reasonably consistent, but they did not match the expected voltage-current curve obtained in the baseline experiment (Figure 5).

5   Discussion

The direct-control data acquisition method for non-volatile memory and the accompanying chip customization workflow involving the iterative method development and final method application phases are logical and technically sound based on the underlying physics and engineering. Clearly, direct-control data acquisition at the transistor level is very challenging. The numerous experiments conducted during the research – many more than the dozen described in this chapter – amply demonstrate this fact. This section discusses the efforts, challenges and opportunities pertaining to the five steps of the data acquisition workflow.

5.1   Chip Preparation

Chip preparation readies a sample chip for viewing under a scanning electron microscope. This task, involving chip package removal and silicon die polishing, is fairly standard. Experiments 1 through 11 involved the same chip preparation process. The lack of good, reproducible results in these experiments influenced the application of the less-common process in Experiment 12 to leave the bond wires and chip leads intact to facilitate the grounding of the silicon substrate, which may have been inadequate. However, this modification did not change the results, which implies that the problems were in the subsequent steps in the workflow.

Memory Cell Reverse Engineering Memory cell reverse engineering seeks to understand the layout and connectivity of memory cells on a chip die. Reverse engineering is as much an art as a science; it is also tedious and time-consuming. Many months were spent investigating microcontrollers containing non-volatile flash memory under a scanning electron microscope to understand memory cell layout and connectivity. Indeed, it was only after a good understanding of the memory cell structure and connectivity was obtained and the memory reverse engineering results were reproducible did Experiment 1 and the subsequent experiments proceed.

Absent details about the silicon-level layout and connectivity from a chip manufacturer, the only option is to progressively cut into chip samples with a focused ion beam and analyze the scanning electron microscope images to obtain a three-dimensional model of the memory cells at the transistor level. The reverse engineering efforts could also benefit from using energy-dispersive x-ray spectroscopy. If this technique is sensitive enough to detect doped silicon, it could provide insights into the types of transistors involved and the signals required to activate them via nano-probing.

Contact Point Identification and Disinterring This important step involves contact point identification and disinterring:

- **Contact Point Identification:** Contact point identification locates the contact points connected to memory cell transistors that accommodate the constraints imposed by the equipment used for data acquisition. After the gate, drain and source of a memory cell were identified via reverse engineering, the experiments progressively improved the focused ion beam edits. The improvements involved reducing the size of the target area to accommodate the limited region of visibility provided by the scanning electron microscope. Subsequent improvements addressed the difficulty of positioning nano-probes by reducing the topographical complexity of the focused ion beam edits. The ATmega328P chip incorporates two connected transistors instead of a single transistor, which rendered the contact point identification task more difficult. Nevertheless, the progressive improvements made in the direct-control data acquisition experiments reduced the difficulty in positioning nano-probes and increased the probability of successful positioning.

- **Contact Point Disinterring:** Contact point disinterring removes the silicon covering the contact points to enable electrical connections to be established between the nano-probe tips and contact points. As in the case of contact point identification, continuous improvements were made to the contact point disinterring process during the series of experiments. Experiments 5 through 9 executed stair-step cuts to the edges of the identified contact lines to improve the chances of uncovering portions of the conductive contacts from under the non-conductive silicon. Other incremental improvements included depositing platinum on the contact points to increase conductivity and facilitate nano-probe positioning.

Unfortunately, the equipment did not support a method for verifying the successful disinterring of nano-probe contact points. Specifically, an energy-dispersive x-ray spectroscope could have been used to identify the materials present on the surfaces of scanning electron microscope samples. This information could have provided valuable feedback in executing additional focused ion beam edits until the successful disinterring of contact points was verified.

Data Acquisition Data acquisition attempts to determine the data stored in a memory cell using a high-precision sourcemeter that applies voltage in a sweeping pattern to the control gate and drain lines of the memory cell while simultaneously measuring the resistance or current flow. The data acquisition experiments involved multiple attempts to mitigate the negative factors that impact resistance and current measurements at the micron scale.

Experiments 6 through 12 progressively increased the spacing of platinum pads to address the lack of success in establishing connections between a nano-probe tip and multiple bit lines. Experiment 11 reduced the contamination due to sample exposure to air by executing focused ion beam edits during the same scanning electron microscope sessions as nano-probing (i.e., samples were maintained in the vacuum chamber of the scanning electron microscope during the entire process). Experiments 11 and 12 reduced the possibility of shorted contact points due to platinum spatter by executing focused ion beam edits to remove excess platinum from the surfaces of samples. Experiments 11 and 12 also facilitated transistor activation by grounding the silicon substrate, the fourth contact point of a transistor. Experiment 11 grounded the exposed chip lead frame directly to the conductive sample holder whereas Experiment 12 left the original bond wires and chip leads intact to ground the silicon substrate using the ground pins of the chip.

The data acquisition efforts could have benefitted from process improvements that remove sample contaminants. The improvements include using xenon difluoride and/or plasma cleaning in an anti-contamination unit, as well as contact point cleaning and parallel chip delayering using a focused ion beam.

The efforts could also have benefitted by employing more sophisticated resistance and current measurement equipment. One solution is to use special measurement equipment that comes with some nano-probers. Another solution involves replacing the single sub-femtoamp sourcemeter for activating transistors and measuring resistance and current with a high-precision power supply for transistor activation and restricting the sourcemeter to resistance and current measurement.

Finally, probe tip modifications that enlarge the contact surface area and improve the mechanical stability of the nano-probe tips could have reduced the resistance created by the probe tips and helped establish better electrical connections between the probe tips and contact points.

It is clear that the experiments were unable to extract data from memory cells in a reliable manner. However, the continuous improvements to the data acquisition process over the experiments are expected to enhance the success of future direct-control data acquisition efforts.

Data Verification Data verification checks the data read via direct-control data acquisition against the data originally stored on a chip. Two patterns were programmed on sample chips at the start of the chip preparation step, repeating `0xFFFF` hex values and repeating `0xFAC0` hex values. The data verification step is technically sound. However, the step could not be completed because the memory cell data reads were non-ideal or inconsistent.

6   Conclusions

The novel direct-control data acquisition method for non-volatile memory described in this chapter directly interfaces with floating-gate transistors on a silicon die using tungsten nano-probes under a scanning electron microscope. The data acquisition method is restricted to non-volatile memory because it is difficult to power volatile memory and/or refresh the stored data when the silicon die is in the chamber of a scanning electron microscope.

The workflow for customizing the data acquisition method to a specific non-volatile microcontroller or memory chip involves a method development phase and a method application phase. During the method development phase, a custom data acquisition method is developed for a specific chip. This phase involves five steps, chip preparation, memory cell reverse engineering, contact point identification and disinterring, data acquisition, and data verification. The five steps are performed iteratively using sample chips until the custom data acquisition method is perfected. During the final method application phase, the custom data acquisition method is applied to the target chip containing evidentiary data.

Numerous direct-control data acquisition experiments were conducted on ATmega328P microcontroller chips. The experimental results reveal that the chip preparation, memory cell reverse engineering and contact point identification steps were successful. However, the contact point disinterring step did not produce good results because the available equipment made it difficult to verify that the contact points were completely exposed and free from contamination and damage. The inability to establish consistent electrical connections between the nano-probe tips and address, bit and ground lines caused the data acquisition step to be generally unsuccessful. The data verification step, while technically sound, could not be completed because the memory cell data reads were non-ideal or inconsistent.

Despite the non-ideal and inconsistent experimental results, the direct-control data acquisition method and the workflow for customizing a data acquisition method to a specific microcontroller or memory chip are technically sound. Future research leveraging more sophisticated equipment and detailed knowledge about the structure and layout of the silicon dies would be expected to demonstrate the success of the data acquisition method and its accompanying workflow.

The views expressed in this chapter are those of the authors, and do not reflect the official policy or position of the U.S. Secret Service, U.S. Department of Homeland Security or the U.S. Government.

Acknowledgment This research was supported by the National Science Foundation under Grant no. DGE 1501177 and by the U.S. Secret Service National Computer Forensics Institute Laboratory.

References

1. Allied High Tech Products, X-Prep Precision Milling/Polishing System, Rancho Dominguez, California (`www.alliedhightech.com/Equipment/x-prep-mechanical-mill`), 2022.
2. J. Autran, D. Munteanu, G. Gasiot and P. Roche, Computational modeling and Monte Carlo simulation of soft errors in flash memories (Chapter 17), in *Computational and Numerical Simulations*, J. Awrejcewicz (Ed.), InTech, Rijeka, Croatia, pp. 367–393, 2014.
3. J. Breier, D. Jap and C. Chen, Laser profiling for the backside fault attacks with a practical laser skip instruction attack on AES, *Proceedings of the First ACM Workshop on Cyber-Physical System Security*, pp. 99–103, 2015.
4. A. Buraga, Protecting microcontrollers. Implementing firmware hardening and secure boot on STM32, *HackMag* (`hackmag.com/security/protec-stm32`), 2022.
5. D. Bursky, Secure microcontrollers keep data safe, Digi-Key Electronics, Thief River Falls, Minnesota (`www.digikey.com/en/articles/secure-microcontrollers-keep-data-safe`), July 8, 2011.
6. F. Courbon, S. Skorobogatov and C. Woods, Reverse engineering flash EEPROM memories using scanning electron microscopy, *Proceedings of the Fifteenth International Conference on Smart Card Research and Advanced Applications*, pp. 57–72, 2016.
7. A. Daga, AVR ATmega16/32 fuse bits, *Engineers Garage*, Jaipur, India (`www.engineersgarage.com/avr-atmega16-32-fuse-bits`), March 28, 2011.
8. C. De Nardi, R. Desplats, P. Perdu, C. Guerin, J. Gauffier and T. Amundsen, Direct measurements of charge in floating gate transistor channels of flash memories using scanning capacitance microscopy, *Proceedings of the Thirty-Second International Symposium for Testing and Failure Analysis*, pp. 86–93, 2006.
9. A. Fievrea, A. Al-Aakhir and S. Bhansalia, Integrated circuit security: An overview, *Journal of the Institute of Smart Structures and Systems*, vol. 4(1), pp. 18–37, 2015.
10. S. Hossain, Chip to chip communication protocols: An overview and design considerations, PCBWay, Hong Kong, China (`www.pcbway.com/blog/PCB_Design_Tutorial/Chip_to_Chip_Communication_Protocols__An_Overview_and_Design_Considerations.html`), April 24, 2021.
11. O. Kommerling and F. Kommerling, Anti Tamper Encapsulation for an Integrated Circuit, U.S. Patent no. 7,005,733 B2, February 28, 2006.
12. K. Magdy, Configuration bits (fuses) for microcontrollers, *DeepBlue* (`www.deepbluembedded.com/configuration-bits-fuses-for-microcontrollers`), April 21, 2021.
13. Microchip Technology, In-Circuit Emulator and Debugger Selection Guide, Chandler, Arizona (`www.microchip.com/en-us/tools-resources/debug/programmers-debuggers`), 2022.

14. S. Mohieldin, Hardware Hacking 101: Introduction to JTAG, *River Loop Security Blog*, Washington, DC (`www.riverloopsecurity.com/blog/2021/05/hw-101-jtag`), May 6, 2021.

15. S. Prado, Extracting firmware from devices Using JTAG, *EmbeddedBits*, Sao Paulo, Brazil (`embeddedbits.org/2020-02-20-extracting-firmware-from-devices-using-jtag`), 2021.

16. S. Rainwater, Physically-Invasive Forensic Data Recovery Techniques, Ph.D. Dissertation in Computer Engineering, Tandy School of Computer Science and Department of Electrical and Computer Engineering, University of Tulsa, Tulsa, Oklahoma, 2014.

17. A. Sguigna, Securing the JTAG interface, *ASSET*, ASSET InterTech, Plano, Texas (`www.asset-intertech.com/resources/blog/2019/07/securing-the-jtag-interface`), July 21, 2019.

18. B. Streetman and S. Banerjee, *Solid State Electronic Devices*, Pearson Education, Harlow, United Kingdom, 2016.

19. J. Tyson, How computer memory works, *HowStuffWorks*, Marina Del Rey, California (`www.computer.howstuffworks.com/computer-memory1.htm`), August 23, 2000.

20. N. Weste and D. Money Harris, *CMOS VLSI Design: A Circuits and Systems Perspective*, Pearson Education, Boston, Massachusetts, 2011.

Image and Video Forensics

Using Perceptual Hashing for Targeted Content Scanning

Leon Twenning, Harald Baier, and Thomas Göbel

Bundeswehr University, Munich, Germany
`thomas.goebel@unibw.de`

Abstract. The Internet is increasingly used to disseminate unethical and illegal content. A grave concern is child sexual abuse material that is often disseminated via end-to-end-encrypted channels. Such encryption defeats network- and server-based scanning measures used by law enforcement. A trade-off is to enable confidential communications channels for users and scanning opportunities for law enforcement by employing perceptual-hashing-based targeted content scanning on user devices. This has generated intense discussions between policymakers, privacy advocates and child protection organizations.

This chapter summarizes the current state of research in perceptual-hashing-based targeted content scanning with a focus on classical metrics such as false positives, false negatives and privacy aspects. Insights are provided into the most relevant perceptual hashing methods and an attack taxonomy for perceptual-hashing-based targeted content scanning is presented. The complexity in generating false negatives is evaluated and the feasibility of evading perceptual-hashing-based targeted content scanning is demonstrated.

Keywords: Perceptual Hashing · Targeted Content Scanning · Child Sexual Abuse Material

1 Introduction

Digital communications channels such as messenger services, discussion boards and social networks are increasingly used for nefarious activities, a trend that appears to have increased during the COVID-19 pandemic [28]. The communications channels are low-cost, highly-scalable and private, and perpetrators leverage them to disseminate illegal, abusive and violent content. The content is often in the form of images and videos that contain hate speech, disinformation, terrorist propaganda and more.

A grave concern is the dissemination of child sexual abuse material (CSAM). According to the German Federal Criminal Police Office [9], the overall numbers of crimes related to child sexual abuse were nearly seven times higher in 2021 compared with 2016. In 2021, the U.S. National Center for Missing and Exploited Children (NCMEC) [20] collected nearly 30 million reports of CSAM from large technology companies such as Meta and Google.

© IFIP International Federation for Information Processing 2023
Published by Springer Nature Switzerland AG 2023
G. Peterson and S. Shenoi (Eds.): DigitalForensics 2023, IFIP AICT 687, pp. 125–142, 2023.
https://doi.org/10.1007/978-3-031-42991-0_7

Several companies have cracked down on the dissemination of illegal content via their online services. While the technical details of their countermeasures are not released, it is clear that image recognition technologies are employed to scan content. Major companies that conduct scanning include Meta [8], Microsoft [19], Apple [2] and Google [26].

Perpetrators are increasingly disseminating illegal content such as CSAM via end-to-end-encrypted channels. Such encryption defeats network- and server-based scanning measures used by law enforcement. A trade-off is to enable confidential communications channels for users and scanning opportunities for law enforcement by employing perceptual-hashing-based targeted content scanning on user devices.

This chapter summarizes the current state of research in perceptual-hashing-based targeted content scanning with a focus on classical metrics such as false positives, false negatives and privacy aspects. Insights are provided into the most relevant perceptual hashing methods and an attack taxonomy for perceptual-hashing-based targeted content scanning is presented. The complexity in generating false negatives is evaluated and the feasibility of evading perceptual-hashing-based targeted content scanning is demonstrated.

2 Related Work

NIST Special Publication 800-168 [7] defines approximate matching as "a generic term describing any technique designed to identify similarities between two digital artifacts." The publication also categorizes a perceptual hash as a semantic hash used primarily for bytewise approximate matching.

Academic research on perceptual hashing is relatively sparse. However, several open-source perceptual hashes have been developed, including bHash [29], aHash [14], dHash [15], pHash [13, 30], wHash [21] and PDQ [17, 18]. Of these perceptual hashes, only pHash and PDQ come with detailed descriptions. In 2010, Zauner [30] provided an extensive description and evaluation of pHash; despite its age, pHash is still relevant today. Meta, which developed PDQ, has released a technical paper [18] covering the inner workings of the hash and a limited evaluation [17].

Closed-source perceptual hashes have also been developed, the most commonly used being PhotoDNA [19] and NeuralHash [2]. While no official document related to PhotoDNA is available, Apple, the NeuralHash developer, has released limited technical information about the perceptual hash [2, 3].

Kulshrestha and Mayer [16] are the only academic researchers to propose a perceptual-hashing-based targeted content scanning system that is designed in a privacy-preserving manner. Their proposal seeks to enforce privacy using cryptographic methods, specifically, private exact membership computation (PEMC) and private approximate membership computation (PAMC). They do not judge whether or not it is ethical to use such a system nor do they take positions on what targeted content should be scanned and the effectiveness of scanning.

Several academic researchers have focused on attacking perceptual hashes. Struppek et al. [25] presented four attacks on NeuralHash that enable detection evasion, hash collision and information extraction. Evaluations of the attacks using a dataset of 10,000 images demonstrate that they are functional and realistic. Importantly, Struppek and colleagues are the only researchers to release the actual code used to evaluate attacks. Jain et al. [11] presented detection evasion attacks on the pHash, aHash, dHash and PDQ perceptual hashes. Their detailed evaluation employed images from the same dataset used by Struppek et al. [25], but their sample size was much larger.

3 Perceptual Hashing

This section explains the general concept of perceptual hashing and presents details about two prominent hash functions.

3.1 Perceptual Hashing Details

Perceptual hashing is an approximate matching technique for comparing the similarity of objects. In this work, the focus is on the perceptual similarity of pictures (images). Perceptual similarity means that a human presented with two images would judge them as being the same or similar. Because images are often modified slightly during their use (e.g., compressed to reduce bandwidth and storage before being uploaded to a digital service), they cannot be identified by cryptographic hashes or other exact matching techniques. In such scenarios, perceptual hashing can be used effectively for approximate matching [16]. Perceptual hashing operates at the semantic level of images, interpreting the internal data structures of image files and using perceptive features of the images for matching [7].

As an approximate matching technique, perceptual hashing has two basic components. One is a similarity digest based on object features and the other is a similarity function that compares similarity digests and computes a similarity score [7].

A feature is the most basic component of an object that is compared and comparing two features yields a binary result [7]. In the case of perceptual hashes, the features should map to data representing the human perceptions of images.

Following the notation of Struppek et al. [25], a perceptual hash function H is given by:

$$H : \mathbb{R}^{h \times w \times c} \to \{0,1\}^k$$

where the three-dimensional array input to function H contains image height h, width w and color channel c data, and the output of function H is a k-bit binary hash. Note that k is a fixed value chosen for a concrete perceptual hash to ensure that hashes produced by the hash function are of equal length. A hash computation involves two parts. First, image features are extracted and stored in an intermediary format (e.g., matrix or vector). Next, the intermediary format is mapped to a k-bit hash.

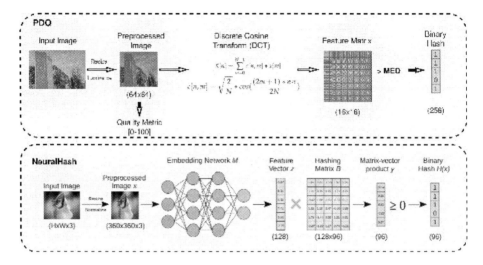

Fig. 1. Overview of PDQ and NeuralHash.

A similarity function $D(h_1, h_2)$ is used to compare two perceptual hashes h_1 and h_2. It produces a similarity score between 0 and 100. The higher the score of images with hashes h_1 and h_2, the more perceptually similar the images. Hamming distance is often used as the basic comparison function. Two images are determined to be perceptually the same, if their similarity score exceeds a preset threshold [30].

3.2   Perceptual Hash Functions

This section describes two prominent perceptual hash functions, PDQ from Meta and NeuralHash from Apple. Figure 1 provides an overview of the main steps in the two functions. Note that the NeuralHash image in Figure 1 is taken from [25].

Although certain differences exist between the two perceptual hash functions, it is possible to generalize the process. Specifically, the input image data is normalized for further processing and the image details are reduced by rescaling and removing color. Next, features representing the perceptions of images are extracted. The features are mapped to a binary hash. While image normalization and the final reduction step have big influences on perceptual hash quality, the main distinction between the two implementations is the feature extraction process. PDQ relies on digital image processing using the discrete cosine transform whereas NeuralHash uses a neural network.

PDQ   PDQ was designed to detect abusive imagery in large-scale contexts in social networks by comparing digital perceptual hashes [17]. While PDQ is claimed to be built from the ground up, it is very similar to the discrete-cosine-transform-based pHash [13].

Figure 1 (top) shows the steps involved in generating a PDQ hash of an image [18]. First, the image is transformed to its luminance representation. To further reduce the image details and render the hash computations less resource intensive, the image is resized to a 64×64 pixel square. The interpolation method employed ensures that each pixel contributes to a down-sampled pixel.

Next, the most perceptually relevant portions of the 64×64 image are extracted. This is accomplished by using the discrete cosine transform to convert the image to a frequency representation and portions of the image that do not contribute much to human perception are discarded. The 64×64 matrix output of the discrete cosine transform is thus reduced to a 16×16 submatrix.

Finally, to generate the hash, the median value of the 16×16 submatrix is computed. Each value in the submatrix is compared against the median to create the 256-bit PDQ hash. Specifically, when a submatrix value is larger than the median, a one is placed in the hash; otherwise, a zero is placed in the hash.

NeuralHash NeuralHash is intended to be a part of a CSAM protection system deployed in Apple's ecosystem of clients and cloud services. Apple released limited information about NeuralHash in a technology description [2] and threat model review [3] before its planned release with iOS 15 in late 2021. Additional details about NeuralHash are described in [25] based on community efforts to extract and reverse engineer its algorithm.

Figure 1 (bottom) shows the steps involved in generating a NeuralHash of an image. First, the input image is preprocessed. This involves transforming the image to the RGB color model, resizing it to a 360×360 pixel square and normalizing the RGB pixel values to $[-1, 1]$ [25]. Next, a neural network is used to extract image features in the form of an array with floating point values. The values serve as descriptors or features of the image [2]. The neural network was previously trained in a self-supervised manner using an unknown dataset to generate close descriptors for images that are perceptually similar. The perceptual similarity is based on angular distance and cosine similarity.

Following this, the array of descriptors is compressed into a much smaller 96-bit hash that preserves similarity using a locality-sensitive hash [2]. Note that NeuralHash was not trained to detect CSAM *per se*, but rather to compare images that are perceptual similar. Therefore, despite the fact that it uses a neural network for feature extraction, NeuralHash is characterized as a perceptual hash function.

4   Targeted Content Scanning

A perceptual-hashing-based targeted content scanning (PHTCS) system comprises three core components, a perceptual hash function, the targeted content database and processes and policies that determine which images are targeted during scanning and how the recognized targeted content is moderated.

The main goal of PHTCS is to find and moderate occurrences of targeted content in a digital service or communications channel. Perceptual hashes are used to scan a flow of images and recognize the images with targeted content [1, 16].

A targeted content database comprising a reference list of perceptual hashes is employed. The database can be viewed as a blacklist. Content subject to PHTCS is examined using perceptual hashing. This enables blacklisted images as well as images that are perceptually similar to be identified. A clear limitation of the blacklisting employed by PHTCS is that only known targeted content can be recognized [1].

Finally, processes and policies must be defined. A PHTCS system is enrolled in a digital service, which feeds it images that it scans to recognize targeted content. Therefore, PHTCS is typically specified for a single service or single service provider that enrolls it in its services. While software is required to implement the image flow, more interesting are the processes and policies that specify how scanning is conducted and how images that match the targeted content are moderated [16].

In general, there needs to be a process that regulates the triggers that cause images to be scanned. For example, scanning could be triggered by a user uploading an image to a social network. Before the image is processed further and displayed in the social network, it would be input to the PHTCS system. This leads to a second process that regulates the actions of the social network if an uploaded image is deemed to have targeted content.

Some of the PHTCS actors have already been mentioned. One actor is the service provider that has enrolled PHTCS in one or more of its services. Another actor is a user of the digital service that has enrolled PHTCS. Aside from triggering scanning due to the presence of targeted content, the user has no active role in PHTCS [1, 16]. Another actor that may not be immediately obvious is a trusted party, which is responsible for creating and curating the targeted content database. In the case of CSAM scanning, child safety organizations, such as the NCMEC in the United States, would curate databases of perceptual hashes and share them with partners. This actor is called a trusted party because the service provider has to trust the actor to include only hashes of targeted content in the database. Of course, this would not be verifiable by the service provider or users because a perceptual hash is a one-way function and the actual targeted content would not be shared [16]. The last PHTCS actor is law enforcement that comes into play when illegal content is detected. The content may be reported by the service provider to the responsible law enforcement agency on a voluntary or mandatory basis [1].

5   Attacking PHTCS

PHTCS relies on perceptual hashes to recognize images that are defined as targeted content. Users intending to circumvent or abuse a PHTCS system would be interested in launching attacks on PHTCS. Some PHTCS systems may implement protection mechanisms against attacks. For example, human review of each matched image can prevent misinterpretations of benign images as targeted content. However, this additional step is expensive and is difficult to scale.

As a result, companies would design their PHTCS systems to have very low (natural) false positive rates (see, e.g., [6]). Errors or adversarial methods that prevent PHTCS from detecting harmful images as targeted content cannot be prevented by human review. Users that manipulate their harmful images to evade detection could significantly reduce PHTCS effectiveness.

Perceptual hashes are more likely to be attacked successfully if they are used in client-side PHTCS. This is because the attacker could gain direct access to key PHTCS components, namely, the targeted content database and the device that performs the scanning. In server-side scanning, attacker access would be much more limited and the perceptual hashes would often be kept secret (e.g., with PhotoDNA [1]).

Based on research described in [22, 25], a taxonomy of attacks on perceptual hashes in the context of targeted content scanning is created. The taxonomy differentiates attacks into three categories, detection evasion, hash collision and data leakage. The following sections describe the attacks and how attackers can use them to combat PHTCS. Additionally, practical examples of attacks on perceptual hashes and their ability to hinder PHTCS are described.

5.1 Detection Evasion

A detection evasion attack seeks to prevent an image containing targeted content from being matched by a PHTCS system. This is accomplished by transforming an image X (hash $H(X)$) with targeted content to a new image X' (hash $H(X')$) that is perceptually similar to X but $H(X') \neq H(X)$. If the PHTCS system to be bypassed employs a threshold T for matching hashes, then the similarity $D(H(X), H(X')) > T$ must hold [10, 11]. For the attack to be effective, changes to the image should have minimal impacts on its perception, but its perceptual hash value would be altered significantly [11]. To carry out the attack, an attacker must have access to the image X that must evade detection and should be able to compute the perceptual hashes $H(X)$ and $H(X')$ [11].

Detection evasion attacks would enable users to store, view and disseminate images with targeted content on services and devices with enrolled PHTCS systems. A successful attack would impact PHTCS effectiveness significantly. The impact on effectiveness is evaluated using three metrics:

- **Success Rate:** This metric assesses how reliably an attack works on images.
- **Perceptual Similarity:** This metric assesses the similarity of an evading image compared with an image with targeted content.
- **Modification Effort:** This metric considers the effort, in terms of time, involved in modifying an image with targeted content. Simple image modifications such as rotating or resizing can be used, as well as more complex modifications such as editing pixels in special positions based on the perceptual hashes [25].

Fig. 2. Detection evasion attacks on NeuralHash (from [25]).

NeuralHash Attacks Struppek et al. [25] describe detection evasion attacks that employ gradient-based modifications of images. The attacks introduce specific perturbations to an original image X with targeted content. The perturbations are obtained by one or more optimization steps using a generic property of the neural network used by NeuralHash to extract image features. Specifically, that hash computations are differentiable and gradient descent can be used to find hash collisions [5].

Struppek et al. [25] demonstrated three levels of the attack that depend on the perturbations that are introduced. In a standard attack, any pixel can be modified. In an edges-only attack, the edges of objects in an image are perturbed. In a few-pixels attack, only a minimum amount of pixels can be manipulated. In general, the greater the restrictions on perturbations, the less the visual discrepancies seen in the modified images.

Figure 2 shows detection evasion attacks on NeuralHash using gradient-based modifications [25]. The top row of images shows the original image with targeted content and three modifications of the original image using standard, edges-only and few-pixels modification attacks, respectively. The row of text between the two rows of images shows the NeuralHash values of the original and modified images. The bottom row of images shows the differences between the original image and modified images where black corresponds to no pixel change and white corresponds to a pixel change.

Struppek et al. [25] define the optimization problem as:

$$\min_{X'} \ L_{\mathrm{MSE}}(X', \tilde{H}) - \lambda * \mathrm{SSIM}(X', X) \quad \text{s.t.} \ d(H(X'), \tilde{H}) > \delta_H$$

where $L_{\mathrm{MSE}}()$ is a negative mean squared error (MSE) function used to increase the hash discrepancy between an image X and its manipulated counterpart X'

$(X, X' \in [-1, 1]^{h \times w \times c})$, $\tilde{H} = H(X)$ and a threshold δ_H expresses the proportion of bits changed in the hash of the modified image.

To minimize visual perturbations, L_{MSE} is influenced by a penalty term based on the structural similarity index measure SSIM between the images weighted by a parameter λ. SSIM values range from zero to one, the closer the SSIM value is to one, the more similar the images. Readers are referred to [27] for details about SSIM. The optimization ends when the Hamming distance $d(H(X'), H(X))$ between the NeuralHash values of the original and perturbed images exceeds the threshold δ_H.

To evaluate the attacks, experiments were conducted on the first 10,000 samples of the ImageNet test split [23]. The optimization steps on the images were performed using Adam [12].

Struppek et al. [25] selected the success rate metric and the SSIM metric for visual similarity. However, they assessed the effort required to modify an image only in terms of the optimization steps required, not the time required for image modification.

All three levels of attacks created visually imperceptible evasion images. To explore the differences, Struppek et al. [25] proceeded to evaluated them using the metrics. The success rates were almost identical for the standard and edges-only attacks, 100% and 99.95%, respectively; in the case of the few-pixels attack, the success rate was slightly lower at 98.21%. The SSIM values were very similar. The standard, edges-only and few-pixels attacks yielded SSIM scores of 0.9999, 0.9996 and 0.9989, respectively. The optimization step metrics varied considerably – about five steps for the standard attack, about 150 steps for the edges-only attack and about 3,095 for the few-pixels attack. These results question whether the edges-only and few-pixels attacks provide any additional value compared with the standard attack. The results also demonstrate that it is very easy to achieve at least a small change in the NeuralHash value of an image.

Struppek et al. [25] only gave detailed metrics for $\delta_H = 0$ (i.e., images are perturbed until one bit in their hashes are flipped). For higher values of δ_H, they only published a single graph showing the relative changes in the evaluation results compared with those obtained with $\delta_H = 0$.

5.2   Hash Collision

A hash collision attack is similar to a second preimage attack in cryptographic hashing. The goal is to modify an image X showing non-targeted content in a way that alters its perceptual hash $H(X)$ to match the perceptual hash in the targeted content database [22, 25]. The perturbed image could be completely synthetic and not show any perceivable content or it could be based on a specific image that is manipulated while keeping its visual perception hash the same.

In this scenario, an attacker must be able to generate $H(X)$ and must know the perceptual hashes in the targeted content database. Access to the targeted content database may be controlled, but an attacker needs to know at least one hash that would lead to a collision.

A hash collision attack could be used in two ways. One use case is denial of service. The attack would generate and disseminate large numbers of non-targeted images that lead to hash collisions. This would induce a PHTCS system to produce numerous false positives, eventually overwhelming the system.

The second use case is framing innocent users. In this case, an attacker could produce collision images and send them to a victim. Depending on the policies in place for the PHTCS system, moderation actions against the victim could range from account deactivation to criminal prosecution. Groups of individuals could also be targeted by sending innocuous images whose hashes collide with those of images containing CSAM. All the members of the group who receive, store or disseminate the images would be flagged by the PHTCS system that is supposed to only flag CSAM [22, 25]. While collision attacks can be leveraged by a variety of actors, a key obstacle for non-government and low-resource actors is gaining access to the targeted content database.

PDQ Attacks Hash collision attacks can be developed to target Meta's PDQ. The attack starts with a known hash $H(X)$ of an image X in a targeted content database. The attack requires the hash $H(X)$, but if only X is known, $H(X)$ would probably be easy to compute. Additionally, an initial image S is required, which is transformed into a new image X' that is perceptually similar to S, but with $d(H(X), H(X')) < T$ where $d()$ computes the Hamming distance between the images and T is a preset threshold.

The perturbations that create image X' are identified by iteratively employing indirect Monte Carlo approximations of the hash function gradients that minimize loss terms over hash distances and perturbation sizes [22]. The perturbations should be minimal so that they do not interfere with the visual perception of the image [22]. Each iteration would identify a perturbation vector δ that makes minimal changes to X' while decreasing the Hamming distance $d(H(X), H(X' + \delta))$. This vector would then be added to X' and the iterative process repeated until $d(H(X), H(X')) < T$ holds.

Since PDQ is not differentiable, the gradient must be estimated for each iteration to proceed. At each step, $H(X'_i)$ is computed for the current candidate image X'_i as well as Δ_i, the current distance to the target hash. Next, q perturbations $p_1, ..., p_q$ are generated where q determines the accuracy of the approximation. In [22], the size changes based on the iteration number. For each perturbation, the change in the hash value c_j is computed according to the target function [22]:

$$c_j = d(H(X), H(X'_i + p_j)) - d(H(X), H(X'_i))$$

Next, the changes c_j are used to compute a weighted average over the perturbations [22]:

$$\delta'_i = \frac{1}{q} \sum_1^q c_j * p_j$$

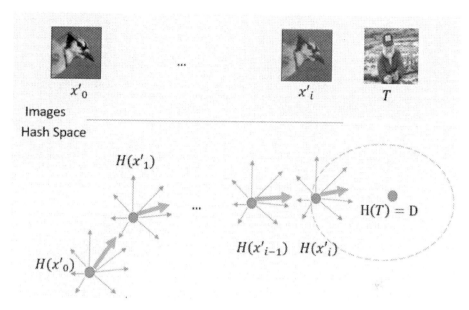

Fig. 3. Gradient estimations leading to a PDQ hash collision (from [22]).

Finally, the gradient δ_i used in the iteration is obtained by normalizing δ_i' and multiplying it by the learning rate λ [22].

Figure 3 shows the iterative process of estimating gradients that lead to collisions. The top portion of the figure shows the changes to the images up to the colliding target image. Below the images are the steps in hash space. The thick arrows in the figure denote the gradients used to move closer to the colliding hash during successive iterations [22].

Prokos et al. [22] used a threshold T of 90 in their experiments. However, in a real system the threshold setting would depend on various factors, especially the likelihood of false positives. The experiments were performed with 30 image pairs randomly selected from the ImageNet validation set [23]. All 30 image pairs had PDQ hash collisions within the threshold, requiring up to 6,350 iterations. The execution time for finding collision hashes for all 30 pairs was about three hours [22].

Figure 4 shows a hash collision attack on PDQ over several iterations [22]. The progression of images in the top row from left to right starts with an image of a bird. Successive images get more perturbed while the Hamming distance between the PDQ hashes of each successive image and the original image is reduced, until the final image of a man is obtained. The bottom row of images shows the differences between the original image and modified images where black corresponds to no pixel change and white corresponds to a pixel change.

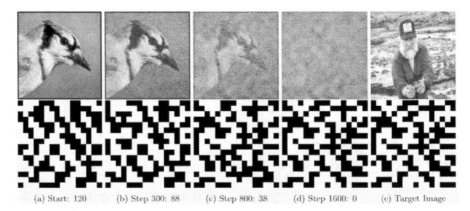

(a) Start: 120   (b) Step 300: 88   (c) Step 800: 38   (d) Step 1600: 0   (e) Target Image

Fig. 4. Hash collision attack on PDQ (from [22]).

5.3 Data Leakage

A data leakage attack seeks to extract information from a perceptual hash. A perceptual hash function extracts image features and converts them to a hash value. This means that a perceptual hash contains some image information [25]. In order to extract information, an attacker would have to collect as many perceptual hashes as possible (to correlate the findings) and would need access to and details about the perceptual hash function [25].

The severity of data leakage depends on how much information can be extracted from a hash. A data leakage attack is less severe if the extracted data only indicates attributes of the original image. Thus, an attacker could derive some general statements about the original image, such the image shows a dog or contains two humans. In a more severe attack, it would be possible to reconstruct portions of the original image from its hash, such as a thumbnail version [22]. Of course, since perceptual hashing compresses a variable-sized image to a fixed size, only a low resolution version of the original image could be reconstructed.

In addition to the amount of information that can be extracted, it is important to consider the potential victims of data leakage. A PHTCS system processes perceptual hashes of two types of images, user images and targeted content images. Both types of perceptual hashes should be protected. Safeguarding user hashes protects user privacy even if only limited image information can be extracted [25]. Therefore, user hashes should always reside on user devices and not be transmitted to servers unless there are targeted content matches. When user hashes are transmitted to servers, the hashes should be safeguarded on the server-side so that only authorized access is possible.

Information leakage from targeted content hashes that enables images to be reconstructed would have disastrous consequences [22]. Therefore, targeted content hashes should have strong protections. Moreover, even during client-side scanning, the hashes should never be stored on user devices. Apple [2, 6] and Kulshrestha and Mayer [16] have provided suggestions about how such a system might work.

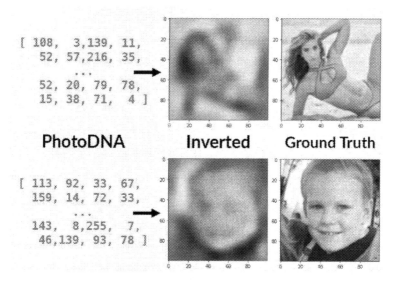

Fig. 5. Image reconstructions from PhotoDNA hashes [4].

PhotoDNA Attack Research on reconstructing images from perceptual hashes is sparse. However, an informal research article in the form of a blog post [4] discusses the reconstruction of images from Microsoft's PhotoDNA perceptual hashes [19]. Since PhotoDNA is not published and can only be used under a strict non-disclosure agreement, the data leakage attack was developed by reverse engineering the PhotoDNA algorithm.

Specifically, the data leakage attack employs a trained neural network that takes a PhotoDNA hash as input and generates a representation of the original image [4]. The neural network training dataset comprised images and their PhotoDNA hashes. In fact, the data leakage attack only became possible because the compiled PhotoDNA code became available and was reverse-engineered to compute PhotoDNA hashes of training images for the training dataset [4]. The results of image reconstruction strongly depend on the similarity between the training dataset and the unknown images to be reconstructed. For example, reconstructing images with faces of celebrities would work best if the neural network was trained on the same type of images [4].

Figure 5 shows examples of image reconstruction (inverted images) from PhotoDNA hashes [4]. The reconstructions, which are very blurry, are deemed "good results." In many cases, the results are much worse [4]. Thus, it is questionable if a data leakage attack could identify a user from a user hash or produce a detailed image from a targeted content hash.

5.4 Evaluation of NeuralHash Detection Evasion

Unfortunately, Struppek et al. [25], who devised the detection evasion attacks on NeuralHash, did not provide detailed evaluations of their results. Specifically,

Table 1. Expanded evaluation of detection evasion attacks on NeuralHash.

$\delta_{\mathbf{H}}$	0	0.05	0.1	0.15
SR	100%	100	100%	100%
Success	10,000	10,000	10,000	10,000
Failure	0	0	0	0
SSIM	0.9998 ± 0.000	0.9991 ± 0.002	0.9976 ± 0.004	0.9953 ± 0.007
(Av. & SD)				
Maximum	0.9999	0.9999	0.9998	0.9997
Minimum	0.9894	0.9593	0.9097	0.8675
Time (s)	3.5 ± 3.3	15.1 ± 14.4	26.7 ± 19.7	38.7 ± 24.2
(Av. & SD)				
Maximum	71.1	152.1	203.3	308.3
Minimum	1.5	1.7	1.8	2.5
Steps	5.4 ± 4.9	20.65 ± 19.5	42.3 ± 29.2	61.9 ± 35.6
(Av. & SD)				
Maximum	102	294	338	393
Minimum	4	4	4	4
Evaluation Time (h)	3.9	13.4	24	34.6

they computed the success rate (SR) and SSIM metrics, but did not provide information about the time requirements for optimizing their gradient-based detection evasion attacks on NeuralHash. The average optimization steps required were provided, but no information about the time required for single steps. The evaluation also focused on finding minimal hash changes (i.e., one flipped bit). Additionally, a brief overview was provided about how the SR and SSIM values and number of optimization steps would change with larger differences in the hash values.

This section builds on the work of Struppek et al. [24] by verifying their SR and SSIM results, expanding their evaluation to include the time needed to create detection evasion images and evaluating the attack efficacy for larger minimum Hamming distances δ_H between the NeuralHash values of the original and modified images. The code provided by Struppek et al. was modified slightly to include time measurements in the logging. Next, the logged metrics were computed and reported. The same image dataset (i.e., first 10,000 images from ImageNet ILSVRC2012 test split [23]) and experimental setup were employed.

Table 1 shows the expanded evaluation of the detection evasion attacks on NeuralHash (see Table 2 in [25] for a direct comparison). The experiments used different Hamming distance thresholds δ_H from the set $\{0, 0.05, 0.1, 0.15, 0.2\}$. Note that threshold $\delta_H = 0$ is the default attack mode where an image is perturbed until only one bit in the hash of the modified image is changed. The threshold $\delta_H = 0.1$ means that at least 10% of the hash bits are flipped. The SR results are provided as percentages as well as the absolute numbers of successful and unsuccessful attacks in the dataset. For the other three metrics, SSIM, time and steps, the average, standard deviation, and maximum and minimum values are provided.

The results show that across the range of experiments, all 10,000 images were successfully perturbed to evade detection determined by varying the δ_H threshold. Furthermore, the average SSIM values are consistently very high over all the experiments. Even in the experiment with $\delta_H = 0.15$, the average SSIM value obtained is 0.9953 with a small deviation, which would correspond to a nearly indistinguishable perturbed image. However, some outliers do exist, starting in the experiments with $\delta_H = 0.1$. These outliers would probably show visible perturbations because the minimum SSIM value drops to 0.9097 and even down to 0.8675 for $\delta_H = 0.15$. The SR and SSIM results in Table 1 confirm the results presented by Struppek et al. [25].

Table 1 shows that the time required for image perturbations increases considerably for high δ_H values. The increase in the time requirement as δ_H goes from zero to 0.05 is large and continues to rise at an average of 38.7 s per image when $\delta_H = 0.15$. The time requirements deviate greatly from the average, which means that the images are very different in how easily they can be perturbed. The trend is also seen in the minimum and maximum values that strongly deviate from the average values. The attack on a single image, in the case of $\delta_H = 0.15$, requires a maximum of 308 s (more than five minutes), which is a long time.

Unfortunately, no patterns are discerned that would provide insights into what makes images easy or hard to perturb in the experimental setup. However, an average of 38.7 s to perturb an image is not very high considering the attack scenarios. The last row in Table 1 lists the evaluation times to provide a sense of how much time an attacker would need to perturb a large image dataset as used in the evaluation. Indeed, the evaluation times show that a determined attacker is definitely capable of executing detection evasion attacks on large datasets. Of course, the time measurements are strongly influenced by the computational resources used in the experiments. Fortunately, the downloadable code available at [25] can execute on graphical processor units (GPUs), which would speed up successful attack development.

6 Conclusions

The dissemination of CSAM on the Internet is a serious problem and technological approaches are required to combat its spread and enable the prosecution of perpetrators. However, it is important to maintain user security and privacy while enabling law enforcement to scan images for illegal content. PHTCS has been suggested as a solution that balances these two requirements. This chapter has discussed the state-of-the-art in PHTCS and conducted an extensive evaluation of potential attacks. Certain problems must be addressed to enable effective PHTCS deployments that would be acceptable to all the stakeholders.

A key problem raised by this research is that PHTCS effectiveness is severely limited by attacks such as detection evasion, hash collision and data leakage. A skilled individual could create and disseminate tools that manipulate CSAM to evade detection, rendering PHTCS systems essentially useless. Hash collision attacks could be used to create innocuous images with the same perceptual hashes as known CSAM images. Large numbers of these innocuous images could be disseminated to cause PHTCS to raise alerts, eventually overwhelming the system to result in denial of service. More insidious is the possibility that innocuous images could be used to frame individuals and groups with possessing and disseminating CSAM, exposing them to criminal investigations and potential prosecution. Data leakage attacks, which invert perceptual hashes to obtain portions or low-resolution versions of the original images, pose privacy risks to subjects who appear in the original images as well as to users. Clearly, additional research is needed to harden perceptual hashes and render them attack-resistant.

Another problem is that perceptual hashing technologies and processes and policies for their use are often developed and deployed in secret. Tech companies, non-governmental organizations, law enforcement, other government agencies and even researchers are cautious about disclosing details fearing that they may help perpetrators evade exposure. While this is understandable, it hinders informed discussion and the lack of transparency spreads mistrust in the research community and user base. A PHTCS solution that balances child safety and security and user privacy concerns can only become operational with mutual trust and collaboration. It is hoped that this chapter will stimulate discussion, research and, eventually, viable PHTCS deployments.

References

1. H. Abelson, R. Anderson, S. Bellovin, J. Benaloh, M. Blaze, J. Callas, W. Diffie, S. Landau, P. Neumann, R. Rivest, J. Schiller, B. Schneier, V. Teague and C. Troncoso, Bugs in our pockets: The risks of client-side scanning, arXiv: 2110.07450v1 (arxiv.org/abs/2110.07450v1), 2021.
2. Apple, CSAM Detection – Technical Summary, Cupertino, California (www.apple.com/child-safety/pdf/CSAM_Detection_Technical_Summary.pdf), 2021.
3. Apple, Security Threat Model Review of Apple's Child Safety Features, Cupertino, California (www.apple.com/child-safety/pdf/Security_Threat_Model_Review_of_Apple_Child_Safety_Features.pdf), 2021.
4. A. Athalye, Inverting PhotoDNA, *Internet Archive*, December 20, 2021.
5. A. Athalye, NeuralHash Collider, GitHub (github.com/anishathalye/neuralhash-collider), 2023.
6. A. Bhowmick, D. Boneh, S. Myers, K. Talwar and K. Tarbe, The Apple PSI System, Apple, Cupertino, California (www.apple.com/child-safety/pdf/Apple_PSI_System_Security_Protocol_and_Analysis.pdf), 2021.
7. F. Breitinger, B. Guttman, M. McCarrin, V. Roussev and D. White, Approximate Matching: Definition and Terminology, NIST Special Publication 800-168, National Institute of Standards and Technology, Gaithersburg, Maryland, 2014.
8. Facebook, Online child protection – Tools and technology, *Internet Archive*, June 21, 2022.

9. Federal Criminal Police Office, Presentation of the Numbers of Child Victims of Violence – Evaluation of the Police Crime Statistics 2021 (in German), Wiesbaden, Germany (`www.bka.de/SharededDocs/Downloads/DE/AktuelleInformationen/Infografiken/Sonstige/kindlicheGewaltopfer_PKS2021.pdf`), 2022.

10. Q. Hao, L. Luo, S. Jan and G. Wang, It's not what it looks like: Manipulating perceptual-hashing-based applications, *Proceedings of the ACM SIGSAC Conference on Computer and Communications Security*, pp. 69–85, 2021.

11. S. Jain, A. Cretu and Y. Montjoye, Adversarial detection avoidance attacks: Evaluating the robustness of perceptual-hashing-based client-side scanning, *Proceedings of the Thirty-First USENIX Security Symposium*, pp. 2317–2334, 2022.

12. D. Kingma and J. Ba, Adam: A method for stochastic optimization, poster paper presented at the *Third International Conference on Learning Representations*, 2015.

13. E. Klinger and D. Starkweather, pHash: The open source perceptual hash library, *Internet Archive*, April 9, 2023.

14. N. Krawetz, Looks like it, *Internet Archive*, May 26, 2011.

15. N. Krawetz, Kind of like that, *Internet Archive*, January 21, 2013.

16. A. Kulshrestha and J. Mayer, Identifying harmful media in (end-to-end) encrypted communications: Efficient private membership computation, *Proceedings of the Thirtieth USENIX Security Symposium*, pp. 893–910, 2021.

17. Meta, Open-sourcing photo- and video-matching technology to make the Internet safer, *Internet Archive*, August 1, 2019.

18. Meta, The TMK+PDQF Video-Hashing Algorithm and the PDQ Image Hashing Algorithm, Menlo Park, California (`raw.githubusercontent.com/facebook/ThreatExchange/main/hashing/hashing.pdf`), 2021.

19. Microsoft, Photo DNA, *Internet Archive*, April 11, 2023.

20. National Center for Missing and Exploited Children, CyberTipline 2021 Report, *Internet Archive*, March 17, 2022.

21. D. Petrov, Wavelet image hash in Python, *Internet Archive*, July 2, 2016.

22. J. Prokos, T. Jois, N. Fendley, R. Schuster, M. Green, E. Tromer and Y. Cao, Squint hard enough: Evaluating perceptual hashing with machine learning, *Cryptology ePrint Archive*, paper no. 2021/1531 (`eprint.iacr.org/2021/1531`), 2021.

23. O. Russakovsky, J. Deng, H. Su, J. Krause, S. Satheesh, S. Ma, Z. Huang, A. Karpathy, A. Khosla, M. Bernstein, A. Berg and F. Li, ImageNet large scale visual recognition challenge, *International Journal of Computer Vision*, vol. 115(3), pp. 211–252, 2015.

24. L. Struppek, Learning-to-Break-Deep-Perceptual-Hashing, GitHub (`github.com/ml-research/Learning-to-Break-Deep-Perceptual-Hashing`), 2022.

25. L. Struppek, D. Hintersdorf, D. Neider and K. Kersting, Learning to break deep perceptual hashing: The use case NeuralHash, *Proceedings of the ACM Conference on Fairness, Accountability and Transparency*, pp. 58–69, 2022.

26. K. Walker, Four steps we're taking today to fight terrorism online, *Internet Archive*, June 18, 2017.

27. Z. Wang, A. Bovik, H. Sheikh and E. Simoncelli, Image quality assessment: From error visibility to structural similarity, *IEEE Transactions on Image Processing*, vol. 13(4), pp. 600–612, 2004.

28. WeProtect Global Alliance, Global Threat Assessment 2021, Sevenoaks, United Kingdom (`www.weprotect.org/wp-content/uploads/Global-Threat-Assessment-2021.pdf`), 2021.

29. B. Yang, F. Gu and X. Niu, Block mean value based image perceptual hashing, *Proceedings of the International Conference on Intelligent Information Hiding and Multimedia*, pp. 167–172, 2006.
30. C. Zauner, Implementation and Benchmarking of Perceptual Image Hash Functions, M.S. Thesis, Secure Information Systems Program, University of Applied Sciences Upper Austria, Hagenberg, Austria, 2010.

Analysis of Document Security Features

Pulkit Garg[1], Saheb Chhabra[2], Garima Gupta[3], Vishal Srivastava[4], and
Gaurav Gupta[5]

[1] Indian Institute of Technology Jodhpur, Karwar, India
[2] Indraprastha Institute of Information Technology, New Delhi, India
[3] Independent Researcher, New Delhi, India
[4] Raj Kumar Goel Institute of Technology, Ghaziabad, India
[5] Ministry of Electronics and Information Technology, New Delhi, India
gauravg@gov.in

Abstract. Document fraud has been rising for several years, severely
impacting individuals, organizations and governments. Security features
in documents change significantly when documents are altered or reproduced, clearly identifying them as fraudulent. However, advancements in
technology and the availability of special hardware and software enable
criminals to create fraudulent documents despite the presence of security
features.

It is important to classify document security features to gain insights
into their unique characteristics, effectiveness and use cases. The classification supports the analysis of the robustness of document security
and steers the development of new and improved security features to
combat document fraud. This chapter classifies document security features based on three criteria, security feature types, inspection levels and
security levels.

Keywords: Fraudulent Documents · Security Features · Classification

1 Introduction

Document fraud [9, 11, 18] is constantly increasing due to technological advances
and the availability of high-resolution printers and scanners. Untrained eyes can
no longer spot high-quality fake documents. Even forensic experts may fail to
identify the fakes, posing significant threats to the economy and society. Figure 1
shows a collage of news items about instances of document fraud.

The most efficient strategy for combating document fraud is to incorporate
multiple security features in documents. The security features are typically generated using unique raw materials and hard-to-mimic manufacturing processes.
When documents with security features are altered or reproduced, the features
exhibit significant modifications, enabling fake documents to be distinguished
from real documents. Several researchers [2, 4] have discussed the changes observed in security features when documents are altered or reproduced. Other

G. Peterson and S. Shenoi (Eds.): DigitalForensics 2023, IFIP AICT 687, pp. 143–159, 2023.
https://doi.org/10.1007/978-3-031-42991-0_8

Fig. 1. News items about document fraud.

researchers [13, 15, 19] discuss various approaches for detecting fake documents based on the changes.

Government organizations around the world print banknotes, passports, bank checks and other high-value documents with security features such as optical fibers, security inks and see-through prints [14, 17]. In India, the Reserve Bank of India and the Security Printing and Minting Corporation of India produce most of India's high-value documents. The raw ingredients and printing processes used to produce the high-value documents are designated as national secrets. In contrast, low-value documents such as product labels, academic transcripts and certificates are printed by individuals or companies utilizing common security features like watermarks and microprinted images. Figure 2 shows a selection of documents commonly targeted for tampering or counterfeiting.

Fraudsters go to great lengths and employ state-of-the-art technologies to tamper with or counterfeit authentic documents, even those with multiple security features. This makes it imperative to upgrade existing security features and develop new features. Specifically, it is necessary to classify document security features to gain insights into their unique characteristics, effectiveness and use cases. The classification facilitates analyses of the robustness of document security and steers the development of new and improved security features to combat document fraud. This chapter classifies document security features based on three criteria, security feature types, inspection levels and security levels. In

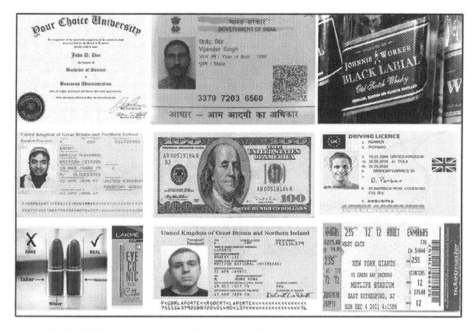

Fig. 2. Documents commonly targeted for tampering or counterfeiting.

addition, it links diverse Indian documents to the security features in order to assess their susceptibility to document fraud.

2   Classification of Document Fraud

Fraudsters use a variety of techniques to generate fake documents. Counterfeiting a product label requires a good color copy of an authentic label on similar paper whereas a fake identity card may require an existing identity card to be modified. Figure 3 classifies document fraud as nature-based, methodology-based and quality-based document fraud.

2.1   Nature-Based Document Fraud

Nature-based document fraud includes static document fraud and dynamic document fraud:

– **Static Document Fraud:** Static documents have the same information inscribed on them from when they are created until they become obsolete. These documents contain a combination of unique and fixed information. Examples include academic transcripts, banknotes, printed invoices, birth certificates, marriage certificates and drivers' licenses. Fraudsters often scan original static documents and may use image editing software to make custom modifications. Following this, they print high-quality fraudulent copies and use them for nefarious purposes.

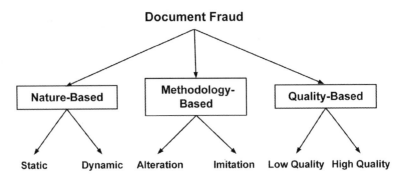

Fig. 3. Classification of document fraud.

– **Dynamic Document Fraud:** Dynamic documents are similar to static documents, except that the issuing and/or receiving parties write or stamp additional information before the documents are useable. Examples include bank checks, optical mark recognition sheets, examination forms, passports and visas. Fraudsters typically alter dynamic document content generated by the issuing/receiving parties for their purposes. For example, a base document (i.e., dynamic document before the issuing/receiving party writes on or stamps it) is created in the same way as a fake static document. Following this, the additional content is imprinted to create the fake document. Alternatively, a fraudster may start with a genuine base document and imprint the additional content. Yet another approach is to physically alter an official dynamic document by erasing, chemical washing and/or overwriting the issuing/receiving party's content.

Tampering detection strategies are employed to detect dynamic document fraud. Because few if any security features are modified, it is more difficult to identify dynamic document fraud than static document fraud.

2.2   Methodology-Based Document Fraud

Methodology-based document fraud includes altered document fraud and imitated document fraud:

– **Altered Document Fraud:** Altered document fraud is the tampering of digitally-printed documents. Software such as Photoshop and high-resolution printers and scanners make it simple even for amateurs to modify digital content and create altered documents. Common targets of altered document fraud include transcripts, certificates, passports, admit cards, identity credentials and legal documents.
– **Imitated Document Fraud:** Imitated documents are replicas of original documents such as banknotes and bank checks that appear to be authentic. The most common method for committing imitated document fraud is to

scan an original document and print it. The availability of inexpensive, high-resolution scanners and printers has significantly increased the opportunities to perpetrate imitated document fraud.

2.3 Quality-Based Document Fraud

Quality-based document fraud includes low-quality document fraud and high-quality document fraud:

- **Low-Quality Document Fraud:** Multiple security features are incorporated in documents to prevent tampering and forgery. It can be difficult for fraudsters to preserve or reproduce all the security features due to lack of expertise, materials and equipment, and cost.
  A fraudulent document is deemed to be of low quality if none or a few security features are preserved or reproduced. These documents may deceive casual users, but they are easily identified by trained professionals. However, casual users can identify low-quality documents with adequate awareness and knowledge.
- **High-Quality Document Fraud:** High-quality fraudulent documents preserve or replicate most or all the security features of the original documents, sometimes even misleading professional examiners who have sophisticated tools at their disposal. Creating high-quality fraudulent documents requires considerable knowledge, expertise and resources. Primary targets of high-quality document fraud are national identification cards, authorization passes and banknotes.

3 Security Feature Classification

Documents incorporate security features with diverse manufacturing techniques, robustness, security levels, verification techniques, cost, etc. Certain security features are chosen although they are susceptible to copying because the features are easily verified without special tools, have low production costs and/or are effective against low-quality document fraud. On the other hand, complex security features utilize special materials and expensive manufacturing techniques, which make them difficult to alter or reproduce.

Developing and improving document security features require considerable knowledge and skills. Additionally, it is essential to comprehend the various security features, their distinctive properties and their application circumstances, which are discussed in this section.

3.1 Security Feature Types

Security features are of diverse types and exhibit distinctive characteristics when exposed to varying lighting conditions or when reproduced. The distinctive characteristics arise from their basic components and production processes. For example, using chemicals visible only under infrared light in the production process provides a security feature with the same characteristics. Table 1 lists the different types of security features along with prominent examples of each type.

Text Endless text constitutes random lines of text that are pre-printed on documents. Attempts at altering information printed over endless text using chemicals also affects the endless text in the background. Pre-printed text is common generic text printed on documents of a certain type. However, the issuing or receiving party writes or prints additional information on a specific document before it is declared usable. Pre-printing also provides an option to hide other security features such as microprints on documents to enhance security.

Machine-Readable Materials It is impractical to manually check every document for tampering or forgery. As a result, machine-readable security features are incorporated on documents that enable automated verification. Magnetic ink character recognition employs magnetizable toner (with iron oxide) during printing, enabling text to be scanned precisely even when it is occluded or overprinted. If document text is printed in standard color ink, the automated reader will not identify it and deem the document to be fraudulent. Barcodes (including QR codes), which encode data in black and white shapes, are a popular security feature. The encoded data is unreadable without special equipment. However, barcode generators are widely available, making it easy to create fake barcodes. As a result, data is encrypted before storing it in barcodes, which prevents the text from being edited after the barcodes are created. However, fraudsters can copy and reuse barcodes.

Radio frequency identification (RFID) tags address this limitation. An RFID tag has a chip that stores information and an antenna that transmits information. RFID tags provide dependable security due to their complexity and high production costs [8]. Nonetheless, barcodes are still favored over RFID tags due to their low cost.

Printing Techniques Printing techniques yield distinctive textures and prints that are difficult to reproduce without the necessary expertise and equipment [3, 10]. For example, inkjet printing propels tiny ink droplets directly on a document substrate causing the ink to penetrate the substrate, creating smooth, high-resolution prints at low cost within a short duration. In contrast, intaglio printing fills the cut region of an intaglio plate with ink after which paper is pressed on the plate at very high pressure, creating a thick raised print on the paper. In offset printing, text and images are transferred from a plate cylinder (with an even surface) to an offset cylinder (with a rubber blanket), following which a print is made on a document substrate. Offset printing uses ink-repellent silicon to protect non-image areas from ink. As a result, offset printing generates high-quality prints, and because of the rubber blanket, it can adapt to different printing surfaces.

Due to the low cost of inkjet and laser printing, most document content is printed using these methods. However, equipment availability and low produc-

Table 1. Security features classified by type.

Feature Type	Examples
Text	Endless text, pre-printed text
Machine-Readable Materials	Magnetic ink characters, barcode, magnetic stripe, RFID tag, EMV chip
Printing Techniques	Background printing, laser printing/copying, miniprinting, gravure printing, inkjet printing, microprinting, intaglio printing, letterpress printing, needle printing, offset printing, rainbow coloring, screen printing, thermal printing, schablon (stencil) multiple coloring
Threads	Security thread, stitching thread
Security Inks	Ultraviolet ink, bleeding ink, fugitive ink, metallic ink, iridescent ink, optically-variable ink, infrared ink, photochromic ink, thermochromic ink
Perforations	Laser perforation, needle perforation, tank tracking perforation, laser perforation with tilting effects, secondary (ghost) laser image perforation, laser fine structure perforation
Multiview Patterns	Hologram, optical stripe, optically-variable ink, latent image, variable laser image, kinegram, identigram, secondary (ghost) image
Stamps	Blind embossed stamp, registered embossed stamp, ink stamp
Security Fibers	Synthetic fiber, security fiber, planchette
Laminates	Hot foil stamp, ultraviolet feature laminate, overprinted laminate, embossed laminate, iridescent laminate, optically-variable ink, retroreflective laminate, integrated bound laminate
Light-Transmitting Materials	Singletone watermark, duotone watermark, multitone watermark, transparent window, see-through register
Identification Data	Serial number, national identification number
Anti-Copy/Anti-Scan Patterns	Microprint, pantograph, fine line, guilloche
Fluoresent Materials	Fluorescent fiber, fluorescent highlight, fluorescent ink, fluorescent overprint, fluorescent planchette, fluorescent security thread, fluorescent serial number, fluorescent stitching thread

tion costs enable fraudsters to reproduce such documents easily. Intaglio and offset printing are used as alternatives because they require advanced machinery, which renders reproduction expensive. Meanwhile, researchers are constantly searching for ways to improve the security of traditional printing processes [5, 7].

Threads Security threads are thin ribbon strips of metal foil or plastic that are woven in a document substrate. They may have fluorescent or ultraviolet properties or may contain microprinted text. The threads are woven such that some portions of the threads appear on the front side of a document and the remaining portions on the rear side. However, when the document is held up against the light, all the threads appear as single lines. Stitching threads are used to tie different pages together. The threads are created using various substrates to provide excellent sewability as well as different colors under different (visible/infrared/fluorescent) lighting conditions.

Security Inks Security inks are often used to enhance security. Various chemicals in the inks incorporated in document substrates exhibit distinct properties when the documents are altered or reproduced. For example, fugitive ink is specially formulated to smudge when exposed to water and other solvents used by fraudsters to modify documents. Penetrating ink contains a red pigment that penetrates paper fibers during production, so that the red coloring remains even after the printed section is removed. Ultraviolet and infrared inks are invisible under visible light and can only be viewed under ultraviolet and infrared light, respectively. Other security inks such as optically-variable, photochromic and thermochromic inks, change color based on the viewing angle, illumination and temperature, respectively. These inks enable document alterations to be detected without using special equipment.

Perforations Perforations are tiny holes or dashes created on the top layers of documents using lasers, needles or blades. Perforated lines are ideal for document security because they are not captured by copy machines and scanners. Security documents may also incorporate laser-perforated serial numbers and secondary pictures that are visible when held up to the light. To increase security, laser perforation with tilting effects is used to perforate images at different angles. The resulting images can be viewed only from certain angles in transmitted light.

Multiview Patterns Advancements in optical technology have contributed to new security features that change based on viewing angle and lighting. Many documents are printed with optically-variable inks containing pigments that change color depending on the viewing angle. Holograms and kinegrams are optical security features that rely on light diffraction and refraction, producing varying three-dimensional effects with changes in angle and illumination. This feature makes them very difficult to replicate in fraudulent documents.

Stamps Ink stamps are impressions created by infusing liquid ink into documents. The stamps, which generally contain the details of the authorized signatories, have complex structures that hinder document reproduction. Direct photocopying produces a deteriorated ink stamp, but it is still a weak security feature. Blind embossed stamps are stamp patterns whose raised and recessed dye surfaces can be felt by touching the documents. It is difficult to replicate the precise alignments and depths of blind embossed stamps.

Security Fibers Synthetic fibers are introduced into document substrates to enhance document durability. However, they also provide security because they have unique compositions that are difficult to mimic. Security fibers are colored or transparent fibers added to a document substrate at random locations and varying depths. They may be customized to be visible or invisible under white light or have magnetic or fluorescent properties. The combination of these features makes the documents difficult to reproduce. Planchettes are tiny 1 mm to 4 mm dots that are randomly distributed in a document substrate during manufacturing. They may have fluorescent, non-fluorescent, chemically-reactive, thermochromic and/or other properties that are lost during reproduction. Due to their minute size and reflectivity, planchettes are not captured by copy machines.

Laminates Laminates have been used to safeguard documents for years. Security laminates incorporate optically-variable or tactile elements to provide document security. Laminates have numerous variations that enhance security. An overprinted laminate has text on the reverse side of the lamination film. An embossed laminate has fine-line patterns that are embossed to be visible in oblique or transmitted light.

Light-Transmitting Materials Documents have long employed security measures that are only visible in transmitted light to enable verification by users with basic expertise and without special devices. Watermarks are embedded figures or patterns created by altering the document substrate density during production – the thicker the substrate at a particular location, the darker it appears under transmitted light. A see-through register is another common security feature involving light-transmitting materials. One half of a pattern is printed on the front of a document and the other half on the back, so the entire pattern is only visible in reflected and transmitted light. If the front and back portions are not aligned perfectly, distortions indicative of counterfeiting are easily seen. Such high precision printing on both sides of a document is not possible with commercial printers.

Identification Data A serial number is unique identification data assigned to and printed on a document. Each document must have a unique serial number that is clearly visible. A national identification number is a unique identifier of a registered individual that is generally printed on an identity document.

The identifier may incorporate personal information such as name and date of birth. A national identification number along with information pertaining to the registered individual is stored in a central database, enabling authorities to quickly verify details about an individual by entering the national identification number.

Anti-Copy/Anti-Scan Patterns A microprint comprises text and/ or symbols printed in a very small font on a document; the microprinted information is not discernible without magnification. Common scanners and copy machines have low resolutions and are unable to recognize microprinted information and reproduce unrecognizable symbols. Pantographs are copy-evident patterns that exploit the limitations of reproduction techniques. Invisible text hidden in a pantograph becomes visible due to aliasing and blurring that occur when a document is reproduced. Guilloches are complex patterns printed using high-resolution printers. They comprise many interwoven shapes created using lines, but appear as solid color patches to the naked eye; however, it is possible to discern the patterns using magnification. Like microprinted text or symbols, scanners and copy machines cannot detect the fine-line patterns and produce distortions that are readily visible.

Fluorescent Materials Fluorescent materials used in security printing change color when exposed to ultraviolet light. Security fibers, inks, overprints, planchettes, threads, serial numbers and stitching threads often incorporate fluorescent materials. The visual effects, which are very difficult to reproduce, provide an additional safeguard against document forgery.

3.2   Security Feature Inspection Levels

According to van Renesse [20], some security features such as intaglio printing, optically-variable inks and holograms are intended to be obvious and visible to the naked eye. These features, which are incorporated to enable the public to identify whether documents are genuine or counterfeit, are classified as Level 1 security features. Level 2 features are semi-covert security features that can be examined by trained examiners using simple equipment such as electronic readers and light microscopes. These features include barcodes, microprinting and planchettes. Level 3 security features are covert security features that are inspected in forensic examinations of documents. Examples include magnetic stripes, RFID tags, EMV chips, ultraviolet inks, infrared inks and fluorescent inks. These features require more sophisticated equipment such as electronic chip readers, high-power microscopes and video spectral comparators for document inspection. Table 2 shows the security feature classification based on document inspection levels.

Table 2. Security features classified by inspection level.

Inspection Level	Examples
Level 1	Pre-printed text, intaglio printing, letterpress printing, needle printing, security thread, stitching thread, bleeding ink, fugitive ink, iridescent ink, optically-variable ink, photochromic ink, thermochromic ink, laser perforation, needle perforation, laser perforation with tilting effects, hologram, optical stripe, latent image, variable laser image, kinegram, identigram, secondary (ghost) image, blind embossed stamp, registered embossed stamp, ink stamp, overprinted laminate, embossed laminate, iridescent laminate, retroreflective laminate, singletone watermark, duotone watermark, multitone watermark, transparent window, see-through register, serial number, national identification number, pantograph
Level 2	Endless text, barcode, background printing, laser printing, miniprinting, gravure printing, inkjet printing, microprinting, offset printing, rainbow coloring, screen printing, thermal printing, schablon (stencil) multiple coloring, laser fine structure perforation, synthetic fiber, security fiber, planchette, hot foil stamp, fine line, guilloche
Level 3	Magnetic ink characters, magnetic stripe, RFID tag, EMV chip, ultraviolet ink, infrared ink, ultraviolet feature laminate, fluorescent fiber, fluorescent ink, fluorescent overprint, fluorescent planchette, fluorescent security thread, fluorescent serial number, fluorescent stitching thread

3.3   Security Feature Security Levels

Incorporating document security features that are highly resistant to fraud is costly due to the raw materials required and the complexity of the manufacturing processes. High-value documents incorporate strong security-level features such as RFID tags, EMV chips, laser perforations with tilting effects, ghost image perforations and latent images.

However, technological advances have made security features that were rare and highly resistant to fraud just a few years ago more ubiquitous and easily replicable [1, 6]. Examples of these features are magnetic stripes, inkjet printing, microprinting, offset printing, thermochromic inks, embossed stamps, digital watermarks and pantographs.

Other security features such as encrypted barcodes, bleeding inks and fugitive inks make documents highly resistant to alteration. However, due to the availability of the inks and barcode generators, these features do not adequately protect against document reproduction. Therefore, these features are deemed to have a weak security level.

Table 3. Security feature classified by security level.

Security Level	Examples
Strong Security Level	RFID tag, EMV chip, miniprinting, intaglio printing, laser perforation with tilting effects, secondary (ghost) laser image perforation, laser fine structure perforation, latent image, variable laser image, kinegram, synthetic fiber, security fiber, transparent window, see-through register, fine line, guilloche, fluorescent fiber, fluorescent planchette, fluorescent security thread
Weak Security Level	Endless text, pre-printed text, magnetic ink characters, barcode, magnetic stripe, background printing, laser printing, gravure printing, inkjet printing, microprinting, letterpress printing, needle printing, offset printing, rainbow coloring, screen printing, thermal printing, schablon (stencil) multiple coloring, security thread, stitching thread, ultraviolet ink, bleeding ink, fugitive ink, metallic ink, iridescent ink, optically-variable ink, infrared ink, photochromic ink, thermochromic ink, laser perforation, needle perforation, hologram, optical stripe, ghost image, blind embossed stamp, registered embossed stamp, ink stamp, planchette, hot foil stamp, ultraviolet feature laminate, overprinted laminate, embossed laminate, iridescent laminate, singletone watermark, duotone watermark, multitone watermark, serial number, national identification number, pantograph, fluorescent highlight, fluorescent ink, fluorescent overprint, fluorescent serial number, fluorescent stitching thread

Table 3 categorizes security features into two classes, strong and weak security levels. In general, a combination of security features of various levels must be employed to reduce costs while achieving appropriate overall levels of document security. For example, a security thread with microprinting and fluorescent ink along with a hologram would provide greater protection than a security fiber alone.

4   Analysis of Security Features

Security features incorporated in documents are tailored to the importance of the documents as well as their sizes, shapes and looks. However, to understand the vulnerabilities of documents to alteration and reproduction, and their security levels and production costs, it is necessary to identify and assess the specific security features that are incorporated.

Table 4 lists a sampling of common Indian documents along with their security features. As mentioned above, high-value documents incorporate more se-

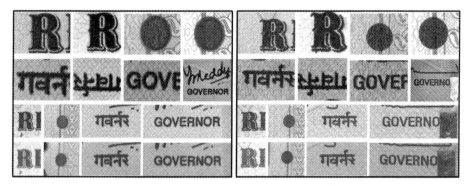

Fig. 4. Security features in genuine (left) and counterfeit (right) Indian banknotes.

curity features with higher levels of security than low-value documents. Clearly, the security of banknotes to a country cannot be overstated. As seen in Table 4, Indian banknotes incorporate numerous security features. The security features are of different types, require different inspection methods and have different security levels. The combination of features renders Indian banknotes notes resistant to counterfeiting.

Figure 4 shows images of security features in genuine and counterfeit Indian banknotes. The genuine banknotes are printed using intaglio printing. As mentioned above, intaglio printing is a strong security feature and is difficult to reproduce, forcing counterfeiters to use offset printing. Offset printing is a weak security feature and, as seen in Figure 4, the visual differences between security features in authentic and counterfeit banknotes are evident [13].

National passports are clearly high-value documents. Table 4 shows that Indian passports incorporate similar security features as Indian banknotes, including magnetic ink characters, microprinting, laser perforations and ink stamps. Figure 5 shows images of the security features in an Indian passport. The use of guilloches, fluorescent inks and fluorescent stitching threads, which are strong security features, makes it difficult to alter or reproduce Indian passports.

On the other hand, Table 4 shows that low-value documents such as insurance certificates and academic transcripts employ few and weak security features such as barcodes and watermarks that are not resistant to tampering and counterfeiting.

Figure 6 shows the security features incorporated in a product label, background printing and offset printing, which are weak security features.

Individuals and organizations that produce such low-value documents are not interested in investing in expensive security features to safeguard them. Barcodes and holograms are commonly used in low-value documents because they are inexpensive and provide protection from alteration and counterfeiting.

Table 4. Common Indian documents and their security features.

Document Type	Documents	Security Features
National Identity Cards	Passport	Magnetic ink characters, barcode, background printing, microprinting, laser perforation, hologram, ink stamp, security fiber, watermark, national identification number, fine line, guilloche, fluorescent ink, fluorescent stitching thread
	Driver's License	EMV chip, ultraviolet ink, national identification number
	PAN Card	Barcode, ultraviolet ink, hologram, watermark
	Voter Card	Hologram
Financial Documents	Banknote	Background printing, laser printing, microprinting, intaglio printing, offset printing, security thread, ultraviolet ink, optically-variable ink, latent image, embossed stamp, watermark, transparent window, see-through register, serial number, fine line, guilloche, fluorescent fiber, fluorescent ink, fluorescent serial number
	Bank Check	Pre-printed text, magnetic ink characters, barcode, background printing, microprinting, ultraviolet ink, bleeding ink, watermark, serial number, pantograph
	Demand Draft	Magnetic ink characters, watermark
Other Documents	Insurance Certificate	Watermark
	Postage Stamp	Background printing, intaglio printing, offset printing
	Legal Stamp Paper	Pre-printed text, microprinting, intaglio printing, rainbow coloring, security thread, ultraviolet ink, watermark, guilloche
	Academic Transcript	Pre-printed text, barcode, microprinting, rainbow coloring, ultraviolet ink, watermark
	Product Label	Barcode, background printing, offset printing, hologram

Fig. 5. Security features in an Indian passport.

Fig. 6. Security features in a product label.

5   Conclusions

Security features are incorporated in documents to safeguard them from alterations and counterfeiting. Security features vary according to their raw materials, manufacturing processes, robustness, alteration and counterfeiting resistance, usability and cost. The value of the documents to be secured dictates the specific combination of features that are employed.

However, advancements in technology and the availability of special hardware and software enable fraudulent documents to be created despite the presence of security features. The classification of document security features based on security feature types, inspection levels and security levels supports the analysis of document security implementations and steers the development of new and improved security features and their combinations to combat document fraud.

The views expressed in this chapter are those of the authors, and do not reflect the official policy or position of the Ministry of Electronics and Information Technology or Government of India.

References

1. A. Ali, Mumbai: Bulgarian ran skimming scam from his room in Andheri, *Times of India (Mumbai)*, December 14, 2021.
2. A. Anjali, A. Abhishek, S. Uttam and P. Verma, Comparison of various security features of genuine, scanned and photocopied Indian currency notes of denomination 2000, *Journal of Forensic Science and Criminology*, vol 5(3), pp. 1–12, 2017.
3. C. Borota, Printing techniques used to secure border-crossing documents, *International Journal of Criminal Investigation*, vol. 2(1), pp. 31–42, 2012.
4. S. Chhabra, G. Gupta, G. Gupta and M. Gupta, Indian currency database for forensic research, in *Advances in Digital Forensics XVII*, G. Peterson and S. Shenoi (Eds.), Springer, Cham, Switzerland, pp. 237–253, 2021.
5. H. Deinhammer, F. Loos, D. Schwarzbach and P. Fajmann, Direct laser engraving of intaglio printing plates, in *Optical Security and Counterfeit Deterrence Techniques V*, R. van Renesse (Ed.), International Society for Optics and Photonics (SPIE), Bellingham, Washington, pp. 184–193, 2004.
6. M. Graham, Fake holograms a 3D crime wave, *Wired*, February 7, 2007.
7. M. Hampden-Smith, S. Haubrich, R. Kornbrekke, J. Shah, R. Bhatia, N. Hardman and R. Einhorn, Overt security features through digital printing, in *Optical Security and Counterfeit Deterrence Techniques VI*, R. van Renesse (Ed.), International Society for Optics and Photonics (SPIE), Bellingham, Washington, pp. 230–239, 2006.
8. A. Juels, RFID security and privacy: A research survey, *IEEE Journal on Selected Areas in Communications*, vol. 24(2), pp. 381–394, 2006.
9. N. Karlikar, Maharashtra: Rs 2,000 fake notes worth Rs 8 crore seized in Thane, two arrested, *Times of India (Thane)*, November 12, 2022.
10. C. Lampert, L. Mei and T. Breuel, Printing technique classification for document counterfeit detection, *Proceedings of the International Conference on Computational Intelligence and Security*, pp. 639–644, 2006.
11. E. Medina, Home Depot worker swapped $387,500 in fake bills for real ones, officials say, *New York Times*, February 6, 2022.
12. J. Mercer, Evaluation of optical security features in ID documents, currency and stamps, in *Optical Security and Counterfeit Deterrence Techniques IV*, R. van Renesse (Ed.), International Society for Optics and Photonics (SPIE), Bellingham, Washington, pp. 323–332, 2002.
13. C. Nakamura, The Security Printing Practices of Banknotes, Senior Project, Department of Graphic Communication, California Polytechnic State University, San Luis Obispo, California, 2010.

14. Reserve Bank of India, Security Features of Indian Banknotes, Mumbai, India (`rbi.org.in/Scripts/ic_banknotessecurity.aspx`), 2023.
15. K. Santhanam, S. Sekaran, S. Vaikundam and A. Mani Kumarasamy, Counterfeit currency detection technique using image processing, polarization principle and holographic techniques, *Proceedings of the Fifth International Conference on Computational Intelligence, Modeling and Simulation*, pp. 231–235, 2013.
16. A. Sarkar, R. Verma and G. Gupta, Detecting counterfeit currency and identifying its source, in *Advances in Digital Forensics IX*, G. Peterson and S. Shenoi (Eds.), Springer, Berlin Heidelberg, Germany, pp. 367–384, 2013.
17. Security Printing and Minting Corporation of India, Security Products, New Delhi, India (`www.spmcil.com/products`), 2023.
18. N. Sharma, Counterfeit medical products increased by 47% from 2020 to 2021, report shows, *Business Today*, March 29, 2022.
19. A. Upadhyaya, V. Shokeen and G. Srivastava, Counterfeit currency detection techniques, *Proceedings of the Eighth International Conference on Cloud Computing, Data Science and Engineering*, pp. 394–398, 2018.
20. R. van Renesse, Paper-based document security – A review, *Proceedings of the European Conference on Security and Detection*, pp. 75–80, 1997.

Deepfake Detection Using Multiple Facial Features

Xinzhe Wang, Duohe Ma, Liming Wang, Zhitong Lu, Zhenchao Zhang and
Junye Jiang

Institute of Information Engineering, Chinese Academy of Sciences, Beijing, China
maduohe@iie.ac.cn

Abstract. Deepfake digital forgery techniques leverage deep learning
to replace faces and modify facial expressions in images and videos. The
techniques have been used to produce fake pornography, spread fake
news and rumors, influence public opinion and even elections. However,
deepfake detection techniques are well behind deepfake generation technology.

This chapter describes a deepfake video detection method that leverages
aspect ratios to express multiple facial features. The aspect ratios of
facial features are computed for every frame in a video and a time window is used to segment processed frame sequences into multiple short
segments, following which pattern matching is employed to identify abnormal expressions that are indicative of deepfakes. Experiments with
the FaceForensics++ and Celeb-DF datasets reveal that the proposed
method detects deepfake videos effectively. Moreover, the aspect ratio
computations improve the ability to detect compressed deepfake videos.

Keywords: Deepfake Detection · Facial Feature Extraction · Aspect
Ratios

1 Introduction

The Internet abounds with deepfake images and videos created by applying deep
learning techniques to replace or modify the original faces and facial expressions.
In the beginning, deepfakes were used to target female celebrities [6]. However,
modern deepfake technologies have advanced significantly by leveraging deep
adversarial networks to produce high-quality fake videos that appear to be real
to human eyes [33]. Deepfake forgery techniques are being used to produce fake
pornography, spread fake news and rumors, influence public opinion and even
elections [14].

Several researchers have focused on detecting deepfake videos [24, 25, 32, 36].
However, while the detection methods differ, they share the common shortcom-
ing of focusing on a specific facial feature, which renders deepfake detection
inefficient.

Since the clues provided by a single facial feature are limited, multiple facial
features should be employed to enhance deepfake video detection. This chapter

Published by Springer Nature Switzerland AG 2023
G. Peterson and S. Shenoi (Eds.): DigitalForensics 2023, IFIP AICT 687, pp. 161–175, 2023.
https://doi.org/10.1007/978-3-031-42991-0_9

proposes a detection method that employs aspect ratios to capture multiple facial features uniquely and easily. Multiple facial features comprise several single facial features such as eye blinking, lip movement and nasal flaring that are essential to deepfake detection.

The proposed method computes the aspect ratios of multiple facial features for every frame in a video and uses a time window to segment processed frame sequences into multiple short segments, following which pattern matching is employed to identify abnormal expressions that are indicative of deepfakes. Experiments with the FaceForensics++ and Celeb-DF datasets reveal that the proposed method detects fake videos more effectively than other deep-learning-based detection methods [4, 8, 17, 19, 25, 29]. Additionally, using the aspect ratio computations improves the ability to detect compressed deepfake videos.

2   Related Work

This section discusses related research on deepfake generation, deepfake video detection and aspect ratios.

2.1   Deepfake Generation

During the past four years, several researchers have employed deep learning to generate fake faces [2, 13, 26, 30]. In particular, the application of generative adversarial networks has greatly advanced the creation of deepfakes [13, 26]. Yang et al. [35] developed a technique that changes faces while improving the resolution of the facial images.

Methods for creating deepfakes fall into three main categories, facial expression manipulation, facial part manipulation and generative adversarial networks. Expression manipulation involves changing a facial expression without changing the face. Facial part manipulation involves replacing a face with another person's face. Generative adversarial network methods create nonexistent persons with random facial expressions.

Deepfakes are mainly based on facial expressions and facial features. Due to the characteristics of deep learning, parts of a face that have insignificant movements are rarely processed. Some improvements have been made to deepfakes, as in the case of the FaceSwap-GAN method [16, 21], which adds adversarial loss and perceptual loss on an original basis. As a discriminator, the adversarial loss makes the generated image close to the real image. Perceptual loss can make the direction of eye rotation more real, which creates a fake face of higher quality.

2.2   Deepfake Video Detection

Deepfake video detection algorithms are broadly divided into two categories, frame-by-frame detection and interframe association detection.

Frame-by-Frame Detection Frame-by-frame detection identifies fake facial features in single video frames. Some of the detection methods focus on simple features that are selected manually. For example, Matern et al. [22] focus on simple artificial defects such as colors, wired shadows on faces and missing details of the eyes and teeth.

Other frame-by-frame detection methods leverage deep features extracted by deep convolutional neural networks. Chollet [5] successfully modified Xception, a deep learning method with depthwise-separable convolutions, to the task of detecting deepfakes. Afchar et al. [1] developed the MesoNet method that leverages mesoscopic properties of images to detect deepfakes. Li et al. [17] employed an advanced architecture named HRNet [28] that detects deepfakes by examining the blending boundaries of manipulated images. These methods employ powerful convolutional neural networks to obtain good detection performance, but they require significant computational resources. However, their principal deficiency is that deepfake detection is based on a single feature, which is difficult to reproduce and lacks robustness.

Interframe Association Detection Interframe association detection examines forged features in series of frames to identify deepfakes. Li et al. [18] leveraged abnormalities in eye blinking frequencies to identify deepfake videos. Yang et al. [34] used outer and central landmarks to capture head and face directions, respectively; inconsistencies in the two directions are indicative of deepfakes. However, these detection methods employ manually-selected features, which renders them less discriminative and limits their performance.

To address the limitation, researchers have developed appearance-based deepfake detection methods that engage expressive deep temporal features. The method of Guerra and Delp [10] employs a convolutional neural network for feature extraction from frames and a long short-term memory network to process feature sequences. Sabir et al. [25] employed a similar architecture, but replaced the long short-term memory network with a bidirectional gated recurrent unit. However, these deepfake detection methods, like the frame-by-frame detection methods, rely on convolutional neural networks and, therefore, have the same limitations.

2.3 Aspect Ratio

The aspect ratio, which is the ratio of the maximum vertical distance to the maximum horizontal distance of an image region, is employed to define the resolutions of electronic device display screens. The eye aspect ratio (EAR) was proposed by Soukupova and Cech [27] to detect eye blinks. Figure 1 shows the landmarks on a human eye that are used to compute the eye aspect ratio. The eye aspect ratio was used by Houssaini et al. [11] to detect automobile driver fatigue in real time.

Eye aspect ratios have the potential to record facial features and represent them uniquely, effectively capturing the states of the eyes in facial images. The

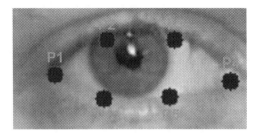

Fig. 1. Human eye landmarks.

aspect ratios are easy to compute and are affected very little by distance and image resolution.

The eye aspect ratio EAR is computed as [27]:

$$\text{EAR} = \frac{\|p_2 - p_6\| + \|p_3 - p_5\|}{2\|p_1 - p_4\|}$$

where p_1 and p_4 are the locations of the landmarks at the extreme right and left corners of the eye in Figure 1, p_2 and p_3 are the locations of the landmarks at the top right middle and top left middle of the eye, and p_5 and p_6 are the locations of the landmarks at the bottom right middle and bottom left middle of the eye.

The proposed deepfake detection method employs aspect ratios computed for seven important facial components, jaw, right eyebrow, left eyebrow, nose, right eye, left eye and mouth. Collectively, the seven aspect ratios concisely and effectively capture the facial expressions of humans.

3   Deepfake Detection Method

Figure 2 shows the proposed deepfake detection method. It involves three steps, data pre-processing, aspect ratio (AR) computation and classification.

3.1   Data Pre-Processing

The data pre-processing step chops a suspected deepfake video into clips, identifies the facial regions and marks key landmarks to obtain high-quality facial features from the facial images. In particular, the data pre-processing step identifies facial regions and their landmarks, and aligns the landmarks.

Facial region detection identifies the regions of interest in the video clips [31]. Next, 68 facial landmarks related to various facial features are identified and marked. Following this, the landmark points are aligned to obtain the best detection positions using an affine transformation, yielding 32 landmark points to compute the aspect ratios of the seven facial features. Finally, the input video is segmented into frames of fixed length to enable frame-level detection.

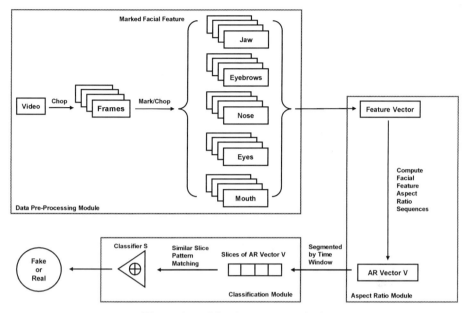

Fig. 2. Deepfake detection method.

3.2 Aspect Ratio Computation

The deepfake detection method employs aspect ratios computed for seven important facial components, jaw, right eyebrow, left eyebrow, nose, right eye, left eye and mouth. The data pre-processing step yields seven facial feature vectors with 32 landmark points:

$$\text{J-AR(Jaw)} = \frac{\|p_1 - p_9\| + \|p_{17} - p_9\|}{2\|p_1 - p_{17}\|}$$

$$\text{REB-AR(Right Eyebrow)} = \frac{\|p_{20} - p_{18}\| + \|p_{20} - p_{22}\|}{2\|p_{18} - p_{22}\|}$$

$$\text{LEB-AR(Left Eyebrow)} = \frac{\|p_{25} - p_{23}\| + \|p_{25} - p_{27}\|}{2\|p_{23} - p_{27}\|}$$

$$\text{N-AR(Nose)} = \frac{\|p_{28} - p_{33}\| + \|p_{28} - p_{35}\|}{2\|p_{32} - p_{36}\|}$$

$$\text{RE-AR(Right Eye)} = \frac{\|p_{38} - p_{42}\| + \|p_{39} - p_{41}\|}{2\|p_{37} - p_{40}\|}$$

$$\text{LE-AR(Left Eye)} = \frac{\|p_{44} - p_{48}\| + \|p_{45} - p_{47}\|}{2\|p_{43} - p_{46}\|}$$

$$\text{M-AR(Mouth)} = \frac{\|p_{51} - p_{59}\| + \|p_{53} - p_{57}\|}{2\|p_{49} - p_{55}\|}$$

where J-AR, REB-AR, LEB-AR, N-AR, RE-AR, LE-AR and M-AR are the aspect ratios corresponding to the jaw, right eyebrow, left eyebrow, nose, right eye, left eye and mouth facial components.

The aspect ratios of the seven facial components computed for each frame are incorporated in feature vectors $\mathbf{V}$:

$$\mathbf{V} = [v_{\text{J-AR}}, v_{\text{REB-AR}}, \ldots, v_{\text{M-AR}}]$$

3.3   Classification

The feature vectors $\mathbf{V}$ created in the aspect ratio computation step are input to a trained recurrent neural network for classification. First, each aspect ratio value sequence is segmented according to the size of the time window. Next, the recurrent neural network performs aspect ratio value repeatability matching on each segmented sequence. If different segmented sequences match multiple times, then the corresponding portions of the video are most likely fake. If the matching of the jth slice is confirmed, the corresponding similarity matching score s_j of the slice is computed; otherwise, s_j is set to zero. The fake score S is computed by summing the individual similarity matching scores s_j over all n slices:

$$S = \sum_{j=1}^{n} s_j$$

The larger the fake score S, the greater the likelihood that the video is a deepfake. After much experimentation, a fake score S of 12 was set as a threshold to deem a video to be a deepfake.

4   Experiments and Results

This section describes the experiments and results.

4.1   Datasets

Two datasets, FaceForensics++ (FF++) and Celeb-DF, were employed in the experiments. FaceForensics++ [24] is a large fake face dataset that is widely used by researchers. It contains more than 1,000 real videos along with their fake versions created using four face-changing algorithms, Face2Face, FaceSwap, Deepfakes and Neural-Textures. However, in the experiments, only fake videos created using the Face2Face, FaceSwap and Deepfakes algorithms were employed.

Each video in FaceForensics++ has an original version (raw), slightly compressed version (c23) and heavily compressed version (c40). The average video length in the FaceForensics++ dataset is 13 seconds. For experimental efficiency and time accuracy, 800 videos with clear and complete faces were selected. The first ten seconds of each video was used as experimental data.

Table 1. General evaluation of methods.

Method	FaceForensics++(raw) AUC Score	Celeb-DF AUC Score
XceptionNet	92.4%	64.7%
CNN+RNN	90.1%	72.1%
LRNet	96.9%	63.7%
DSP-FWA	94.8%	65.1%
ID-Reveal	93.7%	72.6%
Face X-Ray	95.7%	72.9%
Proposed Method	96.3%	73.3%

The Celeb-DF dataset [20] comprises 590 real videos and more than 5,000 fake videos, all of them created by the Deepfakes algorithm. Color conversion and edge softening algorithms were used to optimize the differences between synthetic and original faces, which reduced the synthetic boundary artifacts. This also reduced the jitter of the synthetic videos. The average video length in the Celeb-DF dataset is 11.8 seconds. For experimental efficiency and time accuracy, 150 real videos and 1,500 fake videos were selected. The first ten seconds of each video was used as experimental data.

4.2   Parameters

The Dlib toolkit was used in the data pre-processing step to chop faces and mark landmarks. The fully-connected layers of the recurrent neural network with 64 and 2 units were connected to the output layer. A dropout layer in the recurrent neural network with a dropout rate of 0.2 was inserted between the input and recurrent neural network. Another three dropout layers with dropout rates of 0.4 separated the remaining layers. The length of the time window was set to six. Each video was segmented into clips with a fixed length of 60. The classification model was trained over 400 epochs.

4.3   Comparative Evaluation

The proposed method was compared against six state-of-the-art deepfake detection methods, XceptionNet [5], CNN+RNN [25], LRNet [29], DSP-FWA [19], ID-Reveal [8] and Face X-Ray [17].

Table 1 shows the best-performance area under curve (AUC) scores for the seven methods using the FaceForensics++(raw) and Celeb-D datasets. In the case of the FaceForensics++(raw) dataset, the proposed method yielded the second highest score of 96.3%, just 0.6% less than the LRNet method. LRNet employed a special data pre-processing step to improve its detection rate. This involved marking the facial feature points to obtain the complete facial features and then using a marking point correction method based on optical flow to obtain

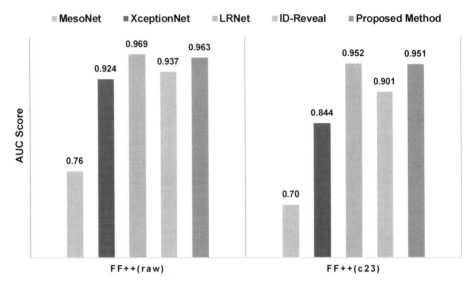

Fig. 3. Area under curve scores for uncompressed and slightly compressed videos.

accurate facial features. However, the method required each video to be corrected twice frame by frame, which is much more computationally expensive than simply computing the aspect ratios as in the proposed method. Additionally, since LRNet mainly relies on pixel information, its detection performance drops for highly compressed videos. LRNet is also less effective at detecting high-quality deepfake videos because of the small differences in correction changes.

Table 1 also shows the best performance area under curve scores for the seven methods using the Celeb-DF dataset. The proposed method yielded the highest area under curve score of 73.3% for Celeb-DF dataset.

The ability of the proposed method to handle compressed videos was also evaluated; this is something that has been overlooked by most current methods. The evaluation compared the performance of the proposed method against four state-of the-art methods, MesoNet [1], XceptionNet [5], LRNet [29] and ID-Reveal [8]. The detection models for all the methods were trained using uncompressed videos from the FaceForensics++(raw) dataset and tested using slightly compressed videos from the FaceForensics++(c23) dataset.

Figure 3 shows the area under curve scores (as fractions instead of percentages) for uncompressed and slightly compressed videos. LRNet and the proposed method have the best scores, however, the reduction in detection performance for slightly compressed videos is less for the proposed method (0.12) than for LRNet (0.17).

Next, the proposed method was compared against XceptionNet [5] to verify the training effect on the performance using different datasets. Specifically, training was conducted using Face2Face, FaceSwap, Deepfakes videos of three

Table 2. Performance on three independent datasets in FaceForensics++.

Deepfake Video	Proposed Method	XceptionNet
Deepfakes(c0)	96.3%	92.4%
FaceSwap(c0)	94.5%	91.3%
Face2Face(c0)	98.7%	93.0%
Deepfakes(c23)	95.1%	84.4%
FaceSwap(c23)	95.0%	88.1%
Face2Face(c23)	93.6%	87.4%
Deepfakes(c40)	94.3%	79.6%
FaceSwap(c40)	93.6%	80.4%
Face2Face(c40)	93.1%	81.3%

different compression factors and the performance was evaluated using three independent datasets from FaceForensics++.

Table 2 shows the results. The methods yield different accuracy values for different compression factors. As expected, the accuracy values drop as the compression factor increases because image details are lost. However, unlike XceptionNet, the proposed method yields greater than 93% accuracy even for highly compressed c40 videos. This demonstrates the robustness of deepfake detection when aspect ratios are used to capture facial features.

4.4   Analysis

Figure 4 shows the fake score values S of real and fake video images. The fake score values computed using aspect ratios tend to be more stable for fake images than real images.

Figure 5 compares the pattern matching results for real and fake video images. The area under score values tend to be more periodic for fake images than real images.

In order to understand the influence of facial features in deepfake detection, the detection performance with individual features and groups of features were evaluated using the FaceForensics++(raw) dataset. Table 3 shows that using more facial features improves detection performance because more information can be matched. Additionally, integrating the two parts of the left and right eyes as one, and doing the same with eyebrows, and the nose or jaw appear to have less effect on detection performance. Clearly, the eyes and mouth are important features because they provide more information that is relevant to deepfake detection.

The effect of input length on detection performance was also evaluated. In this case, the input length corresponds to the number of frames provided to the detection model. Figure 6 shows the area under curve scores for different input

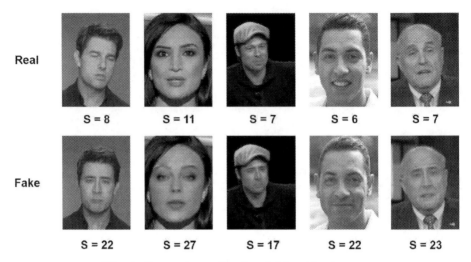

Fig. 4. Comparisons of real and fake video images.

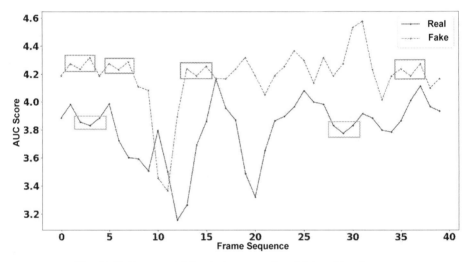

Fig. 5. Pattern matching between real and fake video images.

lengths. Because input length can affect detection performance when using the same dataset for training and testing, a suitable input length can improve the effectiveness and robustness of different data distributions. Figure 6 shows that an input length of 60 yields good detection performance and is also efficient.

The length of the time window is also an important factor in detection. The time window length corresponds to number of frames in a short frame sequence. The time window length is at least one and is at most equal to on-half of the

Table 3. Area under curve scores for various combinations of facial features.

Facial Features	AUC Score
Eyes	68.7%
Mouth	73.9%
Nose	28.4%
Jaw	30.2%
Eyebrows	27.1%
Eyes and Mouth	82.8%
Eyes and Nose	70.1%
Eyes and Jaw	70.1%
Mouth and Nose	74.1%
Mouth and Jaw	83.3%
Eyes, Mouth and Jaw	84.3%
Eyes, Mouth and Nose	86.6%
Eyes, Mouth and Eyebrows	82.2%
All Features	96.3%

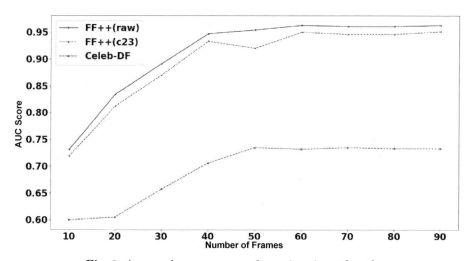

Fig. 6. Area under curve scores for various input lengths.

length of the facial feature vector. Figure 7 shows the area under curve scores for different time window lengths. A time window length of six or seven yields good detection performance. In fact, six was chosen because it exactly divides the total length.

5   Discussion

Although deepfake video detection has been the subject of considerable research, certain problems remain to be addressed. One problem relates to video compres-

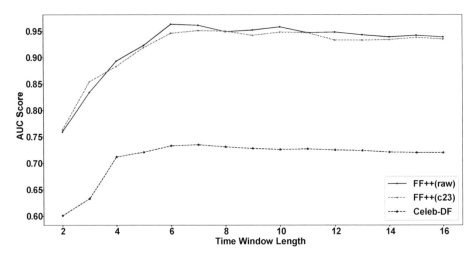

Fig. 7. Area under curve scores for various time window lengths.

sion. Videos on the Internet have varying compression factors and experiments have shown that increased compression negatively impacts deepfake detection performance. The experiments in Section 4 demonstrate that a model trained using low compression data can handle high compression data, but the detection performance is reduced considerably. The noise flow model explored in this research reduces the gap to some extent, but it cannot be eliminated. Even if the H.264 encoding method is not used, different compression factors create large gaps between training and testing. Of course, if a video is highly compressed, its quality is reduced considerably, which would affect the dissemination of deepfake videos [3, 9]. Compression solutions cannot rely solely on data-driven methods, so a trained detection model will depend strongly on the compression of data in the dataset and the generalization ability would be poor. The noise extraction or residual of splicing detection used in traditional forensics would also be compressed, hindering feature extraction [7, 12]. Therefore, it is important to extract features that coexist under different compression factors.

A second problem deals with video resolution. Videos of different resolutions on the web have different face sizes. Large face sizes pose challenges to model testing [15]. After a face is uniformly scaled, the original features are lost to some extent, so that the features used for classification and detection are inconsistent with the distribution method, which reduces the detection rate.

A third problem is algorithm tampering. New generation methods constantly emerge and the drawback of data-based training methods is that they are not robust enough to handle deepfakes created by unknown tampering methods [23]. This is because the distributions of tampered features for different tampering methods are different, making a learning-based model too focused on local features and unable to adapt to the distributions of other tampering methods [22]. One solution is to expand the training set and continuously incorporate new tampering methods as employed in the experiments described in Section 4. While this approach may not handle unknown tampering methods effectively, it can at least detect deepfakes created by as many known tampering methods as possible.

6 Conclusions

Deepfake technologies have advanced significantly by leveraging deep adversarial networks to produce high-quality fake videos that appear to be real to human eyes. Deepfake image and video detection have been the focus of considerable research, but most detection methods engage single facial features with limited clues that reduce deepfake detection performance. The detection method described in this chapter employs aspect ratios to capture multiple facial features uniquely and effectively. The multiple facial features comprise several single facial features such as eye blinking, lip movement and nasal flaring that are essential to deepfake detection. The detection method computes the aspect ratios of multiple facial features for every frame in a video and uses a time window to segment processed frame sequences into multiple short segments, following which pattern matching is employed to identify abnormal expressions that are indicative of deepfakes. Experiments using the FaceForensics++ and Celeb-DF datasets reveal that the proposed method detects fake videos more effectively than other deep-learning-based detection methods. Additionally, using the aspect ratio computations improves the ability to detect compressed deepfake videos.

References

1. D. Afchar, V. Nozick, J. Yamagishi and I. Echizen, Mesonet: A compact facial video forgery detection network, *Proceedings of the IEEE International Workshop on Information Forensics and Security*, 2018.
2. S. Agarwal, H. Farid, Y. Gu, M. He, K. Nagano and H. Li, Protecting world leaders against deep fakes, *Proceedings of the IEEE Conference on Computer Vision and Pattern Recognition Workshops*, pp. 38–45, 2019.
3. J. Bappy, A. Roy-Chowdhury, J. Bunk, L. Nataraj and B. Manjunath, Exploiting spatial structure for localizing manipulated image regions, *Proceedings of the IEEE International Conference on Computer Vision*, pp. 4980–4989, 2017.
4. R. Chesney and D. Citron, Deep fakes: A looming challenge for privacy, democracy and national security, *California Law Review*, vol. 107, pp. 1753–1820, 2019.
5. F. Chollet, Xception: Deep learning with depthwise-separable convolutions, *Proceedings of the IEEE Conference on Computer Vision and Pattern Recognition*, pp. 1801–1807, 2017.
6. D. Citron, How deepfakes undermine truth and threaten democracy, presented at *TEDSummit 2019*, 2019.
7. D. Cozzolino, D. Gragnaniello and L. Verdoliva, Image forgery detection through residual-based local descriptors and block-matching, *Proceedings of the IEEE International Conference on Image Processing*, pp. 5297–5301, 2014.
8. D. Cozzolino, A. Rossler, J. Thies, M. Niessner and L. Verdoliva, ID-Reveal: Identity-aware deepfake video detection, *Proceedings of the IEEE/CVF International Conference on Computer Vision*, pp. 15088–15097, 2021.

9. X. Cun and C. Pun, Image splicing localization via semi-global network and fully-connected conditional random fields, *Proceedings of the Fifteenth European Conference on Computer Vision Workshops, Part II*, pp. 252–266, 2018.

10. D. Guerra and E. Delp, Deepfake video detection using recurrent neural networks, *Proceedings of the Fifteenth IEEE International Conference on Advanced Video and Signal Based Surveillance*, 2018.

11. A. Houssaini, M. Sabri, H. Qjidaa and A. Aarab, Real-time driver's hypovigilance detection using facial landmarks, *Proceedings of the International Conference on Wireless Technologies, Embedded and Intelligent Systems*, 2019.

12. M. Huh, A. Liu, A. Owens and A. Efros, Fighting fake news: Image splice detection via learned self-consistency, *Proceedings of the Fifteenth European Conference on Computer Vision, Part XI*, pp. 106–124, 2018.

13. T. Karras, T. Aila, S. Laine and J. Lehtinen, Progressive Growing of GANs for Improved Quality, Stability and Variation, arXiv: 1710.10196v3 (`arxiv.org/abs/1710.10196v3`), 2018.

14. P. Korshunov and S. Marcel, Deepfakes: A New Threat to Face Recognition? Assessment and Detection, arXiv: 1812.08685v1 (`arxiv.org/abs/1812.08685v1`), 2018.

15. P. Korus and J. Huang, Multi-scale analysis strategies in PRNU-based tampering localization, *IEEE Transactions on Information Forensics and Security*, vol 12(4), pp. 809–824, 2017.

16. M. Kowalski, FaceSwap, GitHub (`github.com/MarekKowalski/FaceSwap`), 2021.

17. L. Li, J. Bao, T. Zhang, H. Yang, D. Chen, F. Wen and B. Guo, Face X-Ray for more general face forgery detection, *Proceedings of the IEEE/CVF Conference on Computer Vision and Pattern Recognition*, pp. 5000–5009, 2020.

18. Y. Li, M. Chang and S. Lyu, *In ictu oculi*: Exposing AI-created fake videos by detecting eye blinking, *Proceedings of the IEEE International Workshop on Information Forensics and Security*, 2018.

19. Y. Li and S. Lyu, Exposing deepfake videos by detecting face warping artifacts, *Proceedings of the IEEE Conference on Computer Vision and Pattern Recognition Workshops*, pp. 46–52, 2019.

20. Y. Li, X. Yang, P. Sun, H. Qi and S. Lyu, Celeb-DF: A large-scale challenging dataset for deepfake forensics, *Proceedings of the IEEE/CVF Conference on Computer Vision and Pattern Recognition*, pp. 3204–3213, 2020.

21. S. Lu, faceswap-GAN, GitHub (`github.com/shaoanlu/faceswap-GAN`), 2022.

22. F. Matern, C. Riess and M. Stamminger, Exploiting visual artifacts to expose deepfakes and face manipulations, *Proceedings of the IEEE Winter Applications of Computer Vision Workshops*, pp. 83–92, 2019.

23. H. Nguyen, F. Fang, J. Yamagishi and I. Echizen, Multi-Task Learning for Detecting and Segmenting Manipulated Facial Images and Videos, arXiv: 1906.06876v1 (`arxiv.org/abs/1906.06876v1`), 2019.

24. A. Rossler, D. Cozzolino, L. Verdoliva, J. Thies and M. Niessner, FaceForensics++: Learning to detect manipulated facial images, *Proceedings of the IEEE/CVF International Conference on Computer Vision*, pp. 1–11, 2019.

25. E. Sabir, J. Cheng, A. Jaiswal, W. AbdAlmageed, I. Masi and P. Natarajan, Recurrent convolutional strategies for face manipulation detection in videos, *Proceedings of the IEEE/CVF Conference on Computer Vision and Pattern Recognition Workshops*, pp. 80–87, 2019.

26. M. Sheng, Z. Ma, H. Jia, Q. Mao and M. Dong, Face aging with conditional generative adversarial network guided by ranking-CNN, *Proceedings of the IEEE Conference on Multimedia Information Processing and Retrieval*, pp. 314–319, 2020.

27. T. Soukupova and J. Cech, Real-time eye blink detection using facial landmarks, *Proceedings of the Computer Vision Workshop* (`vision.fe.uni-lj.si/cvww2016/proceedings/papers/05.pdf`), 2016.

28. K. Sun, Y. Zhao, B. Jiang, T. Cheng, B. Xiao, D. Liu, Y. Mu, X. Wang, W. Liu and J. Wang, High-Resolution Representations for Labeling Pixels and Regions, arXiv: 1904.04514v1 (`arxiv.org/abs/1904.04514v1`), 2019.

29. Z. Sun, Y. Han, Z. Hua, N. Ruan and W. Jia, Improving the Efficiency and Robustness of Deepfakes Detection Through Precise Geometric Features, arXiv: 2104.04480v1 (`arxiv.org/abs/2104.04480v1`), 2021.

30. M. Tan and Q. Le, EfficientNet: Rethinking Model Scaling for Convolutional Neural Networks, arXiv: 1905.11946v5 (`arxiv.org/abs/1905.11946v5`), 2020.

31. M. Tarasiou and S. Zafeiriou, Extracting Deep Local Features to Detect Manipulated Images of Human Faces, arXiv: 1911.13269v2 (`arxiv.org/abs/1911.13269v2`), 2020.

32. J. Thies, M. Zollhofer, M. Stamminger, C. Theobalt and M. Niessner, Face2Face: Real-time face capture and reenactment of RGB videos, *Proceedings of the IEEE Conference on Computer Vision and Pattern Recognition*, pp. 2387–2395, 2016.

33. R. Tolosana, R. Vera-Rodriguez, J. Fierrez, A. Morales and J. Ortega-Garcia, DeepFakes and Beyond: A Survey of Face Manipulation and Fake Detection, arXiv: 2001.00179v3 (`arxiv.org/abs/2001.00179v3`), 2020.

34. X. Yang, Y. Li and S. Lyu, Exposing deep fakes using inconsistent head poses, *Proceedings of the IEEE International Conference on Acoustics, Speech and Signal Processing*, pp. 8261–8265, 2019.

35. X. Yang, Y. Li, H. Qi and S. Lyu, Exposing GAN-Synthesized Faces Using Landmark Locations, arXiv: 1904.00167v1 (`arxiv.org/abs/1904.00167v1`), 2019.

36. P. Zhou, X. Han, V. Morariu and L. Davis, Learning rich features for image manipulation detection, *Proceedings of the IEEE/CVF Conference on Computer Vision and Pattern Recognition*, pp. 1053–1061, 2018.

Novel Applications

Identifying Superspreaders by Ranking System Object Instance Graphs

Rajani Suryavanshi[1], Xiaoyan Sun[2], and Jun Dai[2]

[1] KIOXIA America, Folsom, California, USA
[2] California State University Sacramento, Sacramento, California, USA
xiaoyan.sun@csus.edu

Abstract. Defending enterprise networks is very challenging due to the number of cyber attacks and their complexity. It is critical to understand how attacks occur and propagate in networks. System object instance graphs can reveal attack paths at the system level and help understand attack propagation. The graphs capture dependencies between system object instances such as files, processes and sockets, and help compute the infection probabilities of object instances. Attack paths are revealed by connecting instances with high infection probabilities. However, the graphs can be massive and difficult to comprehend.

Identifying the most important objects in system object instance graphs can enhance the understanding of infection propagation and the impacts. Importance in this context means high infection probabilities and large impacts to other objects. Objects on which other objects are heavily dependent have large impacts and need to be scrutinized. If these objects are infected, they can have huge negative impacts by infecting their dependent objects.

This chapter describes an approach for ranking objects using an extension of the AssetRank algorithm. Security analysts can use the dependency rankings to rapidly identify objects with the greatest impacts. When combined with the infection probabilities, the dependency ranking enables security analysts to prioritize the objects that need attention given limited time and resources. Experimental results demonstrate that the proposed dependency ranking approach successfully determines the objects with the largest impacts.

Keywords: System Object Instance Graph · Dependency Graph · AssetRank Algorithm

1 Introduction

Enterprise networks often incorporate crucial assets and resources that are of considerable interest to malicious entities. Attacks on enterprise networks can lead to security breaches, stolen data, financial losses, disruptions and even business termination. The complete understanding of how attacks occur is indispensable in digital forensics and crucial to recovery and improved cyber defense. However, the increasing numbers and complexity of attacks render attack detection and analysis even more difficult.

© IFIP International Federation for Information Processing 2023
Published by Springer Nature Switzerland AG 2023
G. Peterson and S. Shenoi (Eds.): DigitalForensics 2023, IFIP AICT 687, pp. 179–201, 2023.
https://doi.org/10.1007/978-3-031-42991-0_10

Enterprise networks have complex structures, large sizes and several layers of protection. As a result, malicious entities often have to launch multi-host, multi-stage cyber attacks on the networks [4]. The attacks initially explore enterprise networks to discover their configurations and passively monitor their activities. Next, system vulnerabilities are exploited to gain access and escalate privileges. Systems that have already been compromised are often leveraged as stepping stones to compromise other systems. Eventually, malicious code is embedded and/or sensitive data is exfiltrated.

Determining the various attack paths is effective for detecting attacks and understanding how they occur and propagate in enterprise networks. This is facilitated by the fact that most networks are under constant surveillance by security techniques and tools. Security sensors such as Snort, Tripwire, Wireshark and Ntop are often deployed across networks to capture security events. Alerts from a variety of sensors on hosts reveal malicious activities are chained in the form of attack paths. Additionally, system-level logs, such as system calls, capture the activities of malicious entities as well as legitimate users with fine granularity. This information can contribute significantly to understanding how attacks occur and propagate.

Dai et al. [4] have proposed an approach for identifying attack paths in enterprise networks. The approach represents the network-wide attack context as a superset graph of system objects such as files, processes and sockets called a system object dependency graph. A dependency graph is constructed by analyzing system calls from all the hosts in a network. Since system calls are attack neutral, the superset graph captures the activities of malicious entities as well as legitimate users. Forward and backward tracking is performed on the superset graph to identify the attack paths. However, this approach often identifies numerous attack paths, resulting in path explosion.

To address this problem, Sun et al. [27] proposed the ZePro method that identifies attack paths using probability theory. In particular, ZePro employs a system object instance graph instead of a system object dependency graph. A system object instance graph is constructed in a similar manner as a system object dependency graph, except that nodes in the graph are not objects, but instances of objects with specific timestamps. Each instance is a new version of an object at a different point in time, enabling the infection status of the object to be captured at different times. A Bayesian network is then constructed on top of the system object instance graph so that evidence from security sensors can be incorporated to compute the infection probabilities of object instances. An object instance with high infection probability means that the instance is very likely to be infected. An attack path is then manifested by connecting instances with high infection probabilities.

While these approaches help discover attack paths and identify infection propagation, security analysts find it difficult to use the information for two reasons. One is that the size and complexity of system object instance graphs are overwhelming. For example, a 15-minute system call log in an enterprise network can contain 143,120 system calls that involve 913 system objects, 39,361 object dependencies, 39,840 instances and 74,598 instance dependencies [28]. Even after system call filtering and graph pruning, the size of the system object instance graph can be very large.

The second reason is that a revealed attack path may omit objects that have significant impacts on other objects. This is because attack paths only contain system object instances with high infection probabilities, but these instances do not necessarily propagate infections massively. In a typical system object instance graph, some impactful instances have large numbers of dependents and/or more important dependents, while others do not. Once they are infected, these impactful instances generate much larger negative impacts by infecting other instances. Therefore, identifying and scrutinizing the most impactful instances are critical to understanding the potential risks and attack propagation.

To address the challenges posed by system object instance graph size and complexity, this chapter describes an approach for ranking object instances based on their impacts using an extension of the AssetRank algorithm [25], a modification of Google's PageRank algorithm [23]. Object instances with high dependency ranks are depended on heavily by other object instances and need security analyst attention due to their large impacts. Additionally, the dependency ranks can be used in conjunction with the infection probabilities of object instances computed by ZePro for better analysis.

Instances with high infection probabilities are very likely to be infected, but may not necessarily have massive impacts on other instances, and vice versa. Therefore, based on the instance dependency ranks and their infection probabilities, instances are classified into four categories: instances with high dependency ranks and high infection probabilities, instances with high dependency ranks but low infection probabilities, instances with low dependency ranks but high infection probabilities, and instances with low dependency ranks and low infection probabilities. This can greatly reduce the manual effort on the part of security analysts and help prioritize their work given limited time and resources. Specifically, security analysts would focus first on instances with high dependency ranks and high infection probabilities because they are the most dangerous and most impactful. Next, depending on the situation, security analysts would investigate instances in other categories, namely, those with high dependency ranks or high infection probabilities. The proposed approach is the first to identify the impactful system objects, including files, processes and sockets, that infect large numbers of other objects.

2   Background

This section describes system object dependency graphs and system object instance graphs.

2.1   System Object Dependency Graphs

System calls are usually the interfaces between user applications and the operating system kernel. Applications, whether legitimate or malicious, issue system

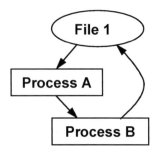

Fig. 1. System object dependency graph.

calls to obtain services provided by the operating system. As a result, system call logs are great resources for revealing and analyzing malicious activities.

In an enterprise network with multiple hosts, system calls can be collected at each individual host. Each system call involves one or more system objects that include files, processes and sockets. Due to the actions produced by system calls, system objects have certain dependencies on each other. For example, when a process reads a file, the process depends on the file for data. Analyzing system calls enables a dependency graph to be constructed for system objects [4].

A system object dependency graph (SODG) is a directed graph with nodes corresponding to operating system objects and edges corresponding to dependencies between objects. A system call is broken down into three components, source object, sink object and dependency relation between the two objects. File, process and socket objects are illustrated as circles/ovals, rectangles and diamonds, respectively.

Consider the following system call log with system calls with timestamps t1, t2 and t3:

```
t1: file 1 read by process A;
t2: process A creates process B;
t3: process B writes to file 1
```

The system call at t1 is parsed as the dependency relation Process A depends on File 1: $File\ 1 \rightarrow Process\ A$. The system call at t2 is parsed as the dependency relation Process B depends on Process A: $Process\ A \rightarrow Process\ B$. The system call at t3 is parsed as the dependency relation File 1 depends on Process B: $Process\ B \rightarrow File\ 1$. Figure 1 shows the system object dependency graph created by connecting the dependency relations.

A network-wide system object dependency graph is created by constructing per-host system object dependency graphs and concatenating them. Concatenation is performed when a directed edge exists between two nodes on different hosts. This usually involves socket communications in which nodes correspond to sockets and the directed edge represents the communications between the two sockets. For example, a send system call may indicate that Socket s1 on Machine X sends data to Socket s2 on Machine Y. In this case, the dependency

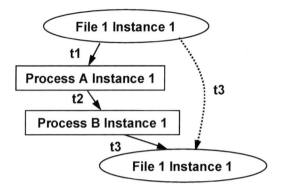

Fig. 2. System object instance graph.

relation *Socket s1 → Socket s2* is generated. Consequently, the per-host system object dependency graphs for Machine X and Machine Y can be concatenated to create a network-wide system object dependency graph.

A network-wide system object dependency graph is a superset graph with a set of paths. It contains the attack paths if malicious activities are involved. Starting from a triggering node, usually a suspicious object involved in a security alert, forward and backward tracking is performed to reveal the attack paths.

2.2 System Object Instance Graphs

ZePro [28] employs a Bayesian network to incorporate attack evidence (security alerts) and infer the infection probabilities of objects. However, as discussed in [28], it is not possible to construct a Bayesian network for a system object dependency graph. This is because a system object dependency graph cannot preserve the temporal information of system calls, which induces incorrect causality inferences. Additionally, a Bayesian network is an acyclic model that does not allow cycles inherited from a system object dependency graph (e.g., cycle involving File 1, Process A and Process B in Figure 1). Therefore, Sun et al. [27] proposed a new type of dependency graph called a system object instance graph for constructing Bayesian networks and computing infection probabilities.

A system object instance graph expresses dependencies between object instances. Each node in a system object instance graph is an instance of the object at a specific point of time. An object may be in a different state (infected or uninfected) at a different point of time. The state of an instance represents the state of an object at a specific time.

Figure 2 shows the system object instance graph generated for the example system call log shown above. The label on each edge shows the time associated with the corresponding system call. Thus, the instance graph reflects correct information flows based on the timestamps. For example, Process B writes to File 1 at time t3. In the system object instance graph, instead of connecting back to File 1, Process B points to the Instance 1 of File 1. The creation of the new

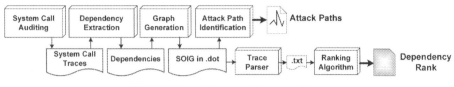

Fig. 3. Dependency rank generation.

instance of File 1 also breaks the cycle created in the system object dependency graph by File 1, Process A and Process B.

Given a system object dependency graph, a Bayesian network can be constructed by assigning a conditional probability table to each node. The conditional probability tables define causality relations among nodes such as how the conditions of parent nodes can impact the conditions of child nodes. For example, in the Bayesian network based on Figure 2, the conditional probability table for node Process A Instance 1 specifies the probability of the node being infected based on the infection status of its parent node File 1 Instance 1. The Bayesian network is able to incorporate the evidence gathered from security sensors such as Snort and Tripwire. For example, if a file is observed to be infected, its probability of infection is set into one. This probability affects the infection probabilities of the other nodes in the Bayesian network. After incorporating all the evidence, the infection probabilities of all the nodes are computed. Object instances with high infection probabilities have higher chances of being infected. Therefore, the infection probabilities can be analyzed together with the dependency ranks of the instances to identify the instances that require security analyst attention and further scrutiny.

3   Proposed Approach

This section describes the proposed approach that incorporates dependency rank generation and system object instance ranking.

3.1   Dependency Rank Generation

Figure 3 shows the steps involved in dependency rank generation. First, system call auditing is performed on each host. The auditing captures malicious and legitimate user activities. Operating-system-aware information such as file inode numbers, process IDs and timestamps are preserved for system calls. Filtering is then applied to remove system calls for redundant and irrelevant objects.

In the next step, dependency relations are extracted by parsing the system calls. An example is a read system call where Process P reads File F is parsed to create the dependency: $File\ F \rightarrow Process\ P$. Having specified the dependencies among system objects, a network-wide system object instance graph is created using the graph generation algorithm described in [28].

Next, the network-wide system object instance graph is employed to identify the attack paths (subset of the system object instance graph) or to generate the dependency ranks of all the instances. To reveal the attack paths, a Bayesian network is constructed and the evidence collected from security sensors is incorporated to compute the infection probabilities of the instances. Instances with high infection probabilities form attack paths.

The dependency ranks are generated by parsing graph information such as node shapes and dependency relations to the node types (AND, OR and SINK) required by AssetRank algorithm. The parsed node type information is written to a TXT file. Finally, the AssetRank algorithm processes the TXT file as input to compute the dependency ranks of all the instances.

3.2   System Object Instance Ranking

Google's PageRank algorithm [23] was developed to compute the importance of web pages based on the number of web pages linked to it. The algorithm uses the web page link structure to compute a rank and evaluate web page importance. The computations involved in the PageRank algorithm are general and can be applied to any problem that is represented in terms of a dependency graph [6].

In the PageRank algorithm, a page has its own intrinsic value that indicates its independent and individual importance. However, the page also gains extrinsic value from the pages linked to it. The page rank can become higher if a page has more links. However, a page that is linked by a few important pages with high intrinsic values may have a higher rank than a page linked by many less important pages.

In order to rank system object instances, the proposed approach applies an extension of the AssetRank algorithm [25], a modification of the generalized PageRank algorithm. The AssetRank algorithm is applicable to graphs that model dependency relationships among vertices. It can be applied to system object instance graphs because they describe dependencies among instances.

The AssetRank algorithm is implemented to suit the semantics of system object instance graphs. The algorithm computes the dependency rank values of system object instances. The rank of an instance reflects how much other system object instances depend on it. The higher the rank, the greater the impact the instance may have on other instances.

In the AssetRank algorithm, every vertex has a numeric value based on its importance in the network. The numeric value is computed by summing the intrinsic value of a vertex and the value that the vertex receives from its dependents [25].

Figure 4 shows the value flow among vertices in the AssetRank algorithm. Vertices v_1 and v_2 depend on v_3, and vertices v_3 and v_4 depend on v_5. If v_1 depends on v_3, which means v_3 is important to v_1, then the value of v_1 flows to v_3 and the value of v_3 is increased. The more nodes depend on v_3, the higher the value of v_3. As a result, v_3 has a darker shade in the figure.

In the case of v_5, some of the values of v_3 and v_4 flow to it and increase its value. However, the value of v_5 is lower than that of v_3 because v_4 has a

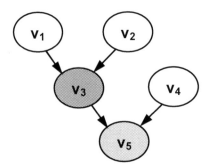

Fig. 4. Value flow in the AssetRank algorithm.

low value. Note that the arrows in Figure 4 show the value flows instead of the dependency relations among vertices. Value flows have the opposite directions of dependencies in a system object instance graph, where v_1 depends on v_3 is denoted as $v_3 \rightarrow v_1$.

In the original PageRank algorithm [23], a vertex can have OR or AND relations. An OR vertex relation requires one of its preconditions (represented as out-neighbors) to be met. An AND vertex relation means all the preconditions present in the out-neighbors must be satisfied to reach the vertex. SINK denotes a vertex that does not have out-neighbors. Considering the special causality relations among vertices in a system object instance graph, vertices will only have OR relations. Specifically, consider a Process A that depends on File B and File C because it reads them. As long as File B or File C is infected, Process A will be infected.

Formally, a graph is defined as $G = (V, A, f, g, h)$ where V is a set of vertices, A is a set of arcs, f is a mapping of weights to vertices, g is a mapping of weights to arcs and h is a mapping of vertices to their types [25]. The out-neighborhood $N^+(v)$ and in-neighborhood $N^-(v)$ of a vertex v are defined as:

$$N^+(v) = \{w \in V : (v, w) \in A\}$$
$$N^-(v) = \{u \in V : (u, v) \in A\}$$

The sum of all the vertex weights is equal to one. If a vertex v has type OR, the sum of all the arc weights is equal to one. If vertex v has type AND, the sum of all the arc weights is equal to the number of out-neighborhoods. If vertex v has type SINK, the sum of all the arc weights is equal to 0:

$$\Sigma_{w \in N^+(v)} g(v, w) = \begin{cases} 1, & \text{if } h(v) = \text{OR} \\ |N^+(v)|, & \text{if } h(v) = \text{AND} \\ 0, & \text{if } h(v) = \text{SINK} \end{cases}$$

where $|N^+(v)|$ denotes the cardinality of set $N^+(v)$.

The value x_v of vertex v is the sum of its intrinsic value and the value it obtains from its dependents:

$$x_v = \delta \Sigma_{u \in N^-(v)} g(u,v) x_u + (1 - \delta) f(v)$$

where δ is a damping factor that defines the ratio between the value a vertex receives from its dependents and its intrinsic value.

The values x_v of all the vertices are placed in a vector X. All the dependencies between vertices are placed in a weighed adjacency matrix D where $D_{vu} = g(u,v)$. Upon applying the Jacobi iteration method to the sequence, vector X becomes:

$$X = \delta D X + (1 - \delta) IV$$
$$X_t = \delta D X_{t-1} + (1 - \delta) IV$$

The ranks of AND and OR vertices are computed differently. When a vertex has an OR type, the value of the vertex is split equally between all its dependents. However, when a vertex has an AND type, the value of the vertex is replicated to all its dependents. Since only OR vertices are considered in this work, the normalized equation becomes:

$$X_{t'} = \delta D X_{t-1} + (1 - \delta) IV$$
$$X_t = \frac{1}{||X_{t'}||} X_{t'}$$

The above sequence is expected to converge to one. However, due to the large scale of a system object instance graph, in rare cases, the sequence may not converge to one in a finite number of iterations. Therefore, the maximum number of iterations in the algorithm is set to 1,000, after which, the algorithm terminates even if the sequence has not converged to one.

4 Implementation

The first step in the implementation is to parse the system calls to generate a network-wide system object instance graph that is stored as a DOT file. DOT is a description language that is used to describe graphs such as flowcharts and dependency trees. The DOT file for a system object instance graph contains information such as node label (instance ID, instance name), shape (correspond-ing to the file, process or socket instance type), color (infection probability or dependency rank) and edge directions (dependencies among instances). In the research, Graphviz software was used to process and visualize DOT files.

A Perl parsing script was developed to process the network-wide system object instance graph. Eclipse IDE (Neon version with the EPIC plugin) was used to code the parser. The script parses node information such as node shape and dependency relations with regular expressions, and converts the information to node type (AND, OR, SINK) with the respective outward nodes. The node type information is stored in a TXT file that is passed as input to a Java program that implements the AssetRank algorithm.

The following is the DOT format representation of the simple system object instance graph shown in Figure 5:

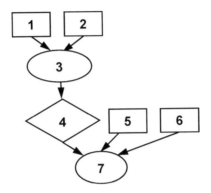

Fig. 5. Simple system object instance graph.

```
Digraph ABC {
1[label = "1", shape = box, fillcolor = white];
2[label = "2", shape = box, fillcolor = white];
3[label = "3", shape = ellipse, fillcolor = white];
4[label = "4", shape = diamond, fillcolor = white];
5[label = "5", shape = box, fillcolor = white];
6[label = "6", shape = box, fillcolor = white];
7[label = "7", shape = ellipse, fillcolor = white];
1->3;
2->3;
3->4;
4->7;
5->7;
6->7;}
```

The Perl script parses the DOT file into a series of node types along with dependent information. The following output produced by the script is stored in a TXT file for input to the Java program that computes the dependency ranks:

```
SINK
SINK
AND, 1, 2
OR, 3
SINK
SINK
AND, 4, 5, 6
OR, 7
```

The Java dependency ranking program stores node information and relative dependencies in an adjacency matrix. Vertex weights are computed by applying the AssetRank algorithm to the adjacency matrix. The results, a list of system object instance graph nodes and their ranks sorted in decreasing rank order, are stored in a CSV file. If desired, the CSV file and the original DOT file containing

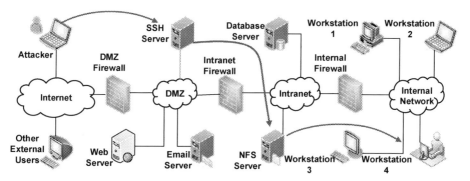

Fig. 6. Attack scenario.

node information could be used to visualize the ranks of instances in the system object instance graph. This is accomplished by invoking another Perl script that parses the node ranks and assigns colors to instances based on their ranks. For example, the top 10% ranked nodes are colored crimson and nodes in the 10% to 50% ranks are colored coral.

5   Attack Scenario and Results

This section presents the network-wide system object instance graph corresponding to an attack scenario, an identified zero-day attack path and detailed results.

5.1   Attack Scenario

A ZePro attack scenario described in [27, 28] is employed to analyze the dependency ranking of system object instances along with their infection rates. This enables the infection rates computed by ZePro to be used in this work.

Figure 6 shows the attack scenario [27, 28]. The malicious entity first gains root privileges on an SSH server by exploiting the CVE-2008-0166 vulnerability [16] and accesses an NFS server using SSH as a stepping stone. Due to an incorrect setup of the export table on the NFS server, the malicious entity uploads an executable containing a Trojan horse that exploits CVE-2009-2692 [17] to a public directory on the file server. The malicious executable is downloaded and installed on a workstation by an unwitting user. The malicious entity is then able to execute arbitrary code on the workstation. Snort, Tripwire, Wireshark and Ntop security sensors are deployed to capture security events that can be used as evidence of attacks.

Given the attack scenario, ZePro is employed to generate a system object instance graph for the network. The system object instance graph captures malicious and legitimate user activities during a 15-minute time period. Since the graph is extremely large, it is not possible to display the entire graph in this chapter. However, Figures 7 through 9 show different portions of the graph for

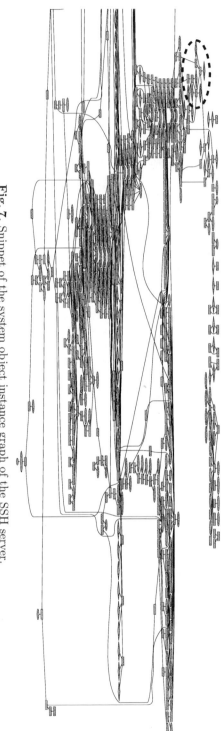

Fig. 7. Snippet of the system object instance graph of the SSH server.

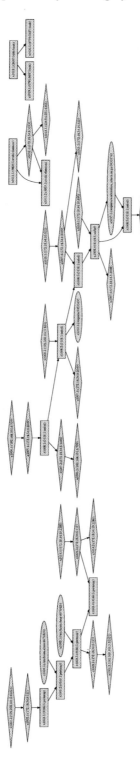

Fig. 8. System object instance graph of the NFS server.

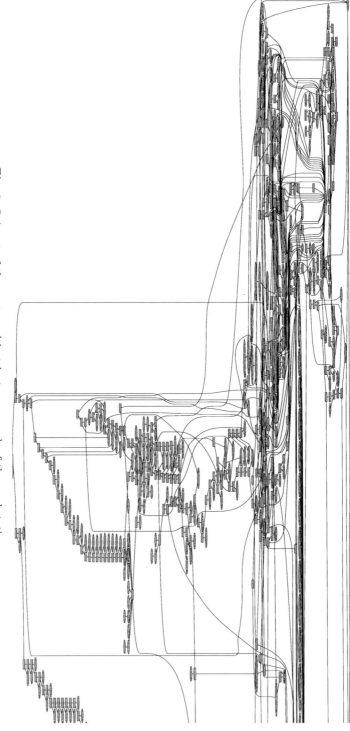

Fig. 9. Snippet of the system object instance graph of the workstation.

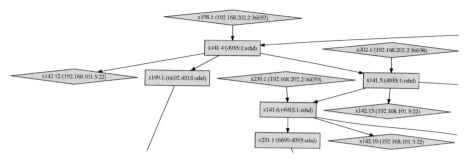

Fig. 10. Magnified view of the dotted oval portion in Figure 7.

each host involved in the attack scenario. Of course, readers are not expected to comprehend the details of these system object instance graphs.

However, to enable readers to visualize nodes and edges in a system object instance graph, Figure 10 shows a magnified view of the dotted oval portion in Figure 7. In this graph, file, process and socket instances are represented using ovals, rectangles and diamonds, respectively. For example, x198.1:(192.168.202.2: 36057) is a socket on the machine with IP address 192.168.202.2 and port number 36057 and x199.1:(6692:4935:sshd) is a process with PID 6692, 4935 and process name sshd.

Table 1. Infection probabilities of representative instances.

Instance	x4.2	x69.1	x142.25	x253.8	x254.7	x259.1	x260.1
Prob.	0.87	0.01	0.99	0.99	0.95	0.92	0.89
Instance	x1007.6	x1008.5	x1017.1	x2005.1	x2006.3	x2083.1	x2082.2
Prob.	0.82	0.84	0.77	0.048	0.81	0.79	0.80
Instance	x2086.5	x2114.2	x2147.2	x2158.5	x2397.21	x2383.3	x2429.14
Prob.	0.82	0.83	0.84	0.77	0.96	0.76	0.99

The ZePro system is able to compute the infection probabilities for all the system object instances in the graphs. Due to the large number of instances, it is not possible to present the infection probabilities for all nodes. However, Table 1 shows the infection probabilities of representative instances.

Of course, readers are not expected to understand the details of the graphs. Indeed, the figures show how difficult it is to identify the system object instances that are depended on the most by other instances and that can infect most system objects. When analyzed together with the infection probabilities, the dependency ranking can help security analysts quickly identify the most important objects that need attention.

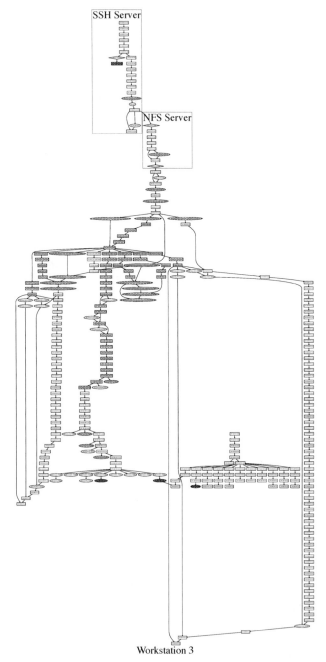

Fig. 11. Identified zero-day attack path [27, 28].

Since a system object instance graph captures malicious activities, instances with high infection probabilities can be identified and revealed. These instances create an attack path, even a zero-day attack path if one or more zero-days are involved [27, 28]. Figure 11 shows a zero-day attack path identified in the system object instance graph that is used for result analysis.

5.2   Results

Dependency ranks were computed for all 1,853 nodes in the network-wide graph created from the system object instance graphs shown in Figures 7 through 9. The damping factor was set to 0.85, the standard value maintained in experiments involving the PageRank algorithm. All the nodes were given equal importance at the beginning of the algorithm and their ranks were computed iteratively until convergence to one or the maximum iteration count of 1,000 was reached.

Due to limited space, Table 2 shows the instances with the top 50 dependency rank values. Instances with greater numbers of out-going edges tend to have higher dependency rank values. This is because the AssetRank of an instance comprises two components, its intrinsic value and the value it gains from its dependents. Vertices with multiple dependents tend to have higher ranks. Analysis can be conducted based on the instance ranks and infection probabilities computed in [27, 28]. Examination of Table 2 and Figure 11 reveals that instances with the highest dependency ranks may not have the highest infection probabilities, and vice versa.

The system object instances in the network-wide graph are divided into four categories:

- **High Dependency Rank; High Infection Probability:** Instances in this category deserve the most attention from security analysts. A high dependency rank means that the instance has many dependents connected to it throughout the network. Since the infection probability is also high, an attack will propagate through the network very easily. For example, Instance 2086.5 (Process tar) and Instance 2147.2 (Process exploit.sh) appear in Table 2 and Figure 11 and are, therefore, critical to the success of the attack. Table 1 lists the infection probability of Instance 2086.5 as 0.82, indicating it is very likely to be infected; meanwhile, it is ranked one in Table 2, which means that many instances depend on it and the instance may propagate infections to them very easily. Therefore, security analysts should identify instances of this category as soon as possible and take countermeasures to eliminate or contain attacks. Security analysts should also check potential vulnerabilities associated with these instances and perform network hardening to prevent repeat attacks.
- **High Dependency Rank; Low Infection Probability:** Instances in this category have low likelihood of being infected. Their high dependency ranks could be due to multiple dependents contributing to their extrinsic values. Although, their infection probabilities are low, if these instances are attacked, the attack propagation could be severe because they have multiple

Table 2. Dependency ranks of the top 50 instances in the graph.

Rank	Instance	Object	Rank Value
1	2086.5	6763:6719:tar	0.0005927777894456
2	290.1	6729:6724:savelog	0.0005830315634006
3	2005.1	/etc/locale.alias	0.0005746923615380
4	69.1	/etc/nsswitch.conf:8798393	0.0005713089890883
5	25.1	5908:5897:apt	0.0005639606663220
6	2023.2	2816:1:udevd	0.0005630498216020
7	2147.2	6783:6781:exploit.sh	0.0005597664307222
8	101.4	6620:6604:cupsys	0.0005597639076630
9	2124.1	6285:5798:bash	0.0005597588152304
10	2493.12	6815:6813:bash	0.0005581044873810
11	263.2	6709:5897:run-parts	0.0005564425363920
12	223.2	2774:1:udevd	0.0005564349986352
13	2091.1	/etc/nsswitch.conf:1491129	0.0005532248168440
14	2429.14	6811:6803:useradd	0.0005531413877282
15	45.1	/etc/localtime:8798371	0.0005523218315349
16	188.1	/proc/sys/kernel/ngroups_max:12635	0.0005515249821289
17	2026.2	/:2	0.0005514693370436
18	52.1	5897:5896:run-parts	0.0005481961040248
19	183.1	/etc/pam.d/common-account:8799591	0.0005481935267130
20	78.2	6604:6603:sh	0.0005481833960051
21	182.1	/etc/pam.d/common-auth:8799592	0.0005481783462166
22	186.1	/etc/pam.d/other	0.0005481783345730
23	181.1	/etc/pam.d/sshd:8800291	0.0005481783345611
24	184.1	/etc/pam.d/common-session:8799594	0.0005481783345492
25	185.1	/etc/pam.d/common-password:8799593	0.0005481783345434
26	62.1	/proc/filesystems:4026531844	0.0005481783345433
27	2076.1	/bin/ls:532536	0.0005481783345137
28	2074.1	6719:6718:bash	0.0005481758038124
29	189.1	/home/jun/.ssh/authorized_keys:4636779	0.0005473713971032
30	4.1	6560:6559:mount.nfs	0.0005473562399357
31	2375.1	6796:6793:collect2	0.0005473473551626
32	2390.1	6801:6798:collect2	0.0005473473551626
33	226.2	/:2	0.0005465138528115
34	223.1	2774:1:udevd	0.0005457474421339
35	2023.1	2816:1:udevd	0.0005457335034186
36	144.1	/usr/sbin/sshd:9462668	0.0005457094577282
37	153.7	6687:4935:sshd	0.0005457043885236
38	2006.2	6737:6736:mount	0.0005457031115441
39	152.1	/etc/hosts.deny:8798361	0.0005457018810209
40	2081.1	/proc/filesystems:4026531844	0.0005456993367521
41	2308.3	6793:6783:cc	0.0005456968001993
42	2383.3	6798:6783:cc	0.0005456968001993
43	123.1	/etc/hosts:8798410	0.0005456967964019
44	301.1	/bin/mv:966724	0.0005456967963309
45	194.16	6690:4935:sshd	0.0005456942656000
46	162.1	6679:4935:sshd	0.0005456942578573
47	2397.1	6803:6783:wunderbar_empor	0.0005456917348751
48	231.16	6699:4935:sshd	0.0005456892041560
49	160.1	6680:4935:sshd	0.0005456892041382
50	164.1	6682:4935:sshd	0.0005456892041382

dependents. For example, some instances have high ranks in Table 2 but are not included in Figure 11. These instances may have very high impacts on other objects, but low infection probabilities. One example is Instance 69.1 (File /etc/nsswitch.conf), which is used by applications to determine the sources for obtaining name-service information in a range of categories as well as their order. Although the file has a low infection probability of 0.01 (Table 1), security analysts must examine it carefully due to its significant impact (rank four in Table 2).

– **Low Dependency Rank; High Infection Probability:** Instances in this category have high likelihoods of being infected despite their low dependency ranks. Analyzing these objects can help security analysts understand which objects are impacted by malicious activities and how the impacts occur. It would also be helpful to check the dependency ranks of these instances to ensure that the negative impacts do not propagate. Table 3 shows the dependency ranks of the top 50 instances in the zero-day attack path. Many instances, such as Instance 2114.2 (File /home/user/testbed/workstation_attack/wunderbar_emporium/pwnkernel.c), have high infection probabilities but relatively low dependency ranks. The infection probability of Instance 2114.2 is 0.83, but its dependency rank is not among the top 50 instances in the attack path. Such instances do not have many dependent instances, but they need to be carefully checked by security analysts due to their high infection probabilities.

– **Low Dependency Rank; Low Infection Probability:** Instances in this category have very low likelihoods of being infected. Their low dependency ranks imply that they do not have many dependent instances. Thus, if these instances are infected, the propagation will occur in a controlled manner. Security analysts should give these instances the lowest priority when resources are limited.

The proposed approach enables security analysts to identify the most critical object instances in terms of their dependency ranks and infection probabilities. The two perspectives enable the prioritization of object instances for investigation, enabling security analysts to focus their limited time and scarce resources to good effect.

6   Related Work

This research has drawn on previous work on zero-day attack path detection [4, 27, 28] that utilizes dependency relations among system objects to capture malicious activities at the system level. Dai et al. [4] proposed the construction of system object dependency graphs based on system calls and using them to reveal zero-day attack paths by tracking system objects involved in security alerts. Sun et al. [27, 28] subsequently proposed the creation of Bayesian networks on top of system object instance graphs, enabling the computation of object instance infection probabilities, and connecting object instances with high infection probabilities to reveal zero-day attack paths. These approaches focus on recognizing

Table 3. Dependency ranks of the top 50 instances in the zero-day attack path.

Rank	Instance	Object	Rank Value
1	2086.5	6763:6719:tar	0.0005927777894456
2	2147.2	6783:6781:exploit.sh	0.0005597664307222
3	2493.12	6815:6813:bash	0.0005581044873810
4	2429.14	6811:6803:useradd	0.0005531413877282
5	4.1	6560:6559:mount.nfs	0.0005473562399357
6	2006.2	6737:6736:mount	0.0005457031115441
7	2383.3	6798:6783:cc	0.0005456968001993
8	2308.3	6793:6783:cc	0.0005456968001993
9	2397.101	wunderbar_empor	0.0005456917348751
10	2429.7	6811:6803:useradd	0.0005440424297800
11	1008.4	5118:1:unfsd	0.0005440411760642
12	2397.8	wunderbar_empor	0.0005440411760287
13	2397.11	wunderbar_empor	0.0005440399068096
14	1008.2	5118:1:unfsd	0.0005440373838006
15	253.8	6706:6703:sshd	0.0005432279583837
16	2144.4	6781:6285:bash	0.0005432128164641
17	2086.4	6763:6719:tar	0.0005424676923594
18	1008.1	5118:1:unfsd	0.0005423956554335
19	2493.11	6815:6813:bash	0.0005423906095075
20	2429.9	6811:6803:useradd	0.0005423906094453
21	2429.101	6811:6803:useradd	0.0005423906055799
22	2429.11	6811:6803:useradd	0.0005423906055798
23	2397.201	wunderbar_empor	0.0005423880748490
24	2114.2	...wunderbar_emporium/pwnkernel.c	0.0005423868133430
25	2397.14	wunderbar_empor	0.0005423855518548
26	2397.9	wunderbar_empor	0.0005423855479953
27	2397.19	wunderbar_empor	0.0005423855479894
28	10.1	/etc/mtab:8798397	0.0005415710300122
29	1007.1	172.18.34.5:2049	0.0005415659839528
30	259.1	/mnt/workstation_attack.tar.gz:9453574	0.0005415634378076
31	2114.1	...wunderbar_emporium/pwnkernel.c:	0.0005415634281084
32	2082.2	/home/..attack.tar.gz	0.0005415622864635
33	1008.5	5118:1:unfsd	0.0005415609225679
34	2397.21	wunderbar_empor	0.0005415608993991
35	2006.3	6737:6736:mount	0.0005415608993162
36	2503.1	6818:6815:bash	0.0005415608993102
37	2385.301	6799:6798:cc1	0.0005415608993102
38	2385.3	6799:6798:cc1	0.0005415608993102
39	2311.401	6794:6793:cc1	0.0005415608993102
40	2152.3	...wunderbar_emporium/pwnkernel1.c	0.0005415608993102
41	2452.1	/etc/shadow+:1493108	0.0005415608954389
42	2388.2	/tmp/ccUZcd3t.o:2984227	0.0005415608954389
43	2372.2	/tmp/ccfRR34r.o:2984223	0.0005415608954389
44	2527.3	6830:6815:bash	0.0005415583685793
45	2458.1	/etc/gshadow+:1493110	0.0005415583685793
46	2455.1	/etc/group+:1493109	0.0005415583685793
47	2449.1	/etc/passwd+:1493107	0.0005415583685793
48	2443.1	/etc/gshadow.6811:1493106	0.0005415583685793
49	2440.1	/etc/group.6811:1493105	0.0005415583685793
50	2437.1	/etc/shadow.6811:1493104	0.0005415583685793

objects and instances that are potentially compromised, but they do not investigate objects and instances that have large impacts and may infect more objects or instances.

This research is also related to system-level provenance tracking that monitors system activities for intrusion forensics and recovery. Several works have tracked malicious activities at the system level [2, 3, 5, 7–9, 13–15, 18, 24]. Like these works, this research leverages the dependencies among system objects such as files, processes and sockets. However, its main purpose is to determine high-impact system instances based on their dependencies instead of merely tracking malicious activities.

The research on capturing dependencies and ranking dependency graphs is related to work on logical attack graphs [1, 10–12, 19–22]. Attack graphs are used to generate potential attack paths by analyzing the causality relations involved in vulnerability exploitation. Dependency attack graphs are essentially attack graphs that capture dependencies among facts. For example, a fact that "vulnerability X is exploited" may depend on the facts: "a host runs a service" and "the service has vulnerability X." Some researchers [4, 26] have proposed the ranking of attack graphs to identify the critical attack assets in enterprise networks, such as servers with key vulnerabilities. This research also ranks the dependency graphs, but the dependency graphs are of a different type and are at a different abstract level. In particular, work on logical attack graphs is at the application level and identifies critical attack assets associated with applications and services whereas this research is at the system level and identifies impactful object instances in enterprise systems.

7 Conclusions

System object instance graphs reveal attack paths by connecting object instances with high infection probabilities. However, the graphs can be very large and overwhelming, which makes them difficult for security analysts to comprehend. In the experiments, system calls were collected over a small timeframe, but the number of calls was still huge. Indeed, the complexity of system object instance graphs keeps increasing as more and more instances are created when objects are accessed by other objects.

Combining the dependency ranks of object instances with their infection probabilities significantly reduces the time and resources needed for security analysts to understand complex system object instance graphs. Indeed, this approach can be used in combination with other intrusion detection techniques and tools to narrow down the suspicious system objects and focus on the most critical objects in attack paths.

Acknowledgment This research was supported by the National Science Foundation under Grant no. DGE 2105801.

References

1. P. Ammann, D. Wijesekera and S. Kaushik, Scalable graph-based network vulnerability analysis, *Proceedings of the Ninth ACM Conference on Computer and Communications Security*, pp. 217–224, 2002.
2. A. Bates, D. Tian, K. Butler and T. Moyer, Trustworthy whole-system provenance for the Linux kernel, *Proceedings of the Twenty-Fourth USENIX Security Symposium*, pp. 319–334, 2015.
3. U. Braun, S. Garfinkel, D. Holland, K. Muniswamy-Reddy and M. Seltzer, Issues in automatic provenance collection, in *Provenance and Annotation of Data*, L. Moreau and I. Foster (Eds.), Springer, Berlin Heidelberg, Germany, pp. 171–183, 2006.
4. J. Dai, X. Sun and P. Liu, Patrol: Revealing zero-day attack paths through network-wide system object dependencies, *Proceedings of the Eighteenth European Symposium on Research in Computer Security*, pp. 536–555, 2013.
5. A. Gehani and D. Tariq, SPADE: Support for provenance auditing in distributed environments, *Proceedings of the Thirteenth ACM/ IFIP/USENIX International Middleware Conference*, pp. 101–120, 2012.
6. D. Gleich, PageRank beyond the web, *SIAM Review*, vol. 57(3), pp. 321–363, 2015.
7. A. Goel, W. Feng, D. Maier, W. Feng and J. Walpol, Forensix: A robust high-performance reconstruction system, *Proceedings of the Twenty-Fifth IEEE International Conference on Distributed Computing Systems*, pp. 155–162, 2005.
8. A. Goel, K. Po, K. Farhadi, Z. Li and E. de Lara, The Taser intrusion recovery system, *ACM SIGOPS Operating Systems Review*, vol. 39(5), pp. 163–176, 2005.
9. M. Hossain, S. Milajerdi, J. Wang, B. Eshete, R. Gjomemo, R. Sekar, S. Stoller and V. Venkatakrishnan, SLEUTH: Real-time attack scenario reconstruction from COTS audit data, *Proceedings of the Twenty-Sixth USENIX Security Symposium*, pp. 487–504, 2017.
10. H. Huang, S. Zhang, X. Ou, A. Prakash and K. Sakallah, Distilling critical attack graph surface iteratively through minimum-cost SAT solving, *Proceedings of the Twenty-Seventh Annual Computer Security Applications Conference*, pp. 31–40, 2011.
11. K. Ingols, R. Lippmann and K. Piwowarski, Practical attack graph generation for network defense, *Proceedings of the Twenty-Second Annual Computer Security Applications Conference*, pp. 121–130, 2006.
12. S. Jajodia, S. Noel and B. O'Berry, Topological analysis of network attack vulnerability, in *Managing Cyber Threats*, V. Kumar, J. Srivastava and A. Lazarevic (Eds.), Springer, Boston, Massachusetts, pp. 247–266, 2005.
13. X. Jiang, A. Walters, D. Xu, E. Spafford, F. Buchholz and Y. Wang, Provenance-aware tracing of worm break-in and contaminations: A process coloring approach, *Proceedings of the Twenty-Sixth IEEE International Conference on Distributed Computing Systems*, 2006.
14. S. King and P. Chen, Backtracking intrusions, *ACM SIGOPS Operating Systems Review*, vol. 37(5), pp. 223–236, 2003.
15. S. Ma, X. Zhang and D. Xu, ProTracer: Towards practical provenance tracing by alternating between logging and tainting, *Proceedings of the Twenty-Third Annual Network and Distributed System Security Symposium*, 2016.
16. MITRE Corporation, CVE-2008-0166, Common Vulnerabilities and Exposures, Bedford, Massachusetts (cve.mitre.org/cgi-bin/cvename.cgi?name=CVE-2008-0166), January 9, 2008.

17. MITRE Corporation, CVE-2009-2692, Common Vulnerabilities and Exposures, Bedford, Massachusetts (cve.mitre.org/cgi-bin/cvename.cgi?name=CVE-2009-2692), August 5, 2009.
18. K. Muniswamy-Reddy, D. Holland, U. Braun and M. Seltzer, Provenance-aware storage systems, *Proceedings of the USENIX Annual Technical Conference*, pp. 43–56, 2006.
19. S. Noel and S. Jajodia, Managing attack graph complexity through visual hierarchical aggregation, *Proceedings of the ACM Workshop on Visualization and Data Mining for Computer Security*, pp. 109–118, 2004.
20. S. Noel, S. Jajodia, B. O'Berry and M. Jacobs, Efficient minimum-cost network hardening via exploit dependency graphs, *Proceedings of the Nineteenth Annual Computer Security Applications Conference*, pp. 86–95, 2003.
21. X. Ou, W. Boyer and M. McQueen, A scalable approach to attack graph generation, *Proceedings of the Thirteenth ACM Conference on Computer and Communications Security*, pp. 336–345, 2006.
22. X. Ou, S. Govindavajhala and A. Appel, MulVAL: A logic-based network security analyzer, *Proceedings of the Fourteenth USENIX Security Symposium*, 2005.
23. L. Page, S. Brin, R. Motwani and T. Winograd, The Page-Rank Citation Ranking: Bringing Order to the Web, Technical Report SIDL-WP-1999-0120, Stanford Digital Library Technologies Project, Stanford University, Palo Alto, California, 1998.
24. D. Pohly, S. McLaughlin, P. McDaniel and K. Butler, Hi-Fi: Collecting high-fidelity whole-system provenance, *Proceedings of the Twenty-Eighth Annual Computer Security Applications Conference*, pp. 259–268, 2012.
25. R. Sawilla and X. Ou, Googling Attack Graphs, DRDC Ottawa TM 2007-205, Defence Research and Development Canada, Ottawa, Canada, 2007.
26. R. Sawilla and X. Ou, Identifying critical attack assets in dependency attack graphs, *Proceedings of the Thirteenth European Symposium on Research in Computer Security*, pp. 18–34, 2008.
27. X. Sun, J. Dai, P. Liu, A. Singhal and J. Yen, Towards probabilistic identification of zero-day attack paths, *Proceedings of the IEEE Conference on Communications and Network Security*, pp. 64–72, 2016.
28. X. Sun, J. Dai, P. Liu, A. Singhal and J. Yen, Using Bayesian networks for probabilistic identification of zero-day attack paths, *IEEE Transactions on Information Forensics and Security*, vol. 13(10), pp. 2506–2521, 2018.

A Dynamic Malicious Document Detection Method Based on Multi-Memory Features

Yuanyuan Wang[1], Gengwang Li[1], Min Yu[1], Kam-Pui Chow[2], Jianguo Jiang[1], Xiang Meng[1], and Weiqing Huang[1]

[1] Institute of Information Engineering, Chinese Academy of Sciences, Beijing, China
yumin@iie.ac.cn
[2] University of Hong Kong, Hong Kong, China

Abstract. The massive use of Microsoft Office documents underscores the need for effective malicious document detection techniques. Most detection methods characterize document behavior using application programming interface traces or other descriptive information, but ignore memory information due to inherent difficulties. Since many malicious behavior patterns are only manifested in memory, these detection methods are vulnerable to ubiquity evasion attacks. One difficulty in extracting malicious behavior information from memory is that only high-coverage memory dump sequences are meaningful, but no established methods can be employed. Another difficulty is that no efficient method exists for representing the numerous long memory dump sequences associated with malicious document samples.

This chapter describes a multi-memory-feature-based method that leverages memory information to detect malicious documents. The detection method employs a high-coverage memory dump service and a multiple memory dump sequence reduction approach. The memory dump service hooks system application programming interfaces to cover the entire lifetimes of processes while also monitoring the initial Office process and every spawned subprocess. The multiple memory dump sequence reduction approach efficiently represents each memory dump in terms of the difference from its adjacent dump. Ablation experiments demonstrate that the memory dump sequence reduction approach performs best using a long short-term memory classifier, yielding an accuracy of 98.27%. Experiments also demonstrate that the detection method outperforms state-of-the-art methods based on application programming interfaces in terms of accuracy and precision.

Keywords: Malicious Document Detection · Microsoft Office · Application Programming Interfaces · Dynamic Memory Analysis · Neural Networks

1 Introduction

The massive use of Microsoft Office documents worldwide makes them attractive targets for attacks that exploit various vulnerabilities to inject malicious

G. Peterson and S. Shenoi (Eds.): DigitalForensics 2023, IFIP AICT 687, pp. 203–218, 2023.
https://doi.org/10.1007/978-3-031-42991-0_11

code. Kaspersky North America [9] reported that, during the second quarter of 2022, Microsoft Office vulnerabilities accounted for 82% of all exploited vulnerabilities [9]. Not surprisingly, malicious Office documents account for a large proportion of all types of malware.

Considerable research has focused on detecting malicious documents. The methods employ static analysis or dynamic analysis. Static analysis methods usually extract statistical features from Office document byte sequences [12, 19, 23, 27], content [10, 11, 15] and document structures [2, 14, 24, 26]. Static methods have high efficiency, but they are easily circumvented by structural changes, code obfuscation and other countermeasures. Dynamic methods are designed to address the limitations of static methods. They typically open documents in a deployed sandbox and observe and record their malicious behavior at runtime. Most dynamic methods rely on recorded application programming interface (API) sequences or reconstructed API callgraphs [16, 29, 31] to profile the runtime behavior of malicious documents. However, many malicious document behaviors are only manifested in memory, especially when decrypting sensitive text or unpacking control instructions.

Researchers have begun to analyze memory dumps to enhance detection, but their methods are designed to detect malware, not malicious documents. Moreover, the methods lack generalization capabilities for two reasons. One reason is that the dumped memory does not cover the entire lifetimes of malware samples. For example, many methods only analyze a single dump, which greatly increases the likelihood that they will miss malicious behavior [1, 6, 17, 20]. Javaheri et al. [8] dump memory at opportune times to increase the probability of capturing the malicious behavior, but the approach does not cover spawned subprocesses. The other reason is that an efficient technique is not available for reducing multiple long memory dump sequences to a suitable format for training classifiers. Some methods take pictures of entire memory dumps [1, 6] whereas others employ two-pass analyses of memory dumps [18, 20]. However, these approaches are not computationally efficient for processing long sequences of memory dumps.

The proposed multi-memory-feature-based method addresses the two limitations of existing memory dump methods. This is accomplished by leveraging a high-coverage memory dump service and a multiple memory dump sequence reduction approach. The dump service, which is implemented as a dynamic-linked library, hooks system APIs to ensure that it is automatically loaded into the process space of every subsequent spawned subprocess. After it is loaded, the service dumps memory from process space at a preset interval. Thus, the service creates dump sequences that cover the entire lifetimes of all the involved process and their spawned subprocesses.

The memory dump reduction approach processes each set of memory dump sequences. First, it transforms each dump to a token set and computes the token set difference for each pair of chronologically-adjacent dumps. Next, the memory differences associated with a single malicious document sample are concatenated to create a single document. Following this, the memory dump documents corresponding to the samples are fed to classifiers for training and testing.

An ablation experiment conducted to evaluate the memory dump sequence reduction approach compared it against three other dump reduction strategies using three common classifiers; the highest accuracy of 99.27% was obtained using the memory dump sequence reduction approach in conjunction with a long short-term memory (LSTM) classifier. Experiments also demonstrate that the proposed detection method outperforms the best state-of-the-art API-trace-based method [31] in terms of accuracy and precision.

2   Related Work

This section discusses static and dynamic analysis methods for detecting malicious documents. Static analysis methods, which extract features from byte sequences, code content and document structure, do not involve malicious document execution. Dynamic analysis methods execute and monitor malicious documents in instrumented environments.

2.1   Static Analysis Methods

Static analysis methods are divided into three categories based on the malicious document features they employ, statistical features, content features and structural features.

Statistical-Feature-Based Methods These methods directly extract character-level information from documents. The methods typically extract n-gram data from documents and compute the similarity [27], distribution change [23] or entropy [12, 19] of the data as features.

Content-Feature-Based Methods These methods focus on code contained in documents. Examples include counting the legal token sets in document code [10], extracting specific keywords [11] and computing the semantic similarity between codes [15] for use as features.

Structural-Feature-Based Methods These methods extract structural information from documents and then leverage keywords with the highest frequency [14], quantitative similarities of specific structural paths [2, 24] or integrated or abstracted structural information [26] as features.

2.2   Dynamic Analysis Methods

Although static methods are useful for detecting malicious documents, they are easily evaded by adversarial tactics such as adding benign features [25] or reducing unnecessary malicious features [30]. Dynamic analysis methods address the limitations of static methods by executing and monitoring malicious documents in instrumented environments. Depending on the features they leverage, dynamic analysis methods are characterized as script-based, API-based and memory-data-based:

Script-Based Methods These methods locate, extract and execute code in documents to determine if they are malicious. For example, MD-Scan [28] extracts JavaScript and runs it in a simulation environment. ZOOZLE [5] extracts and analyzes features from an abstract syntax tree constructed from JavaScript through dynamic execution. BISSAM [22] employs dynamic binary tools to automatically identify embedded malicious code. MPScan [13] dynamically executes samples to extract JavaScript code after de-obfuscation. Cujo [21], JSand [4] and Lux0r [3] are detection methods based on script code. However, these methods have two limitations. One is the difficulty of accurately locating and extracting code in documents. The other is that they typically target a specific language and cannot detect other types of attacks.

API-Based Methods These methods mainly monitor and record the operations performed by documents in virtual environments. Sandboxes such as CWSandbox [29] and Cuckoo Sandbox [7] are commonly used by API-based methods. With the help of a sandbox, Zhang et al. [31] extracted API names and their parameters as features and Mohammed et al. [16] extracted API sequences as features, which they used to train malicious document classifiers. However, these methods have some limitations. Since sandboxes can only track and record system APIs, malware can evade detection by imitating the behavior of non-malicious samples. Also, the extracted APIs only have time-order relationships and do not incorporate call-order relationships that are often used by experts to manually identify malicious document activity. Additionally, these methods cannot discern important malicious behaviors that only exist in memory, such as decrypting sensitive text and unpacking control instructions.

Memory-Data-Based Methods These methods are gaining popularity because they address the limitations of script-based and API-based methods. The memory forensics component of the malware detection framework developed by Rathnayaka et al. [20] employed Cuckoo Sandbox to dump the entire memory of a virtual machine, following which Volatility was used to extract information such as the malware source, registry and dynamic link library. Nissim et al. [17] collected 3,000 memory dumps and represented each dump as a vector with 200 minhash values to train a machine-learning-based classifier. Dai et al. [6] transformed memory dump files into grayscale images in the PNG format and extracted histograms of oriented gradient (HOG) features of the images to train an artificial neural network. Bozkir et al. [1] employed two image descriptors, global image (GIST) and HOG, to analyze the images created from memory dumps.

However, the above methods only dump memory once during a sample run, so there is no guarantee that malicious behavior has already occurred or is occurring at the time of dumping. Also, after the detection mechanism is understood, detection can be evaded by controlling the time of attack and packing or encrypting malicious code. Javaheri et al. [8] employed considerable empirical analysis to determine the right time to dump memory, but only achieved a success rate of 53.88% for unpacking packed files.

To address this limitation, some methods rely on multiple memory dumps during a sample run. For example, Panker et al. [18] acquired 100 memory dumps from a running Linux server every ten seconds and used Volatility to extract 171 features. However, dumping memory multiple times to ensure coverage of malicious code execution is expensive in terms of space and processing time [18, 20]. Additionally, dumped memory cannot be used directly to train classifiers. In fact, current memory dump processing methods that represent dumps as pictures [1, 6] cannot handle multiple memory dumps at the same time.

Unlike the methods discussed in this section, the proposed malicious document detection method considers the entire execution of samples, including their subprocesses. Additionally, it efficiently handles multiple memory dumps while reducing noise.

3   Proposed Detection Method

This section describes the proposed multi-memory-feature-based malicious document detection method that relies on memory dumps. The implementation incorporates two modules, one implementing a high-coverage memory dump service and the other implementing an efficient algorithm for representing long memory dump sequences. The high coverage property is vital to a memory-dump-based method because the goal is to capture malicious document behavior to the maximal extent. The efficient representation algorithm is vital because it makes the utilization of the method possible.

3.1   Overview

Figure 1 shows the malicious document workflow. Given an Office document sample, Cuckoo Sandbox launches the Office document process in a separate sandbox environment. Meanwhile, the memory dump service is automatically loaded into process space for the initial Office document process as well as for all the processes in its control flow. Once it is loaded, each memory dump service periodically dumps the memory of its process. After all the processes have completed their execution, multiple sequences of memory dumps are generated for the document sample. Each dump sequence corresponds to a single process and the multiple sequences are sorted in chronological order.

The representation algorithm transforms the multiple memory dump sequences associated with a single document sample into a compact form for classifier model training. Specifically, each memory dump is tokenized to a word bag. Next, each word bag is replaced by the set distance between itself and its temporally-adjacent word bag. Following this, all the word bags are concatenated in chronological order into a compact raw representation of the document sample. Finally, the document sample representation is fed to pre-trained downstream classifiers that output the probability that the sample Office document is malicious.

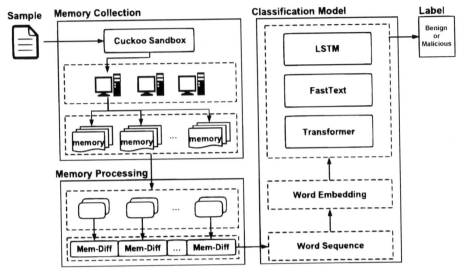

Fig. 1. Malicious document detection workflow.

3.2   High-Coverage Dump Service

Existing memory-based dynamic detection methods create very few memory dumps during the execution of Office document processes; consequently, they have high probabilities of missing malicious document behaviors. Indeed, the efficacy of memory-based malicious document detection is enhanced by dumping memory multiple times to achieve high coverage. High coverage is measured in two dimensions. One is the time domain, meaning that the entire lifetime of every process is covered. The other is the spatial domain, meaning that every process starting with the initial Office document process and all the processes spawned by the control flow of the initial process are covered.

To achieve maximal coverage, the memory dump service is designed to have high coverage in the time and spatial domains. The memory dump service injects into each process a procedure that dumps its memory space periodically using a background thread.

High Time Domain Coverage The memory dump procedure is injected into each process space to dump its memory periodically until it terminates. To ensure that malicious behavior is not missed before the injection, each process is started in the pending mode and resumed only after the dump procedure is injected. Once the process is resumed, the dump procedure dumps memory at a preset interval. Each memory dump is labeled with the process PID and dumping timestamp. Thus, the dump procedure generates a memory dump sequence for each process sorted in chronological order.

The system API MiniDumpWriteDump was selected from among several dump utilities because it provides rich dump functionality with a flexible interface and is accessible on any Windows platform. Additionally, the utility supports various dump types, each of which dumps different areas of process memory space. Experiments revealed that the MiniDumpNormal type dumps small amounts of memory while achieving good performance in downstream tasks. By invoking MiniDumpWriteDump with the argument MiniDumpNormal, only the information necessary to capture stack traces for all existing threads of a process was dumped.

High Spatial Domain Coverage The spatial domain refers to the set of processes spawned by the control flow of the initial Office document process. Since Office processes may launch subprocesses with malicious behavior, the dump service should cover them too. This is achieved by hooking CreateProcess, the system API used to create processes for Office executables. By hooking CreateProcess, a subprocess is created in the pending mode and the dump procedure is injected into the subprocess before it is resumed. The system APIs of created subprocesses are hooked similarly so that their spawned subprocesses are also injected with the dump procedure before they are resumed. Thus, the dump procedure is propagated along the control flow of the initial Office process with high coverage.

Another system API, CreateRemoteThread, which runs a piece of local code in remote process space, is also hooked. This enables the dump service to cover malicious behavior by the local code.

Cuckoo Sandbox The dump service is implemented using Cuckoo Sandbox, an open-source dynamic analysis platform. Cuckoo Sandbox comprises a host and clients connected via a virtual network. The core of Cuckoo Sandbox is its hooking mechanism, which is implemented by `monitor.dll` and `inject.exe` compiled by CucMonitor (Cuckoo Sandbox Monitor).

Figure 2 shows the Cuckoo Sandbox workflow. The host starts the virtual machine after receiving the analysis task submitted by the user and transmits the sample and analysis code to the client. The client executes the analysis code, starts the specified process to run the sample according to the sample type, calls `inject.exe` to suspend the new process and injects `monitor.dll` into it. The injected `monitor.dll` hooks the process to monitor its function calls and intercept and modify its execution process. After the analysis is completed, the client submits the analysis results to the host and restores itself to the original snapshot state.

The hooking mechanism of Cuckoo Sandbox is exactly what is needed by the proposed detection method, so it is leveraged to achieve high coverage of the spatial domain. The memory dump service is coded in CucMonitor and compiled into `monitor.dll`, enabling the memory dump service to be injected into process space within `monitor.dll`. In addition to Cuckoo Sandbox's original operation of API functions, attention is paid to calling the CreateProcess API. By hooking this API, it is possible to dynamically obtain parameters such as the IP address

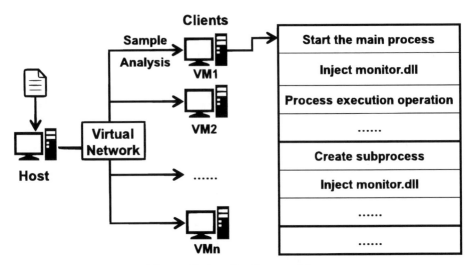

Fig. 2. Cuckoo Sandbox workflow.

and name of the process that are used to bind the process to the memory dump service.

Memory Dump Sequence Reduction The set of memory dump sequences for each malicious document sample must be transformed to a representation suitable for classifier training. As mentioned earlier, methods described in the literature only employ one memory dump for each malicious document sample. In contrast, in the proposed method, each malicious document sample yields a set of memory dump sequences where each sequence corresponds to one involved process. It is non-trivial to efficiently represent a malicious document sample in terms of such memory dump sequences.

Inspired by contrast learning and ResNet, the differences between chronologically-adjacent dumps are employed to create an efficient representation for classifier training. This notion is incorporated in the memory dump sequence reduction approach specified in Algorithm 1. The algorithm takes a set of memory dump sequences S from the same malicious document sample as input. For each memory dump sequence S_{pid} from the same process, the difference D_t is computed for each pair of adjacent memory dumps, which are concatenated in chronological order to create a single document R_{pid}. All the concatenated documents R_{pid} of all the spawned processes (subprocesses) are eventually merged in spawned order to create a single document R.

The dump difference D_t is created by first tokenizing each memory dump m_t into a meaningful token set. Next, the token frequencies are computed and stored in $Table_t$ for each memory dump m_t. Following this, the difference between two adjacent counting tables $Table_t$ and $Table_{prev}$ is computed as the memory dump

---

Algorithm 1: Memory dump sequence reduction.

Data: Sample $S = \{S_{pid} \mid pid$ is the process id$\}$ where
$S_{pid} = \{m_t \mid t$ is the dump time$\}$ is a memory dump sequence and
m_t is the memory dump at time t.
Result: Sample Representation R

$R \leftarrow EmptyString$
foreach $S_{pid} \in S$ **do**
  $\quad R_{pid}, Table_{prev} \leftarrow EmptyString, EmptyTable$
  $\quad$**foreach** $m_t \in S_{pid}$ **do**
    $\quad\quad Tokens \leftarrow \text{TOKENIZE}(m_t)$
    $\quad\quad Table_t \leftarrow \text{COUNT}(Tokens)$
    $\quad\quad D_t \leftarrow Table_t \setminus Table_{prev}$
    $\quad\quad R_{pid} \leftarrow R_{pid} \oplus \text{JOIN}(D_t)$
    $\quad\quad Table_{prev} \leftarrow Table_t$
  $\quad$**end**
  $\quad R \leftarrow R \oplus R_{pid}$
end

---

difference D_t. Finally, all the tokens in the difference tables are concatenated to create the document R.

The effectiveness and efficiency of the memory dump sequence reduction algorithm are assessed later in this chapter by comparing it with three other memory dump reduction strategies:

- **RandMemDump Strategy:** This strategy randomly selects exactly one memory dump from the initial Office process for each sample and uses the memory dump as a document without any further processing. This strategy is similar to the one used in [1, 6, 17, 20] that only considers the memory state at a certain time.
- **AllMemDumps Strategy:** This strategy is like the RandMemDump strategy, except that it concatenates all the memory dumps of one sample into an oversized document. This strategy is the simplest way to represent long sequences of memory dumps. While the strategy effectively uses multiple memory dumps, the oversized documents it produces are much too large for classifier training.
- **ByteByByteDiff Strategy:** This strategy computes memory dump differences in a byte-by-byte manner. It employs the same representation created by Algorithm 1.

4   Experimental Evaluation and Results

This section describes the experimental dataset, experimental setup, evaluation metrics, experiments and experimental results.

Table 1. Experimental dataset.

Label	File Type	Number
Malicious	DOC	1,2847
	DOCX	2,483
	XLS	5,082
	XLSX	852
Total		21,264
Benign	DOC	3,302
	DOCX	3,608
	XLS	2,734
	XLSX	3,164
Total		12,808

4.1 Experimental Dataset

The experimental dataset employed to evaluate the proposed multi-memory-feature-based malicious document detection method comprised 21,264 malicious samples and 12,808 benign samples. Table 1 shows details about the samples, which included DOC, DOCX, XLS and XLSX files. The malicious samples were drawn from Virus Share, a relatively authoritative malicious file sharing website that has published multiple malicious sample datasets. The benign document samples were collected using crawlers with Google, Bing, Baidu and other search engines.

The experiments employed subsets of the dataset, 12,500 malicious samples and 12,500 benign samples. The training, verification and testing sets were obtained by dividing the subsets in the ratio 6:2:2.

4.2 Experimental Setup

Sample analysis, memory extraction and memory preprocessing employed computers equipped with an Intel(R) Xeon (R) CPU E5-2620 v2 2.10 GHz and AS-PEED Graphics Family (rev. 21). Cuckoo Sandbox, which was deployed on a computer, controlled 12 Windows XP clients with the help of VirtualBox. After a sample was submitted, Cuckoo Sandbox performed sample analysis for a duration of one minute. The time interval for memory dumps was set to 500 s.

After analysis was completed, multiple memory dumps, grouped by the processes related to each sample, were transferred to the host. For each memory dump, the `strings` command was used to extract valid strings in memory. Subsequently, all the memory dumps of a single process were sorted by time and inserted in a set. Finally, Algorithm 1 was executed to extract the memory features. It was possible to decide whether or not to process the memory files of subprocesses. The processing of a subprocess was the same as that of its process and the extracted features were spliced after the process sequence.

Table 2. Performance comparison against an API-feature-based method.

Method	Accuracy	Precision	Recall	F1-Score
API-Feature-Based Method	0.9758	0.9849	0.9664	0.9756
Proposed Method	**0.9874**	**0.9927**	**0.9820**	**0.9873**

4.3 Evaluation Metrics

The accuracy, precision, recall and F1-score metrics were employed in the evaluation:

$$\text{Accuracy} = \frac{\text{TP} + \text{TN}}{\text{TP} + \text{TN} + \text{FP} + \text{FN}}$$

$$\text{Precision} = \frac{\text{TP}}{\text{TP} + \text{FP}}$$

$$\text{Recall} = \frac{\text{TP}}{\text{TP} + \text{FN}}$$

$$\text{F1-Score} = 2 \times \text{Precision} \times \frac{\text{Recall}}{\text{Precision} + \text{Recall}}$$

where true positives TP is the number of malicious samples identified as malicious, false negatives TN is the number of benign samples identified as benign, false positives FP is the number of benign samples identified as malicious and false negatives FN is the number of malicious samples identified as benign.

4.4 Experiments and Results

Four sets of experiments were performed. This section describes the experiments and the experimental results.

Detection Effectiveness This set of experiments compared the performance of the proposed method against the performance of the traditional dynamic analysis method of Zhang et al. [31], which extracts API functions and their parameter information. The method is by far the most commonly used detection method with the richest feature extraction. To eliminate the impact of memory extraction on the original Cuckoo Sandbox analysis report, the samples were analyzed using a clean Cuckoo Sandbox for a duration of one minute. After obtaining the analysis report for a sample, the API and its parameters were extracted from the report as the feature representation of the sample. In the experiments, the sample features based on API functions and parameters and the sample features based on memory dump differences employed the same word vector representations and the same three network models for training.

Table 2 compares the performance of the proposed method against the performance of an API-feature-based method [31]. For each detection method, the

Table 3. Performance comparison of memory dump processing strategies.

Method	Accuracy	Precision	Recall	F1-Score
RandMemDump	0.9614	0.9788	0.9432	0.9607
AllMemDumps	0.9754	0.9873	0.9632	0.9751
ByteByByteDiff	0.9818	0.9934	0.970	0.9816
Proposed Method (Main Process)	**0.9888**	**0.9900**	**0.9876**	**0.9888**
Proposed Method	**0.9874**	**0.9927**	**0.9820**	**0.9873**

table presents the best performance metric results from among the three network models. The results demonstrate that the proposed method outperforms the API-feature-based method. This is because the API-feature-based method only records the system APIs called by the samples whereas the proposed method extracts all the operations performed by the samples by way of memory differences. Since the proposed method effectively incorporates more information, it has better accuracy. Additionally, the API-feature-based method leverages API parameter information and time relationships, which correspond to the dependencies between APIs. In the case of the proposed method, code statements dynamically change the memory stack by pushes and pops, and the dependencies between code statements become obvious.

Feature Selection This set of experiments compared the performance of the memory features used by the proposed method against the performance of three other memory features, RandMemDump, AllMemDumps and ByteByByteDiff. The performance of the proposed method for the main process and its subprocesses and the performance for the main process alone are also presented for comparison purposes.

Table 3 compares the performance of five memory dump processing strategies used in the experiments. The performance metrics of the proposed method with the main process and subprocesses and with the main process alone are superior to the performance metrics of the three other memory features.

RandMemDump uses a single memory dump and, therefore, incorporates too little effective information. AllMemDumps uses multiple memory dumps, but incorporates too much noisy information. Thus, RandMemDump and AllMemDumps do not represent the samples well and have lower performance metrics. The comparisons with RandMemDump and AllMemDumps demonstrate that the high-coverage multiple memory dumps of the proposed method incorporate more useful information that enhances detection.

ByteByByteDiff uses multiple memory dumps and has high accuracy but low recall, resulting in a lower F1-score than the proposed method. This is because the byte relationships in memory dumps were destroyed when valid strings were collected, leading to deviations in feature extraction by ByteByByteDiff and, ultimately, reduced accuracy. The comparisons with ByteByByteDiff and

Table 4. Performance comparison of deep learning models.

Model	Accuracy	Precision	Recall	F1-Score
Fasttext	0.9790	0.9914	0.9664	0.9787
LSTM	**0.9874**	**0.9927**	**0.9820**	**0.9873**
Transformer	0.9680	0.9899	0.9456	0.9673

AllMemDumps demonstrate the efficiency of multiple memory dump sequence reduction.

Curiously, the proposed method executed with only the main process is slightly superior to the proposed method with the main process and subprocesses for all the performance metrics except for recall. A possible reason is that the merging of subprocess differences may have resulted in the loss of subprocess timing relationships. Another possibility is that the dataset may not be rich enough because the subprocesses mostly executed legal operations instead of malicious operations.

Model Selection This set of experiments compared the performance of three commonly-used deep learning models, FastText, LSTM and Transformer, to determine the best model for learning memory features. FastText is a leading neural network model that greatly reduces training time while maintaining classification accuracy. An LSTM is a special recurrent neural network structure that learns long-term correlations and effectively processes samples comprising long sequences. A transformer employs a self-attention mechanism to connect an encoder and decoder with good parallelism.

Table 4 compares the performance of the three deep learning models. The LSTM model has the best performance across the four metrics, indicating that its training was the most effective. This is because each sample is represented in terms of the differences between multiple memory dumps with temporal relationships. The LSTM model is designed to learn long-term dependencies and effectively processes samples with temporal relationships. The model is best suited to handle the proposed memory features and makes good use of them.

Processing Efficiency The fourth set of experiments analyzed the time performance of four memory dump processing strategies, RandMemDump, AllMemDumps, ByteByByteDiff, and the proposed multiple memory dump reduction approach. The proposed multiple memory dump reduction approach was used with the LSTM model, the deep learning model with the best detection effectiveness and performance. In the case of the proposed approach, only the time required for partitioning memory dumps and memory feature extraction was recorded. Since memory collection and sandbox analysis occurred synchronously and were set to durations of one minute, memory collection did not affect the time performance.

Table 5. Time comparison of memory dump processing strategies.

Feature	Time (s)
RandMemDump	190.36
AllMemDumps	1,215.02
ByteByByteDiff	1,451.53
Proposed Method	**609.10**

Table 5 shows the times required by the four strategies for processing memory dumps and presenting samples. As expected, RandMemDump, which uses a single dump is the fastest but, as shown in Table 3, its detection performance is not good. Merging dumps in the AllMemDumps strategy requires considerable system resources, so the time requirement is high but, as shown in Table 3, the detection performance is not greatly improved. ByteByByteDiff is the slowest because it requires one more traversal compared with the other strategies. The multiple memory dump sequence reduction algorithm used in the proposed method requires less time than the two other multiple memory dump strategies, AllMemDumps and ByteByByteDiff, but, as shown in Table 3, has the best detection performance.

5   Conclusions

The multi-memory-feature-based malware detection method for Microsoft Office documents leverages a high-coverage memory dump service and a multiple memory dump sequence reduction approach. By hooking specific APIs, the memory dump service covers the entire lifetimes of the processes and subprocesses in the control flow of the initial Office process. This effectively extracts more information from memory that is leveraged to improve detection accuracy. The multiple memory dump sequence reduction approach efficiently represents memory dumps in terms of the differences from their chronologically-adjacent dumps. The approach concatenates all the differences between all the pairs of adjacent memory dumps into a compact, trainable format that embodies rich behavior information. The approach also can process multiple memory dumps at the same time while reducing noise and the training time.

Experiments demonstrate that the proposed malicious document detection method has an accuracy of 98.74%, which is 1.16% higher than the best traditional API-based detection method. Also, the method yields excellent results with an accuracy rate of at least 0.56% higher than other memory features with a time requirement of just 609.10 s.

References

1. A. Bozkir, E. Tahillioglu, M. Aydos and I. Kara, Catch them alive: A malware detection approach through memory forensics, manifold learning and computer

vision, *Computers and Security*, vol. 103, article no. 102166, 2021.

2. A. Cohen, N. Nissim, L. Rokach and Y. Elovici, SFEM: Structural feature extraction methodology for the detection of malicious Office documents using machine learning methods, *Expert Systems with Applications*, vol. 63, pp. 324–343, 2016.

3. I. Corona, D. Maiorca, D. Ariu and G. Giacinto, LuxOR: Detection of malicious PDF-embedded JavaScript code through discriminant analysis of API references, *Proceedings of the Workshop on Artificial Intelligence and Security*, pp. 47–57, 2014.

4. M. Cova, C. Kruegel and G. Vigna, Detection and analysis of drive-by-download attacks and malicious JavaScript code, *Proceedings of the Nineteenth International Conference on the World Wide Web*, pp. 281–290, 2010.

5. C. Curtsinger, B. Livshits, B. Zorn and C. Seifert, ZOZZLE: Fast and precise in-browser JavaScript malware detection, *Proceedings of the Twentieth USENIX Security Symposium*, 2011.

6. Y. Dai, H. Li, Y. Qian, R. Yang and M. Zheng, SMASH: A malware detection method based on multi-feature ensemble learning, *IEEE Access*, vol. 7, pp. 112588–112597, 2019.

7. C. Guarnieri, M. Schloesser, J. Bremer and A. Tanasi, Cuckoo Sandbox open-source automated malware analysis, presented at *Black Hat USA*, 2013.

8. D. Javaheri and M. Hosseinzadeh, A framework for recognition and confronting of obfuscated malware based on memory dumping and filter drivers, *Wireless Personal Communications*, vol. 98(1), pp. 119–137, 2018.

9. Kaspersky North America, Eight times more users attacked via an old Microsoft Office vulnerability in Q2, Press Release, Woburn, Massachusetts (www.kaspersky.com/about/press-releases/2022_eight-times-more-users-attacked-via-an-old-microsoft-office-vulnerability-in-q2), August 15, 2022.

10. P. Laskov and N. Srndic, Static detection of malicious JavaScript-bearing PDF documents, *Proceedings of the Twenty-Seventh Annual Computer Security Applications Conference*, pp. 373–382, 2011.

11. J. Lin and H. Pao, Multi-view malicious document detection, *Proceedings of the Conference on Technologies and Applications of Artificial Intelligence*, pp. 170–175, 2013.

12. L. Liu, X. He, L. Liu, L. Qing, Y. Fang and J. Liu, Capturing the symptoms of malicious code in electronic documents by file entropy signals combined with machine learning, *Applied Soft Computing*, vol. 82, article no. 105598, 2019.

13. X. Lu, J. Zhuge, R. Wang, Y. Cao and Y. Chen, De-obfuscation and detection of malicious PDF files with high accuracy, *Proceedings of the Forty-Sixth Hawaii International Conference on System Sciences*, pp. 4890–4899, 2013.

14. D. Maiorca, G. Giacinto and I. Corona, A pattern recognition system for malicious PDF file detection, *Proceedings of the Eighth International Workshop on Machine Learning and Data Mining in Pattern Recognition*, pp. 510–524, 2012.

15. M. Mimura and T. Ohminami, Using LSI to detect unknown malicious VBA macros, *Journal of Information Processing*, vol. 28, pp. 493–501, 2020.

16. T. Mohammed, L. Nataraj, S. Chikkagoudar, S. Chandrasekaran and B. Manjunath, HAPSSA: Holistic approach to PDF malware detection using signal and statistical analysis, *Proceedings of the IEEE Military Communications Conference*, pp. 709–714, 2021.

17. N. Nissim, O. Lahav, A. Cohen, Y. Elovici and L. Rokach, Volatile memory analysis using the minhash method for efficient and secure detection of malware in private clouds, *Computers and Security*, vol. 87, article no. 101590, 2019.

18. T. Panker and N. Nissim, Leveraging malicious behavior traces from volatile memory using machine learning methods for trusted unknown malware detection in Linux cloud environments, *Knowledge-Based Systems*, vol. 226, article no. 107095, 2021.
19. H. Pareek, P. Eswari and N. Babu, Entropy and n-gram analysis of malicious PDF documents, *International Journal of Engineering and Technology*, vol. 2(2), 2013.
20. C. Rathnayaka and A. Jamdagni, An efficient approach for advanced malware analysis using a memory forensic technique, *Proceedings of the Sixteenth IEEE International Conference on Trust, Security and Privacy in Computing and Communications, Eleventh IEEE International Conference on Big Data Science and Engineering and Fourteenth IEEE International Conference on Embedded Software and Systems*, pp. 1145–1150, 2017.
21. K. Rieck, T. Krueger and A. Dewald, Cujo: Efficient detection and prevention of drive-by-download attacks, *Proceedings of the Twenty-Sixth Annual Computer Security Applications Conference*, pp. 31–39, 2010.
22. T. Schreck, S. Berger and J. Gobel, BISSAM: Automatic vulnerability identification of Office documents, *Proceedings of the International Conference on Detection of Intrusions and Malware, and Vulnerability Assessment*, pp. 204–213, 2012.
23. M. Shafiq, S. Khayam, and M. Farooq, Embedded malware detection using Markov n-grams, *Proceedings of the Fifth International Conference on Detection of Intrusions and Malware, and Vulnerability Assessment*, pp. 88–107, 2008.
24. N. Srndic and P. Laskov, Detection of malicious PDF files based on hierarchical document structure, *Proceedings of the Twentieth Annual Network and Distributed System Security Symposium*, 2013.
25. N. Srndic and P. Laskov, Practical evasion of a learning-based classifier: A case study, *Proceedings of the IEEE Symposium on Security and Privacy*, pp. 197–211, 2014.
26. N. Srndic and P. Laskov, Hidost: A static machine-learning-based detector of malicious files, *EURASIP Journal on Information Security*, vol. 2016(1), article no. 45, 2016.
27. S. Stolfo, K. Wang and W. Li, Towards stealthy malware detection, in *Malware Detection*, M. Christodorescu, S. Jha, D. Maughan, D. Song and C. Wang (Eds.), Springer, Boston, Massachusetts, pp. 231–249, 2007.
28. Z. Tzermias, G. Sykiotakis, M. Polychronakis and E. Markatos, Combining static and dynamic analysis for the detection of malicious documents, *Proceedings of the Fourth European Workshop on System Security*, article no. 4, 2011.
29. C. Willems, T. Holz and F. Freiling, Toward automated dynamic malware analysis using CWSandbox, *IEEE Security and Privacy*, vol. 5(2), pp. 32–39, 2007.
30. W. Xu, Y. Qi and D. Evans, Automatically evading classifiers: A case study on PDF malware classifiers, *Proceedings of the Twenty-Third Network and Distributed Systems Symposium*, vol. 10, 2016.
31. Z. Zhang, P. Qi and W. Wang, Dynamic malware analysis with feature engineering and feature learning, *Proceedings of the Thirty-Fourth AAAI Conference on Artificial Intelligence, Thirty-Second Innovative Applications of Artificial Intelligence Conference and Tenth AAAI Symposium on Educational Advances in Artificial Intelligence*, pp. 1210–1217, 2020.

Traceable Transformer-Based Anomaly Detection for a Water Treatment System

Shenzhi Qin[1], Yubo Lang[2], and Kam-Pui Chow[1]

[1] University of Hong Kong, Hong Kong, China
chow@cs.hku.hk
[2] Criminal Investigation Police University of China, Shenyang, China

Abstract. As industrial control system malfunctions caused by attacks become more complex and frequent, anomaly detection and subsequent forensic analyses are more important than ever. When an anomaly is detected, security professionals need to accurately identify the components that are under attack. However, traditional methods do not provide enough traces, which makes it difficult to identify the targeted components.

This chapter describes a traceable anomaly detection method that leverages unsupervised learning using industrial control system component time series data. The method generates customized transformer-encoder classifiers for industrial control system components. The final detection result is ensembled from all the classifier outputs. Experiments with water treatment testbed data indicate that the method achieves good performance with low false positive rates and delays, and strong traceability.

Keywords: Industrial Control Systems · Time Series Data · Anomaly Detection · Transformer-Encoder Classifier

1 Introduction

The umbrella term "industrial control systems" covers various control systems and their instrumentation, including systems, devices, networks and controls that collectively operate industrial processes. Industrial control systems are widely used in critical infrastructure sectors such as electricity, water and wastewater, oil and gas, transportation, chemicals, pharmaceuticals, aerospace and automotive manufacturing [12]. Internet connectivity has increased the potential of attacks on industrial control systems. Meanwhile, the scale and complexity of industrial control systems renders system exceptions more frequent. The anomalies induced by attacks and exceptions can cause serious harm to infrastructure assets. Reliable detection of anomalies is vital because there can be no mitigation without detection.

Deep learning is a promising approach for anomaly detection. A deep learning model can identify anomalies that are not present in training data. Due to the absence of high-quality attack data and the difficulty obtaining data pertaining to normal operation, unsupervised training is more practical than unsupervised training for industrial control systems.

G. Peterson and S. Shenoi (Eds.): DigitalForensics 2023, IFIP AICT 687, pp. 219–234, 2023.
https://doi.org/10.1007/978-3-031-42991-0_12

Traditional anomaly detection methods can also be effective at detecting anomalies in industrial control systems. Methods that rely on data distributions may be inflexible and find it difficult to model the features of complex patterns encountered in industrial control systems. However, they are suitable for detecting anomalies in components such as backup pumps that are rarely enabled and/or whose data values are very stable during normal operation. Once these components are enabled or the data fluctuates, the system is likely to be abnormal. In these situations, traditional methods based on data distributions are more suitable than deep learning methods because they have very low training costs and provide fast anomaly detection with low false positive rates.

A key requirement imposed on anomaly detection systems is reporting the sources of anomalies, a feature referred to as traceability. Traceability is important to handle anomaly alerts and mitigate negative impacts as well to conduct forensic investigations. However, the vast majority of anomaly detection solutions focus on detection metrics such as the F1-score and do not provide adequate traceability.

This chapter describes a traceable time series prediction anomaly detection (TTPAD) method that performs unsupervised real-time anomaly detection based on time series data from industrial control system components. Anomalies reported by TTPAD enable forensic practitioners to pinpoint the components that act abnormally so that investigations can focus on specific components instead of the entire industrial control systems.

The proposed TTPAD method combines data distribution and deep learning approaches to perform anomaly detection. Industrial control system components are categorized into two groups according to their stability. Components with very stable values are assigned static thresholds to identify anomalies whereas components with less stable values are monitored by customized transformer-encoder classifiers. The final detection result is ensembled from all the classifier outputs. Experiments using water treatment testbed data demonstrate the effectiveness of the TTPAD method with respect to anomaly detection (low false positive rates and delays) and traceability.

2   Related Work

Conventional anomaly detection techniques employ statistical methods, time series analysis and signal processing. Krishna et al. [6] presented an autoregressive integrated moving average (ARIMA) model [5] for detecting electricity theft perpetrated by tampering with smart meter readings. Autoregressive integrated moving averaging is a classic time series analysis method. However, the time series data should be stationary. In the case of industrial control system components, time series data may not be stationary.

Data-driven techniques such as machine learning and deep learning have been used in anomaly detection. Wei et al. [14] designed an unsupervised multi-autoencoder that detects insider threats by analyzing system log files. The multi-autoencoder increased the model depth, which enhanced detection performance.

Zhou et al. [17] employed an informer model to perform long-sequence time series forecasting. Informer is an adjusted version of a transformer model that decreases the complexity of the transformer via self-attention and self-attention distilling. The adjusted transformer-decoder can output entire long-sequence predictions instead of one prediction at a time.

Malhotra et al. [7] proposed a long short-term memory (LSTM) network-based encoder-decoder scheme for anomaly detection. The training goal involved reconstructing normal time series behavior. The approach assumes that a model trained using normal data is unable to reconstruct the sequence well when an anomaly occurs. Therefore, the reconstruction error is used to detect anomalies.

Chauhan and Vig [3] proposed an LSTM method for detecting anomalies in electrocardiogram signals. An LSTM is created as a predictive model of electrocardiogram signals and the predicted errors are indicators of anomalous signals.

Real-world industrial control system data is hard to obtain. This is a problem because anomaly detection techniques need high-quality real data for model training and testing. Secure Water Treatment (SWaT) [4, 8] is an open-source water treatment testbed that has been employed by several industrial control system researchers.

Wijaya et al. [15] have implemented supervised learning models using traces of normal and abnormal SWaT operations. They compared several classifiers such as one-class support vector machine (OCSVM), multilayer perceptron and decision tree classifiers, noting that supervised methods yielded lower false positive rates compared with unsupervised methods.

Raman et al. [11] proposed a supervised probabilistic neural network for detecting anomalies. Balaji et al. [2] created ensemble classifiers using Random Forest, bagging with k-nearest neighbor and Gaussian Naive Bayes algorithms to detect anomalies in SWaT data. However, these supervised learning methods need high-quality labeled industrial control systems data, including real-world attack data, that are hard to obtain. As a result, unsupervised methods are better suited to anomaly detection in industrial control systems.

Raman et al. [10] proposed a method that identifies anomalies in the process dynamics of industrial control systems. Complex relationships between components are modeled in operational data using a deep convolutional neural network. However, the work only considers a small subset of SWaT testbed components.

Aoudi et al. [1] proposed a process-aware stealthy attack detection (PASAD) method that monitors time series sensor measurements in real-time for structural changes in process behavior. PASAD detects attacks by checking if current sensor values diverge from previous values due to generating mechanism changes. However, in its SWaT experiments, PASAD produced numerous false positives on AIT-202, one of the two demonstration components.

Yau et al. [16] utilized OCSVMs to detect attacks in the SWaT testbed. Six models were trained for six filtration processes so that alerts could be traced at the filtration process level. However, the approach is not detailed enough because each filtration process has many components and a forensic practitioner would have to investigate all the components without any guidance provided by

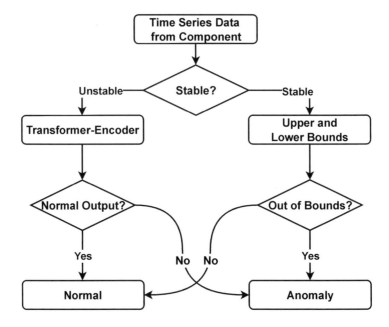

Fig. 1. TTPAD classifier generation workflow.

the model. The training process also did not engage time sequence information, which affected detection performance.

Raman et al. [9] proposed deep autoencoder based anomaly detection using reconstruction error as the anomaly indicator. Different depths in the hidden layer were investigated to enhance performance. The best performance model was achieved when each process stage had an independent autoencoder classifier. The method only provides traces at the filtration process level and, thus, exhibits the same problems as the approach of Yau et al. [16].

The methods described in this section do not satisfy the strong traceability requirement that is crucial in forensic investigations. Additionally, they tend to use metrics such as accuracy, precision, recall and F1-score that are not generally employed by the digital forensics community. In contrast, the TTPAD method described in this chapter is verified using the SWaT dataset with forensic metrics such as detection delay, detection rate and traceability. As described later in this chapter, the experimental results are also very satisfying.

3   TTPAD Method

The traceable time series prediction anomaly detection (TTPAD) method generates a classifier for each industrial control system component, which enhances traceability. Figure 1 shows the classifier generation workflow for a single component.

TTPAD first filters the stable features. Some components in industrial control systems, such as backup pumps in water treatment systems, are rarely enabled or have very stable values during normal system operation. These stable components are special because when their values change, an industrial control system is almost certain to have anomalies.

Component data sampled during normal industrial control system operation is input to the TTPAD method. After minimum-maximum normalization, the standard deviation of each component is computed. The standard deviation reflects the stability of the component. If the component standard deviation is less than a threshold, the component is considered to be stable. The threshold is determined based on prior knowledge about the system and the standard deviation distribution (discussed in Section 4). This data distribution based detection method is adopted for stable industrial control system components. Less stable and unstable components are fitted using transformer-encoder models.

3.1   Data Distribution Based Detection

Classifier generation for a stable industrial control system component involves three steps. In the first step, component data collected during normal operation is normalized using the z-score method. Next, the maximum value Max, minimum value Min and standard deviation SD of the normalized data distribution are computed. In the third step, the data distribution based method learns the upper and lower bounds from the normal data to generate the classifier. The upper and lower bounds are computed as:

$$\text{Upper Bound} = Max + SD$$
$$\text{Lower Bound} = Min - {}^{\vee}SD$$

When a detection classifier is testing or monitoring a stable component, the real-time component value is normalized by the z-score. The mean and standard deviation used to evaluate normalization are computed from normal system operation data, not testing data. An anomaly is detected when the normalized data value is not within the upper and lower bounds.

3.2   Transformer-Encoder Based Detection

Transformer-encoder models are employed to detect anomalies in unstable industrial control system components. Figure 2 shows the transformer-encoder detection model. If an industrial control system reads a component value once a second, the model input is the component value for n consecutive seconds and the output is the component value predicted by the model for time $n + 1$. The input embedding layer is a fully-connected network that maps the input value to an eight-dimensional vector for each second. Positional encoding information

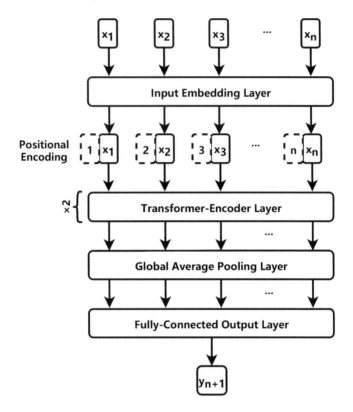

Fig. 2. Transformer-encoder detection model.

is added to the output of the input embedding layer. This step encodes the sequence of time in the embedding so that it incorporates timing information.

Inputting the embedding results of n-second time series data to two transformer-encoder [13] layers produces n outputs. The training process of the encoder causes the output generated each second to be based on the inputs during the previous n seconds. Thus, the encoder learns the pattern of the n-second time series data corresponding to its component. The output of the encoder layer is passed to a global average pooling layer that reduces the data dimension from eight to one. Next, the reduced output is sent to a fully-connected network layer to produce the final output, which is the component value at time $n+1$ predicted by the encoder.

Data collected during normal industrial control system operation is employed for model training. The training goal is to make the model output and the real value at time $n+1$ as close as possible. Mean squared error is employed as the loss function:

$$\text{Loss} = (y_{n+1} - y'_{n+1})^2$$

where y_{n+1} and y'_{n+1} are the real and predicted values at time $n+1$, respectively.

Components with low training loss are well fitted by their detection models. Components with high training loss are not used for real-time detection. During the detection phase, real-time data is input to the transformer-encoder model. An anomaly is detected when the difference between the output predicted by the model and the real value is greater than a threshold; otherwise, the component value at time $n + 1$ is normal.

A transformer-encoder uses self-attention to process time sequence information. The mechanism computes the attention score for all the inputs in a sequence that could encode contextual information. The encoder is adopted because the self-attention mechanism can fit the time series well, which benefits the task of predicting the next value.

The original transformer model designed for natural language processing has six encoder layers and an embedding dimension of 512. However, the model has high complexity and too many parameters, which render it unsuitable for time series predictions for a single component. Therefore, the model structure was customized to the time series data characteristics. The resulting slimmed-down model speeds up training and avoids overfitting. Additionally, the time complexity of the model inference process is reduced to enable faster predictions that meet real-time industrial control system requirements. The slimmed-down model also handles longer input sequences, which increases its scalability and adaptability.

For detailed adjustments, the embedding dimension was reduced to eight in the input layer. The depth of the encoder layer was reduced to two. Global average pooling was used to reduce the output dimension of the encoder layer concisely and efficiently. The replacement of multiple fully-connected layers by the combination of the global average pooling layer and a single fully-connected layer reduced the number of model parameters.

4   TTPAD Method Evaluation

This section describes the evaluation of the TTPAD method using the SWaT dataset. The metrics employed to assess TTPAD performance include detection delay, precision, recall, F1-score, detection rate and traceability.

4.1   SWaT Dataset

The SWaT testbed is a scaled-down version of a real-world industrial water treatment plant that filters five gallons of water per minute. SWaT has six sub-processes: Process 1 stores raw water, Process 2 assesses water quality, Process 3 performs membrane-based ultrafiltration, Process 4 performs dechlorination using ultraviolet lamps, Process 5 reduces inorganic impurities using reverse osmosis and Process 6 distributes the treated water. SWaT has a total of 51 components. Table 1 shows the five main SWaT component types and their functions.

Table 1. Main SWaT component types and functions.

Component	Function
LIT	(Sensor) Level Transmitter
AIT	(Sensor) Chemical Composition Analyzer
FIT	(Sensor) Flow Meter
MV	(Actuator) Motorized Valve
P	(Actuator) Pump

Table 2. Process 1 components.

Name	Description
FIT-101	Flow Meter: Measures inflow into raw water tank
LIT-101	Level Transmitter: Measures raw water tank level
MV-101	Motorized Valve: Controls water flow to raw water tank
P-101	Pump: Pumps water from raw water tank to second stage
P-102	Pump: Serves as the backup pump for P-101

Table 2 shows the Process 1 component names and their descriptions. Process 1 has a raw water tank and uses pumps to transfer the raw water to Process 2. A component name includes its component type and three digits. The first digit is the process index, the second digit is 0 and the third digit denotes the index within the same component type in the current process. For example, P-102 is the component name of the backup pump in Process 1. The component type is P for pump, the first digit is one because it is in Process 1 and the third digit is two because it is the second pump in Process 1. Readers are referred the original SWaT paper [4] for details about the other five processes and their components.

SWaT operates 24 hours a day without stoppages. Data is recorded each second and it is assumed that an attack on SWaT cannot be launched in less than one second. All the tanks in SWaT are empty when data collection starts. It takes about five hours for SWaT to become stable after it starts operating.

Data was recorded over two periods. The first period lasted seven days with data recorded from 12/22/2015 16:30:00 to 12/28/2015 9:59:59. This period included SWaT initialization and stable operation without any attacks. The second period lasted six days with data recorded from 12/28/2015 10:00:00 to 1/2/2016 14:59:59. During the second period, 36 attacks were launched intermittently.

The data collected during the first period comprises 495,001 timestamped records of 51 component values, all with normal labels. The data collected during the second period comprises 449,919 timestamped records of 51 component values, 54,621 with attack labels and 395,298 with normal labels.

The first attack in the dataset (Attack 1) targeted Process 1 to cause a tank overflow. The process uses a motorized valve MV-101 to control flow to the

Table 3. Effective and discarded SWaT components.

Components		Count
Effective Stable Components	P-102, P-202, P-301, AIT-401, P-401, P-402, P-403, P-404, UV-401, P-501, P-502, P-601, P-603	13
Discarded Stable Components	Mechanical Interlock: P-201, P-204, P-206	3
Effective Unstable Components	LIT-301, AIT-203, AIT-402, LIT-101, AIT-502, AIT-503, AIT-202, FIT-501, FIT-401, FIT-503, PIT-501, PIT-503, DPIT-301, AIT-501, FIT-504, LIT-401	16
Discarded Unstable Components	Huge Training Loss: AIT-504, FIT-201, FIT-101 FIT-301, FIT-502, PIT-502, FIT-601, P-203, MV-101, P-101, P-602, MV-201, MV-301, MV-303, P-205, P-302, MV-302, MV-304 Data Drift After Attack: AIT-201	19

raw water tank. MV-101 was closed before the attack. The attack opened MV-101 and kept water flowing into the tank. Another attack, Attack 4, targeted an unknown component MV-504 and had no impact on SWaT operation. Therefore, the labels of the corresponding records were changed from attack to normal. As a result, the final dataset used in the experiments had 35 attacks. Readers are referred the original SWaT paper [4] for a link to the SWaT dataset with details about all the attacks.

4.2   Evaluation and Results

The normal data collected during the first period was used for TTPAD model training. The data collected during the second period was used for TTPAD model testing.

The first step in the TTPAD method is to identify the stable and unstable components. After min-max normalization, the standard deviation of each component was computed and sorted in ascending order. The 16th standard deviation (Component: AIT-401, SD: 0.000025) was much smaller than the 17th standard deviation (Component: AIT-504, SD: 0.0038). Since the lower standard deviation means that a component is more stable, the 16 components with low standard deviations were designated as stable components.

Table 3 shows the effective and discarded SWaT components. The first two rows in the table list the 16 stable components. Thirteen components are effective stable components classified by their upper and lower bounds. Three stable components, P-201, P-204 and P-206, were discarded due to mechanical interlock logged in the attack list.

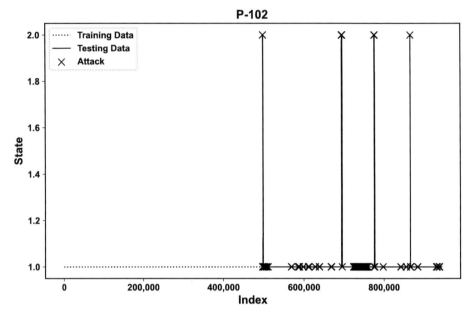

Fig. 3. Stable backup pump P-102 state visualization.

Stable components have unique advantages with regard to anomaly detection. Figure 3 shows the state visualization of stable component P-102, the backup pump for P-101. During normal operation, the backup pump P-102 remained off (state = 1). During the testing phase, after P-102 was turned on (state = 2), it is clear that the system came under attack. Redundancy is a basic rule in industry and industrial control systems always have backup components. The TTPAD method leverages the redundancy in industrial control systems to improve its detection capabilities.

Transformer-encoder models were created for the 35 unstable components. During the training process, a sliding window (window size = 19 and step size = 1) was used to process component data to generate the training samples. The sliding window contained 19 consecutive component readings as model input and the model predicted the component value for the next second. Mean squared error was used as the loss function to evaluate the prediction error, perform gradient backpropagation and update the model parameters. During the training process for each component, the training epoch was set to 50, batch size to 512, optimizer to Adam and learning rate to 0.01. Training was terminated when the training error did not decrease over five consecutive epochs and the model with the smallest training error was selected as the final model for the component.

After model training for all the unstable components was completed, the effective models were selected based on their training losses. A large training loss indicates that the information learned by a model is incomplete, which results in a high false positive rate and reduced traceability. Therefore, components whose models had small training losses were selected as effective components and were used for anomaly detection. Components whose models had large training losses were discarded.

After sorting the training losses, 17 component models had training losses on the order of $10^{-6} \sim 10^{-5}$ and 18 components had training losses on the order of $10^{-4} \sim 10^{-3}$. Finally, a threshold of 10^{-4} was selected and components with training losses on the order of $10^{-4} \sim 10^{-3}$ were discarded. The last two rows in Table 3 list the effective and discarded unstable components. Component AIT-201 was discarded due to data drift after attack. This is because the data pattern changed dramatically and it would be difficult for the encoder to predict values based on normal data patterns.

The testing phase used the same sliding window as the training phase. When the model prediction error (i.e., absolute value of the distance between the predicted and real values) exceeded a certain threshold, the model reported an anomaly in the associated component. If one or more models were to report anomalies at the same time, a system-level alert would be raised and the list of components reporting anomalies would be provided for traceability.

The prediction error threshold for detecting anomalies was set based on the training statistics. After model training was completed, the maximum and standard deviation of the prediction error were computed for the training data. The prediction error of effective components was on the order of 0.01 and the maximum prediction error was on the order of 10. Therefore, the standard deviation was multiplied by 100 and added to the maximum value to obtain the prediction error threshold. Each effective unstable component was assigned its own threshold. A prediction error exceeding the prediction error threshold resulted in an anomaly being reported during the testing phase.

Figure 4 shows the TTPAD method performance. The horizontal axis is time and the vertical axis is system state. The system state may be normal or under attack. The first (top) trace shows the attacks detected by the effective stable components. The second trace shows the attacks detected by the TTPAD encoder models. The third trace, which collects the attacks in the first and second traces, expresses the TTPAD method performance. The bottom trace shows the real attacks. The traces demonstrate that the stable and unstable features work well and they collectively improve TTPAD method performance.

Detection delay is a useful anomaly detection metric. It is defined as the latency between when an attack occurs and when the attack is reported. The delay is greater than or equal to zero by default. Figure 5 shows the detection delay statistics. The TTPAD method detects 26 attacks, 13 of them within ten seconds after the attack were launched.

Experiments were conducted to compare the TTPAD method performance against the autoencoder (AE), LSTM, PASAD and OCSVM baseline models. All the models executed in the same computing environment with an Intel I7-7700 CPU, 16 GB memory, Nvidia 3060 12 GB memory GPU, Ubuntu 20.04 LTS system, Python and the PyTorch deep learning framework.

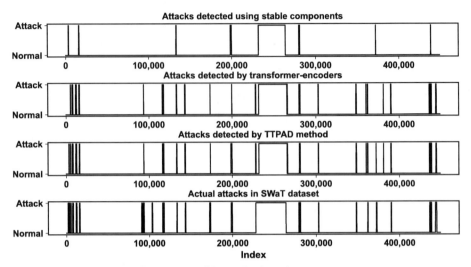

Fig. 4. TTPAD method performance.

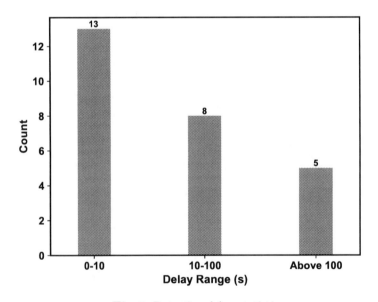

Fig. 5. Detection delay statistics.

The same training and testing data were used to create the TTPAD, AE, LSTM and OCSVM baseline models. The training data used for the PASAD baseline model comprised the last 5,000 data items intercepted from the training data.

The AE and LSTM models employed a sliding window size of 19 and a step size of one to process the training data. The encoder in the AE baseline model incorporated three fully-connected layers with output dimensions of 64, 24 and eight, respectively, and its decoder incorporated three fully-connected layers with output dimensions of 24, 64 and 19, respectively. The LSTM baseline model incorporated two LSTM layers and a hidden layer dimension (hidden size) of eight. The hyper parameters were: training epoch = 50, batch size = 512, loss function = mean squared error, optimizer = Adam and learning rate = 0.1. Training was terminated when the training error did not decrease for five consecutive epochs. The AE loss function computed the reconstruction error whereas the LSTM loss function computed the prediction error.

The PASAD model employed the official implementation [1]. As in the original paper, the length of the initial part of the time series used for training was 30,000 and the statistical dimension was 10.

OCSVM was implemented using scikit-learn, a machine learning toolset for Python. The implementation employed the rbf kernel function with a nu value of 0.0005. Since the results were too poor to be used when OCSVM models were trained by components, all 51 component values at one second were used as input (i.e., feature length = 51). Thus, traceability was not possible at the component level. After the input data was uniformly scaled, the model was trained to produce normal and attack outputs.

The precision, recall and F1-score metrics were used to evaluate anomaly detection performance:

$$\text{Precision} = \frac{\text{TP}}{\text{TP} + \text{FP}}$$

$$\text{Recall} = \frac{\text{TP}}{\text{TP} + \text{FN}}$$

$$\text{F1-Score} = 2 \times \text{Precision} \times \frac{\text{Recall}}{\text{Precision} + \text{Recall}}$$

where true positives TP is the number of attacks identified as attacks, false positives FP is the number of normal conditions identified as attacks and false negatives FN is the number of attacks identified as normal.

Table 4 compares the TTPAD method performance against the AE, LSTM, PASAD and OCSVM baseline models. It also presents the results of an ablation experiment on the TTPAD encoder model (Encoder in Table 4). OCSVM has the best precision whereas TTPAD has the best recall and F1-score. The customized encoder in TTPAD has the best F1-score among the basic classifiers. In the ablation experiment, the contribution of the stable components was incorporated, which improved the recall significantly.

Experiments were also conducted to compare the detection rate and traceability of the TTPAD method against the other baseline models. An attack was deemed to be detected successfully if, during an attack period, a model raised at least one anomaly alert. An attack was deemed to be traceable if the component

Table 4. TTPAD vs. baseline model performance comparisons.

Model	Precision	Recall	F1-Score
AE	0.8654	0.6684	0.7542
LSTM	0.8673	0.6761	0.7598
PASAD	0.7392	0.6727	0.7044
OCSVM	**0.9940**	0.6270	0.7689
Encoder	0.9233	0.6863	0.7873
TTPAD	0.9278	**0.7536**	**0.8317**

models that reported the anomalies corresponded to the components that were, in fact, attacked. The detection rate and traceability were computed as follows:

$$\text{Detection Rate} = \frac{\text{Detected Attacks}}{\text{Total Attacks}}$$
$$\text{Traceability} = \frac{\text{Traceable Attacks}}{\text{Detected Attacks}}$$

Table 5. TTPAD vs. baseline model performance comparisons.

Baseline	Total Attacks	Detected Attacks	Detection Rate	Traceable Attacks	Traceability
AE	35	13	37.14%	4	30.77%
LSTM	35	12	34.29%	7	58.33%
PASAD	35	2	5.71%	0	0.00%
OCSVM	35	5	14.29%	0	0.00%
TTPAD	35	**26**	**74.29%**	**21**	**80.77%**

Table 5 compares the attack detection and traceability results for the TTPAD method against the four baseline models. The results reveal that the TTPAD method has by far the best attack detection ability and traceability.

5   Conclusions

The TTPAD method leverages unsupervised learning using industrial control system component time series data. Customized transformer-encoder classifiers are created for unstable industrial system components and the classifier outputs are ensembled to identify anomalies. Features of stable components such as backup pumps are also leveraged to enhance anomaly detection. Experiments with SWaT testbed data indicate that the method achieves good performance compared with baseline models with respect to false positive rates, detection delays and traceability. However, the current transformer-encoder model design is not good at fitting discrete data. Future research will attempt to address this issue.

References

1. W. Aoudi, M. Iturbe and M. Almgren, Truth will out: Departure-based process-level detection of stealthy attacks on control systems, *Proceedings of the ACM SIGSAC Conference on Computer and Communications Security*, pp. 817–831, 2018.
2. M. Balaji, S. Shrivastava, S. Adepu and A. Mathur, Super detector: An ensemble approach for anomaly detection in industrial control systems, *Proceedings of the Sixteenth International Conference on Critical Information Infrastructures Security*, pp. 24–43, 2021.
3. S. Chauhan and L. Vig, Anomaly detection in ECG time signals via deep long short-term memory networks, *Proceedings of the IEEE International Conference on Data Science and Advanced Analytics*, 2015.
4. J. Goh, S. Adepu, K. Junejo and A. Mathur, A dataset to support research in the design of secure water treatment systems, *Proceedings of the Eleventh International Conference on Critical Information Infrastructures Security*, pp. 88–99, 2017.
5. J. Hamilton, *Time Series Analysis*, Princeton University Press, Princeton, New Jersey, 1994.
6. V. Krishna, R. Iyer and W. Sanders, ARIMA-based modeling and validation of consumption readings in power grids, *Proceedings of the Tenth International Conference on Critical Information Infrastructures Security*, pp. 199–210, 2016.
7. P. Malhotra, A. Ramakrishnan, G. Anand, L. Vig, P. Agarwal and G. Shroff, LSTM-Based Encoder-Decoder for Multi-Sensor Anomaly Detection, arXiv: 1607.00148v2 (arxiv.org/abs/1607.00148), 2016.
8. A. Mathur and N. Tippenhauer, SWaT: A water treatment testbed for research and training in ICS security, *Proceedings of the International Workshop on Cyber-Physical Systems for Smart Water Networks*, pp. 31–36, 2016.
9. M. Raman, W. Dong and A. Mathur, Deep autoencoders as anomaly detectors: Method and case study in a distributed water treatment plant, *Computers and Security*, vol. 99, article no. 102055, 2020.
10. M. Raman and A. Mathur, A hybrid physics-based data-driven framework for anomaly detection in industrial control systems, *IEEE Transactions on Systems, Man and Cybernetics: Systems*, vol. 52(9), pp. 6003–6014, 2022.
11. M. Raman, N. Somu and A. Mathur, Anomaly detection in critical infrastructure using a probabilistic neural network, *Proceedings of the Tenth International Conference on Applications and Techniques in Information Security*, pp. 129–141, 2019.
12. K. Stouffer, J. Falco and K. Scarfone, Guide to Industrial Control Systems (ICS) Security, NIST Special Publication 800-82, Gaithersburg, Maryland, 2011.
13. A. Vaswani, N. Shazeer, N. Parmar, J. Uszkoreit, L. Jones, A. Gomez, L. Kaiser and I. Polosukhin, Attention is all you need, *Proceedings of the Thirtieth Annual Conference on Neural Information Processing Systems*, pp. 5998–6008, 2017.

14. Y. Wei, K. Chow and S. Yiu, Insider threat detection using multi-autoencoder filtering and unsupervised learning, in *Advances in Digital Forensics XVI*, G. Peterson and S. Shenoi (Eds.), Springer, Cham, Switzerland, pp. 273–290, 2020.
15. H. Wijaya, M. Aniche and A. Mathur, Domain-based fuzzing for supervised learning of anomaly detection in cyber-physical systems, *Proceedings of the Forty-Second IEEE/ACM International Conference on Software Engineering Workshops*, pp. 237–244, 2020.
16. K. Yau, K. Chow and S. Yiu, Detecting attacks on a water treatment system using one-class support vector machines, in *Advances in Digital Forensics XVI*, G. Peterson and S. Shenoi (Eds.), Springer, Cham, Switzerland, pp. 95–108, 2020.
17. H. Zhou, S. Zhang, J. Peng, S. Zhang, J. Li, H. Xiong and W. Zhang, Informer: Beyond efficient transformer for long-sequence time-series forecasting, *Proceedings of the Thirty-Fifth AAAI Conference on Artificial Intelligence*, pp. 11106–11115, 2021.

Legal Issues and Applications

Evolution of Global Digital Forensics Laws and Emergent Challenges

Kaushik Thinnaneri Ganesan

Central Board of Indirect Taxes and Customs, Ministry of Finance, Mumbai, India
kaushik.tg@gov.in

Abstract. The proliferation of digital devices in the commission of crimes has presented unique challenges to law enforcement the world over. Academia and industry have developed tools to assist law enforcement in conducting digital forensic investigations. However, inadequate awareness of the legal provisions on the part of law enforcement and the absence of updated laws have resulted in situations where, despite the availability of technological support, offenders could not be prosecuted. It would also be productive if academia and industry could become more aware of the legal provisions governing electronic evidence and the legal challenges to technological solutions.

This chapter discusses the evolution of global laws pertaining to digital forensics with a focus on the admissibility of evidence derived from digital forensic procedures. The chapter also examines emergent challenges in digital forensics and efforts to enhance global cooperation.

Keywords: Laws · Cyber Crime · Electronic Evidence · Law Enforcement · Investigations

1 Introduction

The role of digital forensics in civil and criminal investigations has increased dramatically during the last decade. While law enforcement personnel recognize the importance of digital forensics, there appears to be a significant gap in following procedures laid out in the law for handling digital devices to ensure that the data obtained is admissible as evidence in court. Some of this is because applicable laws enacted some years ago may not address modern scenarios. Meanwhile, countries around the globe handle matters pertaining to electronic evidence in myriad ways.

This chapter pursues a holistic view of laws pertaining to digital forensics and the admissibility of electronic evidence in the United States, United Kingdom and India, with a more detailed analysis of Indian laws. Also, it critically analyzes emergent challenges in digital forensics from a policy perspective and what could be done to address them globally.

G. Peterson and S. Shenoi (Eds.): DigitalForensics 2023, IFIP AICT 687, pp. 237–248, 2023.
https://doi.org/10.1007/978-3-031-42991-0_13

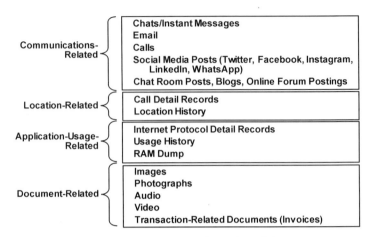

Fig. 1. Information obtained via digital forensics.

2   Legal and Policy Issues

One might question the importance of legal and policy perspectives in digital forensics, which has become an intensely technical field involving state-of-the-art technological developments and cutting-edge research that power innovations in the field. However, the law enforcement perspective can help academicians and researchers better appreciate the challenges in translating technological advancements to perceptible actions by law enforcement, who are the principal beneficiaries of digital forensics research and development. For much too long, the legal and technological domains have not moved forward at the same pace. The unfortunate reality has prevented technological improvements in digital forensics from fully benefiting law enforcement. This chapter attempts to bridge the gap by raising awareness about legal and policy issues that govern the use of digital forensics by law enforcement and exploring legal solutions that could be devised to overcome the technological challenges.

3   Investigations

In an era where technology has become ubiquitous across society, offenses – whether cyber crime, murder, arson, tax fraud or smuggling – invariably involve the use of digital devices. This is because communications are *sine qua non* in the commission of most offenses, which makes it imperative to use digital devices. Indeed, digital forensics helps investigators ascertain one or more of the four key roles in the commission of offenses: planning, coordination, execution and transportation.

Figure 1 shows the information gleaned during investigations via digital forensics. The four information types include communications-related, location-related, application-usage-related and document-related information.

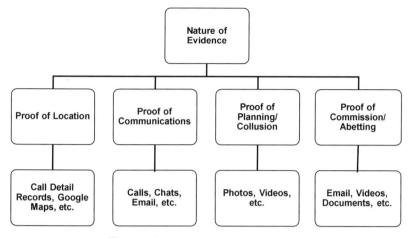

Fig. 2. Nature of electronic evidence.

Figure 2 shows the nature of electronic evidence that is gleaned during investigations via digital forensics. The four main categories are proof of location, proof of communications, proof of planning and/or collusion, and proof of commission and/or abetting.

4   Legal Provisions on Evidence Admissibility

Five fundamental rules relating to electronic evidence must be addressed by legal frameworks:

- **Admissibility:** Can data found on digital devices be used as evidence in a court of law?
- **Authenticity:** Does electronic evidence establish the facts in an indisputable manner?
- **Completeness:** Does electronic evidence convey the complete story without any gaps?
- **Reliability:** Was the manner in which electronic evidence was gathered beyond all doubt?
- **Believability:** Is the theory propounded by electronic evidence persuasive about the facts it represents?

This section examines the legal provisions in the United States, United Kingdom and India with regard to the five fundamental rules pertaining to electronic evidence.

4.1   United States Legal Provisions

Legal issues pertaining to the admissibility of electronic evidence in the United States are primarily governed by the Federal Rules of Evidence [25]. Rules 104(a) and 104(b) provide the underlying principles prior to proceeding to electronic evidence authentication. Rule 104(a) gives the judge the power to decide on the admissibility of evidence and covers questions such as whether a witness is qualified, whether a privilege exists, whether evidence is relevant, whether it constitutes hearsay, etc. Building on Rule 104(a), Rule 104(b) stipulates that "[w]hen the relevance of evidence depends on whether a fact exists, proof must be introduced sufficient to support a finding that the fact does exist. The court may admit the proposed evidence on the condition that the proof be introduced later."

Rule 702 requires that scientific and expert testimony must be reliable with respect to the principles and methods used by experts as well as the application of the principles and methods to the specific facts. The original test for admissibility of scientific evidence is the Frye test (Frye v. United States, 1923) [24]. The Frye test allows scientific evidence to be admitted if the science upon which it rests is generally accepted by the scientific community.

The Federal Rules of Evidence as amended with effect from December 1, 2017 [11] recognize the availability of more than one option to a party seeking to produce electronic records. Under the amended rules, a party can follow the traditional route under Rule 901 or the route of self-authentication under Rule 902 under which a certificate of authenticity is required. If a party chooses not to claim the benefit of self-authentication, the party is free to come under Rule 901, even if the evidence sought to be adduced is stored electronically. To establish that an evidentiary item is authentic, Rule 901(a) requires that a proponent must produce admissible evidence "sufficient to support a finding that the item is what the proponent claims it is." Rule 901(b) provides examples of evidence that satisfy the standard of proof for establishing authenticity, including testimony of a witness with knowledge, circumstantial evidence and evidence describing a process or system that shows it produces an accurate result [10].

Reference is made to Rule 902 [11] – evidence that is self-authenticating and, especially, to sub-rules of Rule 902. Rule 902(13) allows the use of a certification to authenticate evidence generated by an electronic process or system (e.g., website content, data generated by an app or electronic entry/exit records in a security system). Rule 902(14) authorizes a certification to authenticate a digital copy of data taken from a device or system (e.g., mobile phone or hard drive).

The U.S. Rules of Evidence enumerate how electronic records are required to be certified and where certificates are required to make them admissible in a court of law. However, the rules do not specify the types of records that are covered. Furthermore, they leave open the question of who is competent to issue the required certification.

4.2   United Kingdom Legal Provisions

The United Kingdom was one of the first countries in the world to pass legislation pertaining to the admissibility of electronic evidence. Section 5 of the United Kingdom Civil Evidence Act of 1968 deals with the admissibility of statements produced by computers [21]. This act has since been replaced by the United Kingdom Civil Evidence Act of 1995 that permits hearsay evidence [22].

Electronic evidence is accepted in civil and criminal trials in the United Kingdom. With regard to the actual evidence stored on digital devices, computer records are admissible as evidence in court by virtue of Section 3 of the Civil Evidence Act of 1995 [22]. Under the Criminal Justice Act of 2003, the court has the discretion to refuse to admit a business or other document under certain circumstances [14]. In any case, evidence contained in a digital device can be considered to be real evidence and is generally considered to be admissible. Specifically, the Police and Criminal Evidence Act of 1984 defines electronic evidence as "all information contained in a computer" [14].

Pertinent to this discussion is the 1985 case of Castle v. Cross [17], where the court held that a printout from a computerized breath-testing device was admissible evidence. Another is the R v. Shephard case of 1988 [13] in which records from till rolls in a shop linked to a central computer were produced to prove that items in the possession of the accused had not been billed and had, therefore, been stolen by the accused. In fact, the court held that if it could be shown that the computer was functioning properly, the records could be admitted as evidence. Finally, in the Intercity Telecom Limited and Anor v. Sanjay Solanki case of 2015 [2], the court accepted evidence in the form of digital devices such as laptops, iPads and USB drives containing confidential information belonging to the company.

4.3   Indian Legal Provisions

The Indian Evidence Act of 1872 as amended is the country's primary legislation that addresses issues governing the admissibility of evidence [8]. Section 65B of the Indian Evidence Act deals with the admissibility of electronic records. However, a lesser-known fact is that the amended Indian Evidence Act was not the first piece of Indian legislation to address the issue of electronic evidence. The Customs Act of 1962 as amended, which regulates all matters of policies and duties pertaining to the importation and exportation of goods, contains a provision about the admissibility of microfilms, facsimile copies of documents and computer printouts as documents and as evidence [7]. In fact, Section 138 of the Customs Act could be read as a precursor to the current Section 65B of the Indian Evidence Act.

A similar provision exists in the amended Central Excise Act of 1944, which deals with issues pertaining to Central Government excise duties on goods manufactured or produced in certain parts of India [6]. Section 138C of the Customs Act and Section 36B of the Central Excise Act were inserted vide Notification No. 18/88-C.E. (N.T.) dated June 29, 1988 by Section 13 of the Customs and Central Excise Laws (Amendment) Act of 1988 (Act 29 of 1988). However, Section 65B of the Indian Evidence Act was inserted vide Section 92 of the Information Technology Act of 2000 (Act 21 of 2000) [9]. Section 397 of the Companies Act of 2013 was inserted vide S.O. 902(E) dated March 26, 2014 [4].

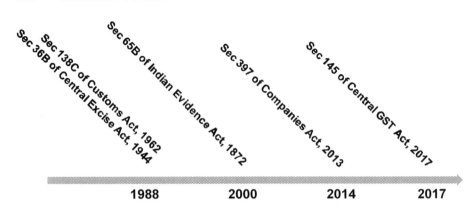

Fig. 3. Evolution of electronic evidence laws in India.

Most recently, the Central Goods and Services Tax Act of 2017, India's federal legislation providing for levy and collection of tax on the intra-state supply of goods and services, introduced a much-improved provision to address the issue of admissibility of electronic documents as evidence [5]. Figure 3 presents a timeline of the evolution of electronic evidence laws in India.

Section 138C of the Customs Act, Section 36B of the Central Excise Act and Section 65B of the Indian Evidence Act as amended have their origins in Section 5 of the United Kingdom Civil Evidence Act of 1968 [21], which was enacted in the era of mainframe computers, when personal computers were rare and the Internet and smartphones were figments of imagination. Of course, the nature of offenses that could be committed using mainframes were drastically different from the cyber crimes of today.

In 2020, the Supreme Court of India delivered a major judgment in the appellate case of Arjun Panditrao Khotkar vs. Kailash Kushanrao Gorantyal and others [19]. Specifically, the court held that "the major jurisdictions of the world have come to terms with the change of times and the development of technology and finetuned their legislations. Therefore, it is the need of the hour that there is a relook at Section 65B of the Indian Evidence Act, introduced 20 years ago, by Act 21 of 2000, and which has created huge judicial turmoil, with the law swinging from one extreme to the other in the past 15 years."

It is worth mentioning here that the most recent legislation passed on the subject of admissibility of electronic evidence, namely Section 145 of the Central Goods and Services Tax Act of 2017 [5], is a much-simplified version of the law that focuses on the main aspect of electronic evidence. In particular, it establishes the authenticity of electronic evidence by placing reliance on a certificate to identify the document containing the statement and describing the manner in which it was produced, and also giving the particulars of any device involved in producing the document. This law provides a simpler and more effective framework for dealing with electronic evidence that could be emulated by other nations to deal with the admissibility of electronic evidence.

5   Indian Challenges and Solutions

This section discusses some challenges imposed on law enforcement agencies by current laws and offers proposals for addressing the challenges.

5.1   Agency Challenges

Key challenges faced by Indian agencies include issues related to primary versus secondary evidence and practical issues encountered during investigations.

Primary and Secondary Evidence   The key provision governing all Indian laws pertaining to the admissibility of electronic evidence is the issuance of a certificate under the relevant section(s) to authenticate and/or certify the generated evidence. The Supreme Court of India has ruled that a certificate is required only when a secondary copy of evidence is relied upon and submitted as evidence in a court of law [19]. Going forward, the submission of original digital devices will be increasingly challenging due to the volatile nature of electronic data. This is exacerbated by the fact that Indian trials commence many months or years after the occurrence and detection of the actions in question.

Relying on the original devices until they are to be exhibited as evidence is problematic. One problem is that there is no guarantee that devices would function properly after the passage of time. After seizure and forensic analysis, digital devices are sealed and maintained in secure locations until trial. Digital devices typically need to be used regularly to function properly. Prolonged non-usage is likely to render the devices unusable and may even lead to data loss.

Another problem is that some courts, upon reviewing applications filed by accused parties whose devices have been seized by law enforcement agencies, have ordered that the original devices be returned to their owners after cloning the devices. The increasing emphasis on the personal rights of individuals will lead to legal challenges to the retention of original devices by law enforcement agencies and the possibility exists that device retention may even be discontinued in time.

Investigations   Prevailing Indian laws related to electronic evidence also pose practical challenges in investigations by law enforcement agencies. These challenges are faced during investigations in other countries as well:

- **Password/PIN Code Sharing:** A common problem faced by law enforcement during investigations is the non-cooperation of accused parties with regard to sharing passwords and PIN codes for unlocking digital devices. This issue came to the fore in the aftermath of the 2015 terrorist attack in San Bernardino, California, and, more recently, in the 2019 terrorist shooting incident at the Pensacola Naval Air Station in Florida. While courts have come to the aid of investigating agencies by issuing orders to enable the unlocking of phones and other digital devices, equipment manufacturers, most notably Apple, have expressed reluctance and have appealed against such orders.

- **Cloud Data Recovery:** Another major challenge faced during investigations is the recovery of data from the cloud. When accused parties refuse to cooperate in providing access to cloud data, law enforcement has no recourse but to request cloud service providers for access. Some major service providers may provide metadata. However, the vast majority of providers are located outside India, and due to the lack of jurisdiction, investigators are forced to resort to tedious and time-consuming procedures such as mutual legal assistance treaties and/or letters rogatory to legally procure cloud data. These procedures often take many years and require persistent follow-up efforts with overseas authorities. Often, even if the data is received, domestic time limits come into play. For example, a chargesheet or show cause notice may have already been filed, which invalidates the cloud data obtained from abroad from being used as evidence.

- **Deleted Data Coverage:** Modern digital forensic software helps in recovering data that has been deleted from digital devices, specifically from instant communications applications used on smartphones. However, the law is silent on whether deleted data that has been recovered is admissible in a court of law because this is due to technological developments that could not be conceived even a few years ago. Often, deleted data plays a crucial role in establishing the involvement of an individual in criminal activity. Moreover, it has been noticed by investigators that, in many cases, offenders tend to delete critical documents/chats from their smartphones to prevent law enforcement from recovering crucial evidence.

6   Proposed Solutions

The challenges and issues discussed above should be addressed more by legal solutions than technical solutions. Some proposals are:

- **Password/PIN Code Sharing:** A commonly-held misconception is that forcing an individual to part with the password or PIN code for unlocking a device is akin to forcing the individual to give evidence against himself/herself (i.e., self-incrimination). In fact, not providing a password or PIN code to enable law enforcement to conduct a legitimate investigation is more akin to withholding the key to a safe that is in the custody of an accused rather than refusing self-incrimination.

  One of the High Courts in India (just below the Supreme Court of India in the judicial hierarchy) has relied on the Indian Code of Criminal Procedure of 1973 pertaining to persons who refuse to provide access to conduct physical searches of property [12]. Using the analogy, the court ruled that a magistrate may order an individual to part with a password or pattern to enable law enforcement to conduct a search of data contained in a digital device. Similar orders have also been issued by U.S. courts to enable law enforcement to access digital devices during the course of their investigations [20].

Be that as it may, it would preferable to enact legal provisions that mandate individuals to provide passwords, PIN codes and biometric information to enable electronic evidence to be accessed during investigations conducted by authorized government agencies. This would eliminate any ambiguity with regard to cooperating with investigating agencies seeking access to evidence residing in digital devices. In the event that a digital device owner or possessor of the password, PIN code or biometric information is unavailable or unable to provide them, the original equipment manufacturer would be required to unlock the device to facilitate the investigation. A global consensus among law enforcement agencies would help achieve an amicable resolution with technology giants such as Apple after impressing upon them the need for cooperation with law enforcement worldwide.

– **Cloud Data Recovery:** Much of the cloud data sought by law enforcement around the world resides in a few countries such as Canada, United States and Ireland. Some countries have enacted or are enacting data protection legislation, but these efforts are focused more on protecting personal data than providing law enforcement with access to data during investigations involving overseas jurisdictions. Some multi-national corporations such as Google and Microsoft have begun to cooperate with overseas law enforcement agencies by providing them access to some basic data and metadata via law enforcement portals. However, this is more polite support than outright cooperation in investigations. Consequently, the utility of the basic data and metadata is limited and law enforcement agencies have to rely on the tedious and time-consuming routes of mutual legal assistance requests and letters rogatory. The U.S. Clarifying Lawful Overseas Use of Data (CLOUD) Act [15] covering cross-border access by law enforcement to electronic communications held by private companies is a major piece of legislation that facilitates U.S. law enforcement access to data located outside the United States. It is important to explore a global data-sharing agreement on the lines of the CLOUD Act to enable law enforcement around the world to access cloud data during investigations. The instruments could be amendments to existing mutual legal assistance treaties or a new multilateral treaty that deals only with the issue of sharing electronic data.

– **Deleted Data Coverage:** The term "electronic record" is defined in India's Information Technology Act of 2000 [9] as "data, record or data generated, image or sound stored, received or sent in an electronic form or microfilm or computer-generated microfiche." A plain reading of this definition seems to imply that deleted data is not covered under the ambit of an electronic record. Therefore, it would be worthwhile to consider amending the definition to include deleted data recovered using digital forensic analysis software on a digital device. Countries should also examine ways to ensure that deleted data is included in their definitions of "data" or "record" that can be used as evidence in courts of law.

7   Enhancing Global Cooperation

At its tenth session in October 2020, the Conference of the Parties to the United Nations Convention against Transnational Organized Crime adopted Resolution 10/4 that "request[ed] the United Nations Office on Drugs and Crime, within its mandate, to continue to provide technical assistance and capacity-building to member states, upon request, to support their capacity to prevent and combat transnational organized crime, including through the following: (...) (d) The updating, as necessary, of model instruments and publications, such as the guide on current practices in electronic surveillance in the investigation of serious and organized crime developed by the United Nations Office on Drugs and Crime in 2009 and the model law on mutual assistance in criminal matters developed by the Office in 2007." Subsequently, the Model Law on Mutual Assistance in Criminal Matters was amended to incorporate a section pertaining to assistance in relation to electronic evidence [23]. New provisions have been inserted about the production of stored computer data in emergency situations and relevant definitions have been updated to reflect the state of the art. New provisions concerning the treatment of electronic evidence by a nation state following a foreign request have also been inserted. This model law could be used as a reference point to amend all mutual legal assistance treaties to encourage and simplify global cooperation with regard to electronic evidence.

8   Conclusions

Information technology and electronic evidence laws are evolving and leave considerable scope for interpretation in various judicial forums. There is a long way to go before the interpretation of electronic-evidence-related aspects is uniform and open issues are settled. Therefore, the onus is on governments to draft laws and provisions that are easy to understand and use, primarily by law enforcement involved in investigations and related activities. Additionally, laws dealing with electronic evidence need to be reviewed regularly and amended to take into account technological developments and ensure that justice is served. Better and closer working relationships between researchers and law enforcement must be instituted to create blended technological and legal solutions that address emergent challenges in the digital forensics domain. It is also important to keep in mind that no matter how advanced technologies may develop, as long as allied laws pertaining to electronic evidence do not keep pace with the developments, it would not be possible for the full benefits of technological advancements to be realized in ensuring that justice is done.

The views expressed in this chapter are those of the author, and do not reflect the official policy or position of the Central Board of Indirect Taxes and Customs, Ministry of Finance or Government of India.

References

1. V. Dubey, Admissibility of electronic evidence: An Indian perspective, *Forensic Research and Criminology International Journal*, vol. 4(2), pp. 58–63, 2017.
2. England and Wales High Court (Mercantile Court), Intercity Telecom Limited and Anor v. Sanjay Solanki, London, United Kingdom, February 27, 2015.
3. S. Goodison, R. Davis and B. Jackson, Digital Evidence and the U.S. Criminal Justice System, RAND Corporation, Santa Monica, California (www.jstor.org/stable/10.7249/j.ctt15sk8v3), 2015.
4. Government of India, The Companies Act, 2013 (as amended), New Delhi, India (www.indiacode.nic.in/bitstream/123456789/2114/1/A2013-18.pdf), July 7, 2022.
5. Government of India, The Central Goods and Services Tax Act, 2017 (as amended), New Delhi, India (www.indiacode.nic.in/bitstream/123456789/15689/1/A2017-12.pdf), October 1, 2022.
6. Government of India, The Central Excise Act, 1944 (as amended), New Delhi, India (www.indiacode.nic.in/bitstream/123456789/19238/1/a1944-01.pdf), 2023.
7. Government of India, The Customs Act, 1962 (as amended), New Delhi, India (www.indiacode.nic.in/bitstream/123456789/2475/1/a1962-52.pdf), 2023.
8. Government of India, The Indian Evidence Act, 1872 (as amended), New Delhi, India (www.indiacode.nic.in/bitstream/123456789/2188/1/A1872-1.pdf), 2023.
9. Government of India, The Information Technology Act, 2000 (as amended), New Delhi, India (www.indiacode.nic.in/bitstream/123456789/1999/1/a2000-21.pdf), 2023.
10. P. Grimm, D. Capra and G. Joseph, Authenticating digital evidence, *Baylor Law Review*, vol. 69(1), pp. 1–55, 2017.
11. G. Joseph, Self-Authentication of Electronic Evidence: New Rules 902(13)–(14) (www.txs.uscourts.gov/sites/txs/files/Self-Authentication%20of%20Electronic%20Evidence%20-%20New%20Rules%20-%20G.Joseph.pdf), 2018.
12. Karnataka High Court, Virendra Khanna vs. State of Karnataka, Writ Petition no. 11759/2020, Bengaluru, India, March 12, 2021.
13. Law Teacher, R v. Shepherd – 1988, Nottingham, United Kingdom (www.lawteacher.net/cases/r-v-shepherd.php?vref=1), June 27, 2019.
14. A. Mohamad, Admissibility and authenticity of electronic evidence in the courts of Malaysia and United Kingdom, *International Journal of Law, Government and Communication*, vol. 4(15), pp. 121–129.
15. S. Mulligan, Law Enforcement Access to Overseas Data Under the CLOUD Act, Report no. LSB10125, Congressional Research Service, Washington, DC, 2018.
16. S. Piasecki, Legal admissibility of electronic records as evidence and implications for records management, *The American Archivist*, vol. 58(1), pp. 54–64, 1995.
17. Queen's Bench Division, Castle v. Cross, *All England Law Reports*, vol. 87, 1985.
18. L. Romano, Electronic evidence and the Federal Rules, *Loyola of Los Angeles Law Review*, vol. 38(4), pp. 1745–1802, 2005.
19. Supreme Court of India, Arjun Panditrao Khotkar vs. Kailash Kushanrao Gorantyal and others, Civil Appeal nos. 20825–20826 of 2017, 2407 of 2018 and 3696 of 2018, New Delhi, India, July 14, 2020.
20. Supreme Court of Minnesota, State of Minnesota v. Matthew Vaughn Diamond, Docket no. A15-2075, Minneapolis, Minnesota, January 17, 2018.
21. United Kingdom Government, Civil Evidence Act 1968, London, United Kingdom (www.legislation.gov.uk/ukpga/1968/64/contents), 1968.

22. United Kingdom Government, Civil Evidence Act 1995, London, United Kingdom (www.legislation.gov.uk/ukpga/1995/38/contents), 1995.
23. United Nations Commission on Crime Prevention and Criminal Justice, Model Law on Mutual Assistance in Criminal Matters (2007) as Amended with Provisions on Electronic Evidence and the Use of Special Investigative Techniques, Document E/CN.15/2022/CRP.6, Vienna, Austria (www.unodc.org/documents/commissions/CCPCJ/CCPCJ_Sessions/CCPCJ_31/CRP/E_CN15_2022_CRP6_e_V2202980.pdf), 2022.
24. United States Circuit Court of Appeals (DC Circuit), Frye v. United States, *Federal Reporter*, vol. 293, pp. 1013–1014, 1923.
25. United States Government, Federal Rules of Evidence, Washington, DC (www.law.cornell.edu/rules/fre), December 1, 2020.

A Blockchain Model for Sharing Information in Criminal Justice Systems

Pardon Ramazhamba[1] and Hein Venter[2]

[1] Council for Scientific and Industrial Research, Pretoria, South Africa
pramazhamba@csir.co.za
[2] University of Pretoria, Pretoria, South Africa

Abstract. Criminal justice systems around the world encounter missing case dockets and digital evidence. Problems are also posed by the mechanisms used to share criminal case data, especially email and paper documents that provide exposure to illegal data alteration.
This chapter describes a blockchain model for sharing criminal case data securely and efficiently with authorized criminal justice system entities. The model is implemented using Hyperledger Fabric and promising results were obtained during the simulation experiments. The model enables entities to access criminal case data in real time, which helps speed up the delivery of justice. Moreover, the model improves collaboration among the various entities, especially when it comes to joint operations and investigations involving law enforcement and prosecutors. The model also stores credible evidence because the underlying data is immutable and cannot be deleted.

Keywords: Criminal Justice System · Digital Evidence Sharing · Blockchain

1 Introduction

Information and communications technologies have significantly advanced the collection, storage, processing and analysis of digital information. Interactions with digital information tend to leave digital footprints or evidence of what happened, when and where. When a crime is committed, a forensic investigator creates a report that seeks to ascertain what occurred, where it occurred, when it occurred and who might be involved, and suggests why it occurred and attempts to explain how it occurred. These issues play critical roles in the criminal justice process because they seek to prove that a subject is linked to a specific criminal activity. Preserving such crucial information that may convict or acquit a subject requires innovative information and communications technology solutions that are secure and efficient.

In parliamentary questioning, the South African Police Service revealed that 688 criminal case dockets went missing in the period between April 2008 and February 2009 [10]. The South African Police Service rolled out its Integrated Case and Docket Management System to address the problems posed by lost

© IFIP International Federation for Information Processing 2023
Published by Springer Nature Switzerland AG 2023
G. Peterson and S. Shenoi (Eds.): DigitalForensics 2023, IFIP AICT 687, pp. 249–266, 2023.
https://doi.org/10.1007/978-3-031-42991-0_14

or stolen case dockets or evidence. In 2020, a docket archive store assessment conducted by the South African Department of Community Safety reported that approximately 63% of the case dockets in the Western Cape were lost in the archiving system and 14% of the dockets were lost in court [17, 25]. Also in 2020, the South African Broadcasting Corporation reported that almost 400 corruption, theft and fraud cases involving the South African Police Service were under investigation [22]. In 2022, Carte Blanche [5] reported that case dockets were sold by a corrupt South African Police Service official before they could be entered into the Integrated Case and Docket Management System.

These reports and others indicate that a different approach is required to ensure that criminal case data and digital evidence are secure and shareable. Indeed, The Sunday Times (South Africa) [10] reported that the Integrated Case and Docket Management System did not curb the loss or theft of case dockets in certain high-profile criminal cases. In other instances, case data was unavailable because the applications were designed to share information in a centralized manner. However, decentralization using gateway ports enables nefarious individuals to secretly share information with interested parties outside organizational boundaries.

This chapter proposes a blockchain model for securely preserving and sharing criminal case data during its lifecycle with all the entities in the South African criminal justice system. The novelty of the model lies in its integration of blockchain technology with the applications used by South African criminal justice system entities.

2   Background

This section presents a conceptual model of the South African criminal justice system and describes the blockchain technology employed in this work.

2.1   Conceptual Model

The South African criminal justice system covers the eight processes shown in Figure 1, where each process may involve one or more entities. The first process is the commission of a crime (1) that is reported to the South African Police Service (2). The South African Police Service then opens a criminal case docket and assigns it to an investigating officer. During the investigation process (3), witnesses are identified, evidence is acquired, secured and analyzed, and the accused individual is identified. The accused individual is then arrested by the South African Police Service and detained or released on bail (4).

The arrest and subsequent detention or release of an accused individual involve other entities as required by the South African Constitution. The participating entities include the National Prosecuting Authority (NPA), Department of Justice and Constitutional Development (DJCD), Legal Aid South Africa (LASA) and Department of Social Development (DSD). The National Prosecuting Authority handles the prosecution. The Department of Justice and Constitutional Development handles the court proceedings [7]. Legal Aid South Africa

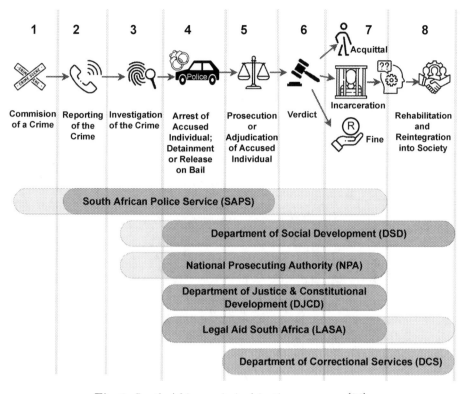

Fig. 1. South African criminal justice processes [24].

assists individuals who cannot afford legal representation. The Department of Social Development handles social support programs for vulnerable individuals such as victims of crime, poor people, elderly people and children.

The fifth process (5) is the prosecution of the accused individual, which may involve adjudication instead of a trial. The National Prosecuting Authority accepts the case for prosecution if the evidence is strong enough for court proceedings. This leads to the accused individual being handed over to the Department of Correctional Services (DCS) for pre-trial detention, if necessary [6]. The next process is the trial in a court of law that concludes with a verdict (6), resulting in one of three outcomes, acquittal, incarceration or fine (7). The Department of Correctional Services is responsible for incarcerating the convicted individual as well as providing post-sentence rehabilitation and reintegration into society (8).

The six entities use various applications to interact with criminal case data:

- The South African Police Service uses its Integrated Case and Docket Management System to maintain and manage case dockets and forensic evidence.
- The National Prosecuting Authority uses its Electronic Case Management System (ECMS) to handle cases that are ready for prosecution.

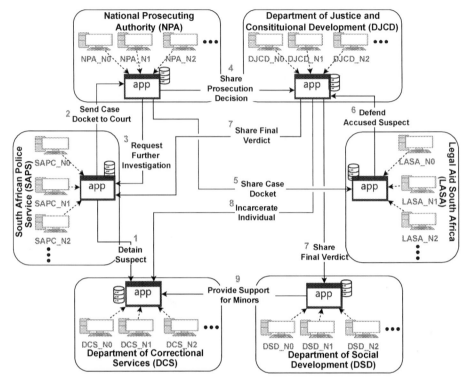

Fig. 2. Integrated South African justice system.

- The Department of Justice and Constitutional Development uses its Integrated Case Management System (ICMS) for court proceedings.
- Legal Aid South Africa uses its Electronic Legal Aid Application (eLAA) to assist individuals who cannot afford legal representation.
- The Department of Social Development uses its Child Protection Register (CPR) to assist individuals younger than 18 years old.
- The Department of Correctional Services uses its Integrated Inmate Management System (IIMS) to manage incarceration and post-sentence rehabilitation and reintegration into society.

Figure 2 presents a conceptual view of the integrated South African justice system. The solid lines represent the information flows in the integrated justice system whereas the dotted lines represent information flows of the applications used by the various entities in the integrated justice system. Key to the integration is a gateway portal that shares criminal case data with authorized entities.

2.2   Blockchain Technology

Blockchain technology is employed to implement distributed shared ledger systems that store diverse assets and transactions [9]. Blockchain technology is part of the larger class of distributed ledger technology (DLT) that employs distributed ledger systems to store and share information with various entities. Specifically, blockchain technology groups transactions into blocks that are linked in a chain-like data structure called a blockchain. The principal advantage of distributed ledger technology is that it automatically eliminates problems associated with single points of failure experienced by centralized systems. In a criminal case data management scenario, distributed ledger technology also eliminates problems posed by an entity with centralized power over the data, especially when the entity is reluctant to share the data with other entities. For example, a prosecutor with the National Prosecuting Authority may be reluctant to share information about an accused individual with a representative from Legal Aid South Africa who is assisting the individual with his/her legal defense.

Another benefit of distributed ledger technology is that it enforces trust among entities even when they do not trust each other. This is because all the network nodes provide access to the same data as identical copies of the ledger containing criminal case data are replicated across multiple geographical locations [23]. Therefore, it would not be possible to alter data without it being detected. Distributed ledger technology employs cryptographic techniques to add and append new transactions to achieve the immutability of data across the network. Every interaction stores information governed by its smart contract that self-executes whenever the conditions associated with a transaction are met.

Several blockchain frameworks such as Bitcoin, Ethereum, Quorum, HydraChain, Hyperledger Fabric (HLF) and MultiChain are used in distributed ledger systems. However, some of the frameworks, namely Bitcoin, Ethereum, Quorum, HydraChain and MultiChain, employ cryptocurrency or mining algorithms to add new transactions to the network. The proposed solution seeks to share criminal case data among entities that are known to each other. Therefore, a private blockchain that does not use cryptocurrency or mining algorithms to add new transactions is adequate.

Hyperledger Fabric was chosen to implement the proposed integrated justice system. Hyperledger Fabric is a private blockchain framework that implements cross-industry blockchain solutions [15]. Hyperledger Fabric employs a membership service provider feature that enrolls participants. Its distributed ledger system incorporates two components, a world state (WS) and transaction log (TL) [13]. The world state stores the data that describes the network state whereas the transaction log records all the transactions that manifest the current state of the ledger.

3   ShareCrimE Model

Figure 3 presents an overview of the proposed blockchain-based ShareCrimE model for sharing criminal case data. The model comprises four components:

- **Users/Agents:** Users and agents are members of the entities that play critical roles in the South African criminal justice system.

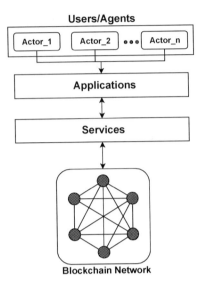

Fig. 3. ShareCrimE model.

- **Applications:** Applications are mechanisms employed by users/agents to interact with the ShareCrimE model.
- **Services:** Services are mechanisms used by applications to interact with the data stored in the blockchain network in the ShareCrimE model.
- **Blockchain Network:** The blockchain network stores and distributes criminal case data to nodes in the ShareCrimE model.

Five steps are involved in creating the ShareCrimE model: (i) identifying users/agents, (ii) establishing applications, (iii) establishing services, (iv) establishing the blockchain network and (v) integrating the four components created in the previous four steps in the ShareCrimE model.

3.1 Identifying Users/Agents

This step identifies the users/agents in the ShareCrimE model. The South African criminal justice system has six types of users/agents (i.e., entities) that have specific roles in the ShareCrimE model:

- **South African Police Service:** Creates or scans criminal case dockets, appends digital evidence, shares and accesses criminal case data.
- **National Prosecuting Authority:** Creates chargesheets, and shares and accesses criminal case data.
- **Department of Justice and Constitutional Development:** Enters verdicts, and shares and accesses criminal case data.
- **Legal Aid South Africa:** Accesses criminal case data and verdicts, and shares some data with the National Prosecuting Authority.

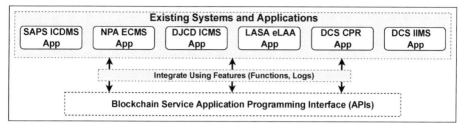

Fig. 4. ShareCrimE model application layer.

- **Department of Social Development:** Accesses criminal case data to identify the victims associated with criminal cases.
- **Department of Correctional Services:** Accesses criminal case data and verdicts.

3.2   Establishing Applications

This step identifies the applications employed by users/agents to interact with criminal case data and digital evidence. Figure 4 shows the applications in the ShareCrimE model application layer. The applications are integrated with the blockchain service application programming interface (API) using features such as functions and logs. Integrating the currently-used applications instead of creating new applications saves considerable time and money. The integration also facilitates the implementation of data security. The data stored in the model can be trusted because it is immutable by default, meaning that it cannot be changed or altered for unauthorized purposes.

3.3   Establishing Services

This step identifies the services that implement the interactions between the application layer and blockchain network. The services include identity management, wallet management and network gateway:

- **Identity Management:** This service manages the identities of various resources (e.g., nodes, applications and administrators) in the ShareCrimE model [14]. Each resource is associated with a digital identity or certificate that is used by the blockchain network to control access. Note that the membership service provider in Hyperledger Fabric uses X.509 certificates as identities that rely on a public key infrastructure (PKI) hierarchical model [14].
- **Wallet Management:** This service manages the identities of users/agents that participate in the blockchain network [11]. The service is embedded in the applications employed by users/agents as they interact with the network. The process is initiated when a user/agent logs into an application

and submits valid credentials to connect with the blockchain network via a specific channel associated with its identity. The channel is essentially a private blockchain overlay that enables a user/agent to share data secretly.

- **Network Gateway:** This service manages all the interactions between the blockchain network and applications employed by users/agents [11]. Note that an application uses a connection profile to configure a gateway that handles its interactions because it describes a set of components associated with various nodes (i.e., peer nodes and ordering nodes) and certificate authorities [11]. Additionally, the connection profile contains the channel and information about users/agents that use the components [11]. The certificate authority issues public key infrastructure certificates to users/agents.

3.4   Establishing the Blockchain Network

Figure 5 shows the blockchain network used by the ShareCrimE model. The network comprises four components, certificate authorities, raft ordering service, main channel and peer nodes:

- **Certificate Authorities:** The ShareCrimE model comprises six certificate authorities corresponding to the six entities: South African Police Service (SAPS_CA), National Prosecuting Authority (NPA_CA), Department of Justice and Constitutional Development (DJCD_CA), Legal Aid South Africa (LASA_CA), Department of Social Development (DCS_CA) and Department of Correctional Services (DSD_CA).
- **Raft Ordering Service:** The ShareCrimE model comprises six ordering nodes (node_1, ..., node_6). The raft ordering service collects all the transactions in the network and groups them into blocks [13].
- **Main Channel:** The ShareCrimE model has one main channel that connects to the raft ordering service and six entity domains, integrating the various peer nodes belonging to the six domains. The main channel provides mechanisms that enable the entities to share criminal case data securely and use the private blockchain configurations efficiently. In particular, the channel uses the raft ordering service to group its transactions into blocks and distribute the blocks to relevant peer nodes in the blockchain network.
- **Peer Nodes:** Each entity has six peer nodes, all six connected with their domains and three of the nodes connected directly to the main channel. The 18 peer nodes connected directly to the main channel are called anchor peer nodes because they can send data outside their domain boundaries (e.g., sharing data in nodes in the South African Police Service domain with nodes in the National Prosecuting Authority domain) [13].

An anchor peer node is like a TV anchor who sits in a studio, collects the latest news feeds from journalists in various locations and broadcasts the news to viewers. For example, nodes SAPS_P1, SAPS_P2 and SAPS_P3 may be anchor peers whereas nodes SAPS_P4, SAPS_P5 and SAPS_P6 may be normal peer nodes. Note that all the peer nodes, including anchor peer nodes, have smart contracts and distributed ledger systems. This setup applies to all the entities in the blockchain network.

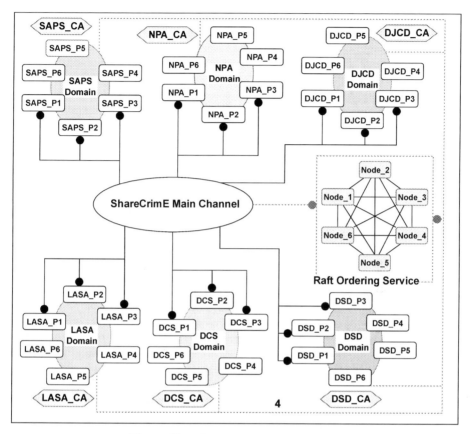

Fig. 5. ShareCrimE blockchain network.

3.5   Integrating Model Components

Figure 6 shows a high-level representation of the ShareCrimE model obtained by integrating the users/agents, applications, services and blockchain network established in the first four steps. The information flows start when users/agents submit criminal case data using various applications. The ShareCrimE model functionality is embedded in these applications via mechanisms such as features and functions. The identities of users/agents that request access to data in the ShareCrimE model are verified by services to ensure data confidentiality, integrity and availability. The blockchain network used by the ShareCrimE model comprises six certificate authorities, a raft ordering service and 36 peer nodes.

4   ShareCrimE Model Design

This section discusses two key elements of the ShareCrimE model design, information flows and main channel sequence diagram.

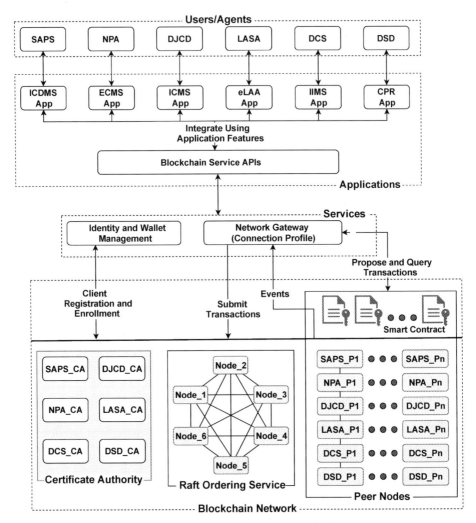

Fig. 6. High-level ShareCrimE model.

4.1   Information Flows

Figure 7 shows the information flows in the ShareCrimE model, including how the components interact with criminal case data and how digital forensic evidence is accessed. The information flows begin when users/agents submit their transactions to the blockchain network in the ShareCrimE model. Transactions are accepted by the ShareCrimE model upon checking that they meet all the predefined conditions stipulated in their smart contracts. Following this, the raft ordering service collects all the accepted transactions, groups them into a block and distributes them to all the nodes in the network. As mentioned above, the distributed ledger system has two components, a world state and a transaction

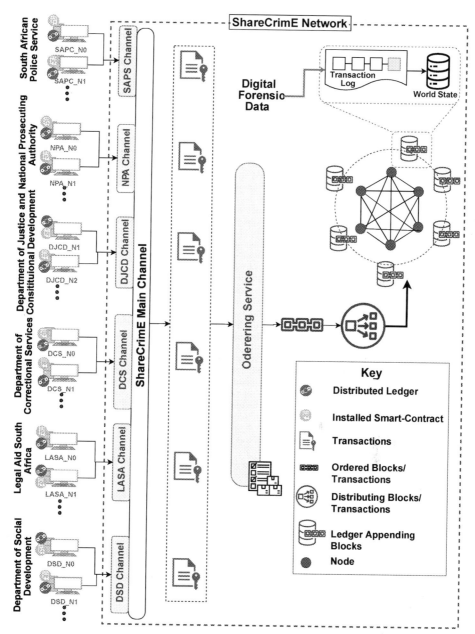

Fig. 7. ShareCrimE model information flows.

log. The world state stores the data that has resulted in the current state of the network whereas the transaction log stores data that can be used by forensic investigators or other actors to verify what has transpired for a particular crim-

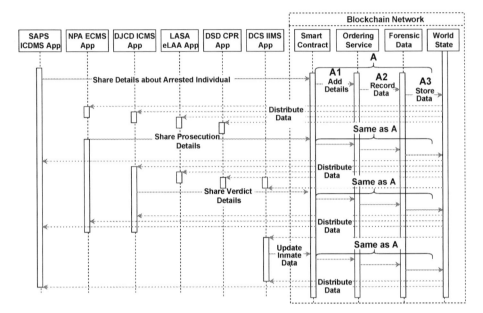

Fig. 8. Main channel sequence diagram.

inal case. Transaction log data is available to law enforcement agencies as well as lawyers and judges.

4.2   Main Channel Sequence Diagram

Figure 8 shows a sequence diagram associated with the main channel. The main channel shares criminal case data among applications used by different entities. The SAPS app in the figure shares criminal case data about arrested individuals. The process of sharing starts when the SAPS app seeks to create or share criminal case data pertaining to an individual under arrest. Note that all the accepted transactions associated with the arrest are grouped into blocks (represented by A1) and distributed to all the nodes in the network. The transactions are stored in transaction logs (represented by A2) and the actual data is stored in the world state (represented by A3). Thereafter, the NPA app shares the prosecution details associated with the same criminal case. The recording and storing of evidence is handled by the blockchain network in the same way as shown for the SAPS app.

After sharing the prosecution details with relevant entities, the DJCD app shares the verdict by submitting it with a smart contract. Next, the blockchain network handles another process involving digital evidence storage and distributes the details to other entities. After the verdict provided by the DJCD app is associated with the incarceration, the details of the individual are shared with the DCS app, including the sentence given to the individual. The DCS app

---

Algorithm 1: ShareCrimE model algorithm.

Data: Criminal Case Reports with Digital Evidence
Result: Criminal Case Data Shared with Authorized Entities
Initialize Criminal Case (Report Crime to SAPS) ← 0
if *Establishing Blockchain Network* **then**
  | Configuration Results
end
if *Interacting with Blockchain Network (Operational Results)* **then**
  | **if** *Criminal Case is not yet opened* **then**
  | | Open/Create Criminal Case and add it to the Blockchain Network
  | **end**
  | **else**
  | | Enable Various Nodes to Access or Query Criminal Case Reports
  | | **if** *Update Criminal Case Data* **then**
  | | | Update Assigned Reporter/Investigator
  | | | Update Criminal Case Reports
  | | **end**
  | | Query Criminal Case History
  | **end**
end

---

then shares its records with all its members and the SAPS app as part of its role to maintain the records of its inmates.

5 ShareCrimE Prototype Results

A ShareCrimE model prototype was implemented using Hyperledger Fabric v2.2 on a virtual machine with two CPU cores, 6 GB RAM and 60 GB secondary storage. Note that Hyperledger Fabric requires the installation of several packages as prerequisites [12]. After all the prerequisites were met and Hyperledger Fabric was executing, the implementation of the ShareCrimE network was initiated and various processes were executed.

Algorithm 1 specifies the processes involved in the ShareCrimE model simulation. Various results are generated during the simulation. Some results are associated with configuring the blockchain network whereas others are associated with the operation of the ShareCrimE model. The algorithm only produces the results generated during the operational testing phase that involves the creation, modification and querying of criminal case data.

Figure 9 shows the results generated by the two types of query operations, query updated criminal case data and query criminal case history. Query updated criminal case data yields the latest results or updates added to the blockchain network whereas query criminal case history yields the results of all the transactions that sought to create or modify criminal case data in the blockchain network. The results of transactions are marked using TxId in the figure. Lines 380–390 in Figure 9 specify a function used by two peer nodes (Peer0 of DCS and

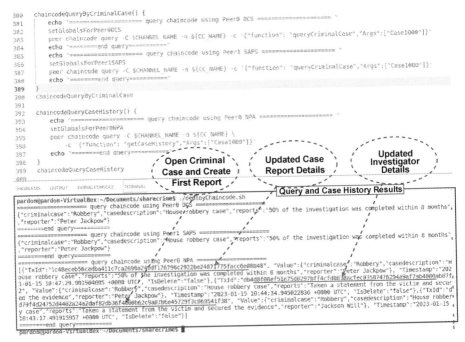

Fig. 9. ShareCrimE model results.

Peer1 of SAPS) to query the latest results of criminal case Case1000. Lines 392–399 specify a function used by Peer0 of NPA to query the entire history of the criminal case Case1000. The results generated by these functions are depicted as query and case history results. The query criminal case history outlines three transactions used to create or modify data stored in the blockchain network.

6   Evaluation

This section discusses the benefits and limitations of the ShareCrimE model.

Benefits The ShareCrimE model provides enhanced information security. The mechanisms used to secure criminal case data from unauthorized parties include the use of a distributed ledger system, cryptography, secure communications channels, timestamps and immutable transactions.

Increased transparency is provided by the distributed nature of the model and the processes used to create and modify criminal case data. Creation or modification of criminal case data by rogue parties would be visible because all the authorized entities have access to the entire criminal case data history. This also ensures the integrity of the stored data and evidence.

The ShareCrimE model supports parallel, real-time investigations by the South African Police Service and National Prosecuting Authority. It reduces delays because the National Prosecuting Authority can rapidly determine if case dockets are ready for trial. Additionally, all the authorized entities have seamless access to criminal case data that enables them to complete their reports quickly, ensuring the timely delivery of justice. Also, the ShareCrimE model supports collaboration by users/agents in different geographical locations.

Limitations A limitation of the ShareCrimE model is the difficulty integrating criminal case data applications used by some entities in the South African criminal justice system. This is especially true for current criminal case data applications that are rendered as services by third parties.

A second limitation is the possible lack of political will. Most of the high-ranking positions in the participating entities are political appointees and it would be a slow process to gain approvals for an advanced technological system from all the stakeholders.

7   Related Work

Lone and Mir [21] have proposed a blockchain-based forensic chain of custody system that is intended to maintain the integrity of criminal case data and evidence. However, their solution employs Hyperledger Composer, which is a deprecated system. Elgohary et al. [8] also employ Hyperledger Composer, but their application is focused on maintaining the chain of custody in image forensic investigations. Other researchers, including Ahmad et al. [1], Bonomi et al. [3], Li et al. [20] and Yunianto et al. [26], adopt the Ethereum framework as their foundation. The problem is that the Ethereum framework employs native cryptocurrency and mining algorithms to add new transactions to their networks, which require considerable computational resources.

The proposed ShareCrimE model bears similarities to the work of Lone and Mir [21], Li et al. [20], Khan et al. [19] and Alruwaili [2] in that they also propose blockchain models for criminal justice systems. The model of Khan et al. [19] is implemented using Hyperledger Sawtooth [16] that employs practical Byzantine fault tolerance and proof of elapsed time consensus algorithms. Hyperledger Sawtooth supports private and public blockchain solutions, but it relies on a third-party (Intel for its Software Guard Extensions) [18].

Table 1 compares the ShareCrimE model with four prominent models in terms of eight key features. The ShareCrimE model stands out from the other models because it accommodates all eight features. Additionally, it is only one of two models that does not rely on cryptocurrency or mining algorithms to add new transactions.

Table 1. Comparison of the ShareCrimE model with related models.

Model Features	Lone and Mir [21]	Ahmad et al. [1]	Bonomi et al. [3]	Khan et al. [19]	ShareCrimE Model
Support of private blockchain	✓	✓	✓	✓	✓
No cryptocurrency/mining algorithms required to add transactions			✓	✓	✓
Integration of existing applications			✓	✓	✓
Support of multiple criminal justice system entities	✓	✓	✓	✓	✓
Based on the South African criminal justice system					✓
Sharing of criminal case data and evidence	✓	✓	✓	✓	✓
No third-party reliance	✓	✓		✓	✓
Use of Hyperledger Fabric				✓	✓

8   Conclusions

The ShareCrimE model demonstrates how blockchain technology can be adapted to securely share criminal case data among the various authorized entities in a criminal justice system. The ShareCrimE model promotes greater transparency and accountability. Creation or modification of criminal case data by rogue parties would be visible because all the authorized entities have access to the entire criminal case data history. The stored evidence and underlying data are immutable and cannot be deleted, ensuring their security, integrity and availability. All the authorized entities have seamless access to criminal case data that enables them to compile reports and complete tasks quickly, ensuring the timely delivery of justice. The model also enhances collaboration especially when it comes to joint operations and investigations involving law enforcement and prosecutors.

The ShareCrimE model was developed using the South African criminal justice system as a case study. However, the model is generic enough to be customized to criminal justice systems in other countries.

Acknowledgment This research was supported by the University of Pretoria.

References

1. L. Ahmad, S. Khanji, F. Iqbal and F. Kamoun, Blockchain-based chain of custody: Towards real-time tamper-proof evidence management, *Proceedings of the Fifteenth International Conference on Availability, Reliability and Security*, article no. 48, 2020.
2. F. Alruwaili, CustodyBlock: A distributed chain of custody evidence framework, *Information*, vol. 12(2), article no. 88, 2021.
3. S. Bonomi, M. Casini and C. Ciccotelli, B-CoC: A Blockchain-Based Chain of Custody for Evidence Management in Digital Forensics, arXiv: 1807.10359v1 (arxiv.org/abs/1807.10359v1), 2018.
4. A. Carstensen and J. Bernhard, Design science research – A powerful tool for improving methods in engineering education research, *European Journal of Engineering Education*, vol. 44(1-2), pp. 85–102, 2019.
5. Carte Blanche, Dockets for sale, YouTube (`www.youtube.com/watch?v=s1L8j 50Sgz0`), April 10, 2022.
6. Department of Correctional Services, Mission/Vision/Values, Republic of South Africa, Pretoria, South Africa (`www.dcs.gov.za/?page_id=174`), 2023.
7. Department of Justice and Constitutional Development, Strategic Plan for the Period 2011-2016: Annual Review 2011/12, Document no. RP45/2011, Republic of South Africa, Pretoria, South Africa (`www.gov.za/sites/default/files/gcis_document/201409/mtsf0.pdf`), 2011.
8. H. Elgohary, S. Darwish and S. Elkaffas, Improving uncertainty in chain of custody for image forensic investigation applications, *IEEE Access*, vol. 10, pp. 14669–14679, 2022.
9. Hong Kong Applied Science and Technology Research Institute, Whitepaper on Distributed Ledger Technology, Hong Kong, China (`www.astri.org/tdprojects/whitepaper-on-distributed-ledger-technology`), 2022.

10. G. Hosken and S. Masombuka, A hole in Pistorius conman case docket, *Sunday Times (South Africa)*, March 23, 2016.
11. Hyperledger Fabric, Application Design Elements, San Francisco, California (`hyperledger-fabric.readthedocs.io/en/release-2.2/developapps/desi gnelements.html`), 2023.
12. Hyperledger Fabric, Getting Started – Install, San Francisco, California (`hyperledger-fabric.readthedocs.io/en/release-2.5/getting_started. html`), 2023.
13. Hyperledger Fabric, Glossary, San Francisco, California (`hyperledger-fabric. readthedocs.io/en/latest/glossary.html?highlight=ledger\#`), 2023.
14. Hyperledger Fabric, Identity, San Francisco, California (`hyperledger-fabric. readthedocs.io/en/release-2.2/identity/identity.html?highlight=certif icate\%20authority\#what-is-an-identity`), 2023.
15. Hyperledger Foundation, About Hyperledger Foundation, San Francisco, California (`www.hyperledger.org/about`), 2023.
16. Hyperledger Foundation, Hyperledger Sawtooth, San Francisco, California (`www. hyperledger.org/use/sawtooth`), 2023.
17. L. Isaacs, DA demands in-field training for SAPS officers in the Western Cape, *Eyewitness News (Cape Town)*, March 4, 2022.
18. S. Kaur, S. Chaturvedi, A. Sharma and J. Kar, A research survey on applications of consensus protocols in blockchain, *Security and Communication Networks*, article no. 6693731, 2021.
19. A. Khan, M. Uddin, A. Shaikh, A. Laghari and A. Rajput, MF-ledger: Blockchain Hyperledger-Sawtooth-enabled novel and secure multimedia chain-of-custody forensic investigation architecture, *IEEE Access*, vol. 9, pp. 103637–103650, 2021.
20. M. Li, C. Lal, M. Conti and D. Hu, LEChain: A blockchain-based lawful evidence management scheme for digital forensics, *Future Generation Computer Systems*, vol. 115, pp. 406–420, 2021.
21. A. Lone and R. Mir, Forensic-chain: Blockchain-based digital forensics chain of custody with PoC in Hyperledger Composer, *Digital Investigation*, vol. 28, pp. 44–55, 2019.
22. L. Matya, Almost 400 corruption cases involving SAPS members being investigated, *SABC News (South Africa)*, November 3, 2020.
23. H. Natarajan, S. Krause and H. Gradstein, Distributed Ledger Technology and Blockchain, FinTech Note no. 1, World Bank, Washington, DC (`hdl.handle.net/ 10986/29053`), 2017.
24. Select Committee on Security and Justice, Progress Report: Integrated Justice System (IJS) Programme, Department of Justice and Constitutional Development, Republic of South Africa, Pretoria, South Africa (`static.pmg.org.za/ 170531IJSReport.pdf`), 2017.
25. Republic of South Africa, MEC Albert Fritz on e-docket software not being effectively used by SAPS and courts, Media Statement, Pretoria, South Africa, March 5, 2020.
26. E. Yunianto, Y. Prayudi and B. Sugiantoro, B-DEC: Digital evidence cabinet based on blockchain for evidence management, *International Journal of Computer Applications*, vol. 181(45), pp. 22–29, 2019.

Printed in the United States
by Baker & Taylor Publisher Services